Additional copies of *Fundamentals of Instructing FAA Written Exam* are available from

Gleim Publications, Inc.
P.O. Box 12848, University Station
Gainesville, Florida 32604
(352) 375-0772
(800) 87-GLEIM or (800) 874-5346
FAX: (352) 375-6940
Internet: www.gleim.com

The price is $12.95 (subject to change without notice). Orders must be prepaid. Use the order form on page 164. Shipping and handling charges will be added to telephone orders. Add applicable sales tax to shipments within Florida.

Gleim Publications, Inc. guarantees the immediate refund of all resalable texts returned in 30 days. Shipping and handling charges and software are nonrefundable.

REVIEWERS AND CONTRIBUTORS

Karen A. Hom, B.A., University of Florida, is our book production coordinator. Ms. Hom coordinated the production staff and reviewed the final manuscript.

Barry A. Jones, ATP, CFII, MEI, B.S. in Air Commerce/Flight Technology, Florida Institute of Technology, is our aviation project manager and also a flight instructor and charter pilot with Gulf Atlantic Airways in Gainesville, FL. Mr. Jones drafted answer explanations, incorporated numerous revisions, assisted in assembling the text, and provided technical assistance throughout the project.

Joshua B. Moore, B.A., University of Florida, is our aviation technical research assistant and an instrument-rated private pilot. Mr. Moore researched questions, edited answer explanations, and incorporated revisions into the text.

Travis A. Moore, M.B.A., University of Florida, provided production and editorial assistance throughout the project.

John F. Rebstock, B.S., Fisher School of Accounting, University of Florida, reviewed portions of the edition and composed the page layout.

Jan M. Strickland is our book production assistant. Ms. Strickland reviewed the final manuscript and provided assistance throughout the project.

The many FAA employees who helped, in person or by telephone, primarily in Gainesville, FL; Jacksonville, FL; Orlando, FL; Oklahoma City, OK; and Washington, DC.

The many CFIs, pilots, and student pilots who have provided comments and suggestions about *Fundamentals of Instructing FAA Written Exam* during the past 10 years.

A PERSONAL THANKS

This manual would not have been possible without the extraordinary effort and dedication of Jim Collis and Terry Hall, who typed the entire manuscript and all revisions, as well as prepared the camera-ready pages.

The author also appreciates the proofreading and production assistance of Svetlana Dzyubenko, Jennifer Forrester, Rob Gallardo, Jamie Gentile, Melissa Guinand, Lynn Li, Jessica Medina, Shane Rapp, Wendy Rice, McKenzie Rogers, and Jenna Zirkel.

Finally, I appreciate the encouragement, support, and tolerance of my family throughout this project.

Groundwood Paper and Highlighters -- This book is printed on high quality groundwood paper. It is lightweight and easy-to-recycle. We recommend that you purchase a highlighter specifically designed to be non-bleed-through (e.g., Avery *Glidestick* ™) at your local office supply store.

SEVENTH EDITION

FUNDAMENTALS OF INSTRUCTING

FAA WRITTEN EXAM

for the FAA Computer-Based Pilot Knowledge Test

by Irvin N. Gleim, Ph.D., CFII

with the assistance of
Barry A. Jones, ATP, CFII, MEI

ABOUT THE AUTHOR

Irvin N. Gleim earned his private pilot certificate in 1965 from the Institute of Aviation at the University of Illinois, where he subsequently received his Ph.D. He is a commercial pilot and flight instructor (instrument) with multiengine and seaplane ratings, and is a member of the Aircraft Owners and Pilots Association, American Bonanza Society, Civil Air Patrol, Experimental Aircraft Association, and Seaplane Pilots Association. He is also author of Practical Test Prep and Flight Maneuvers books for the private, instrument, commercial, and flight instructor certificates/ratings, and study guides for the private/recreational, instrument, commercial, flight/ground instructor, fundamentals of instructing, and airline transport pilot FAA pilot knowledge tests. Three additional pilot training books are *Pilot Handbook*, *Aviation Weather and Weather Services*, and *FAR/AIM*.

Dr. Gleim has also written articles for professional accounting and business law journals, and is the author of widely used review manuals for the CIA exam (Certified Internal Auditor), the CMA exam (Certified Management Accountant), the CFM exam (Certified in Financial Management), and the CPA exam (Certified Public Accountant). He is Professor Emeritus, Fisher School of Accounting, University of Florida, and is a CFM, CIA, CMA, and CPA.

Gleim Publications, Inc.
P.O. Box 12848 • University Station
Gainesville, Florida 32604

(352) 375-0772
(800) 87-GLEIM or (800) 874-5346
FAX: (352) 375-6940

Internet: www.gleim.com
E-mail: admin@gleim.com

ISSN 1078-2087
ISBN 1-58194-129-3
First Printing: December 2000

This is the first printing of the seventh edition of *Fundamentals of Instructing FAA Written Exam*.

Please e-mail update@gleim.com with FOI 7-1 in the subject or text. You will receive our current update as a reply.

EXAMPLE:

To: update@gleim.com
From: your e-mail address
Subject: FOI 7-1

HELP !!

This is the Seventh Edition, designed specifically for pilots who aspire to the flight instructor certificate and/or ground instructor certificate. Please send any corrections and suggestions for subsequent editions to the author, c/o Gleim Publications, Inc. The last page in this book has been reserved for you to make comments and suggestions. It can be torn out and mailed to Gleim Publications, Inc.

A companion volume, *Flight/Ground Instructor FAA Written Exam,* is available as is *Flight Instructor Flight Maneuvers and Practical Test Prep*, which focuses on the FAA practical test, just as this book focuses on the FAA pilot knowledge test. Save time, money, and frustration -- order both books today! See the order form on page 164. Please bring these books to the attention of flight instructors, fixed-base operators, and others with a potential interest in acquiring their flight instructor certificates. Wide distribution of these books and increased interest in flying depend on your assistance and good word. Thank you.

NOTE: ANSWER DISCREPANCIES and UPDATES

Our answers have been carefully researched and reviewed. Inevitably, there will be differences with competitors' books and even the FAA. If necessary, we will develop an UPDATE for *Fundamentals of Instructing FAA Written Exam*. Send e-mail to update@gleim.com as described at the top right of this page, and visit our Internet site for the latest updates and information on all of our products. To continue providing our customers with first-rate service, we request that questions about our books and software be sent to us via mail, e-mail, or fax. The appropriate staff member will give each question thorough consideration and a prompt response. Questions concerning orders, prices, shipments, or payments will be handled via telephone by our competent and courteous customer service staff.

TABLE OF CONTENTS

SEVENTH EDITION CHANGES (12/00)

1. This new edition has been revised to reflect the new *Aviation Instructor's Handbook* (FAA-H-8083-9), dated 1999.

2. Recent changes and additions to the fundamentals of instructing knowledge test question bank have been incorporated throughout.

PREFACE

This book has three purposes:

1. To provide you with the easiest and fastest means of passing the Fundamentals of Instructing (FOI) Knowledge Test.

2. To help both experienced and inexperienced aviation instructors improve their instruction techniques.

3. To assist flight and/or ground instructors in organizing and presenting aviation ground schools which prepare individuals to pass the FAA pilot knowledge tests.

FOI Knowledge Test

Successful completion of the FOI knowledge test is required by the FAA for those seeking the flight instructor or ground instructor certificates. Chapter 1 of this book (beginning on the next page) contains a discussion of the requirements to obtain the flight instructor and ground instructor certificates, and a description of the FOI knowledge test, how to prepare for it and take it, and how to maximize your score with minimum effort. Chapters 2 through 7 contain outlines of exactly what you need to know to answer the FAA knowledge test questions, as well as all of the actual FAA test questions, each accompanied by a comprehensive explanation.

NOTE: Appendix A contains a practice test consisting of 50 questions from this book which reflects the subject matter composition of the FAA knowledge test.

Improving Instruction Methods

The FAA has published *Aviation Instructor's Handbook* (FAA-H-8083-9), which explains the basic principles and processes of teaching and learning. This is the subject matter of the FOI knowledge test. The first 72 pages of the *AIH* set forth these general concepts. This material is more easily presented and studied in outline format, as it appears in Chapters 2 through 7 of this book. Both experienced and inexperienced aviation instructors will find the study of these outlines very useful in improving their instruction methods.

Appendix B of this book (46 pages in length) is a reprint of chapters 8, 9, and 10, which specifically concern flight instruction, of *Aviation Instructor's Handbook*. It is useful reading and periodic review for CFIs. It consists of three chapters:

1. Instructor Responsibilities and Professionalism
2. Techniques of Flight Instruction
3. Planning Instructional Activity

Ground School Course Suggestions

Many aviation instructors would like to increase the general public's interest in learning to fly. These instructors also enjoy teaching. Appendix C of this book consists of suggestions on how to find (or become) a sponsor for a "ground school." It also contains suggestions on course organization, lecture outlines, and class presentation.

Enjoy Flying -- Safely!

Irvin N. Gleim

December 2000

CHAPTER ONE
THE FAA PILOT KNOWLEDGE TEST

The beginning of this chapter provides an overview of the process to obtain a flight instructor certificate. The ground instructor certificate is also addressed. The remainder of this chapter explains the content and procedure of relevant Federal Aviation Administration (FAA) tests. Becoming a Certificated Flight Instructor (CFI) and/or a Certificated Ground Instructor is fun. Begin today!

Fundamentals of Instructing FAA Written Exam is one of four related books for obtaining a flight and/or ground instructor certificate. The other three are *Flight/Ground Instructor FAA Written Exam*, which is in a format similar to this book, and *Flight Instructor Flight Maneuvers and Practical Test Prep* and *Pilot Handbook*, each in outline/illustration format.

Flight/Ground Instructor FAA Written Exam prepares you to pass the FAA's flight and/or ground instructor knowledge test. If you are planning to obtain both the flight and ground instructor certificates, you only need to pass the Fundamentals of Instructing (FOI) test once.

Flight Instructor Flight Maneuvers and Practical Test Prep is a comprehensive, carefully organized presentation of everything you need to know to prepare for your flight training and for your flight instructor practical (flight) test. It integrates material from over 100 FAA publications and other sources.

Pilot Handbook is a complete pilot reference book that combines over 100 FAA books and documents including *AIM*, FARs, ACs, and much more. This book, more than any other, will help make you a better and more proficient pilot.

Also available is Gleim's *FAR/AIM*, an easy-to-read reference book containing all of the Federal Aviation Regulations (FARs) applicable to general aviation flying, plus the full text of the FAA's *Aeronautical Information Manual* (*AIM*).

If you are planning on purchasing the FAA books on aviation weather, purchase Gleim's *Aviation Weather and Weather Services*, which combines all of the information from the FAA's *Aviation Weather* (AC 00-6A), *Aviation Weather Services* (AC 00-45E), and numerous FAA publications into one easy-to-understand book. It will help you study all aspects of aviation weather and provide you with a single reference book.

1.1 WHAT IS A FLIGHT INSTRUCTOR CERTIFICATE?

A flight instructor certificate is similar in appearance to your commercial pilot certificate and will allow you to give flight and ground instruction. The certificate is sent to you by the FAA upon satisfactory completion of your training program, two pilot knowledge tests, and a practical test. A sample flight instructor certificate is reproduced below.

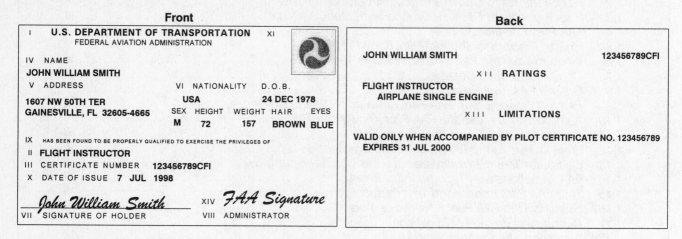

1.2 REQUIREMENTS TO OBTAIN A FLIGHT INSTRUCTOR CERTIFICATE

1. Be at least 18 years of age.

2. Be able to read, write, and converse fluently in English (certificates with operating limitations may be available for medically related deficiencies).

3. Hold a commercial or airline transport pilot (ATP) certificate with an aircraft rating appropriate to the flight instructor rating sought (e.g., airplane, glider).

    a. You must also hold an instrument rating to be a flight instructor in an airplane.

4. Use this book, *Flight/Ground Instructor FAA Written Exam*, *Flight Instructor Flight Maneuvers and Practical Test Prep*, and *Pilot Handbook* to learn

    a. Fundamentals of instructing

    b. All subject areas in which ground training is required for recreational, private, and commercial pilot certificates and for an instrument rating

5. Pass both the FOI and the flight instructor knowledge tests with scores of 70% or better. All FAA knowledge tests are administered at FAA-designated computer testing centers. The FOI test consists of 50 multiple-choice questions selected from the 192 FOI-related questions among the 1,303 questions in the FAA's flight and ground instructor knowledge test bank; the balance of 1,111 questions are for the flight and ground instructor tests. Each of the FAA's 192 FOI questions is reproduced in this book with complete explanations to the right of each question.

    a. You are not required to take the FOI knowledge test if you

        1) Hold an FAA flight or ground instructor certificate

        2) Hold a current teacher's certificate authorizing you to teach at an educational level of the 7th grade or higher

        3) Are currently employed as a teacher at an accredited college or university

6. Demonstrate flight proficiency (FAR 61.187).

    a. You must receive and log flight and ground training and obtain a logbook endorsement from an authorized instructor in the following areas of operations for an airplane category rating with a single-engine or multiengine class rating:

        1) *Fundamentals of instructing*
        2) *Technical subject areas*
        3) *Preflight preparation*
        4) *Preflight lesson on a maneuver to be performed in flight*
        5) *Preflight procedures*
        6) *Airport and seaplane base operations*
        7) *Takeoffs, landings, and go-arounds*
        8) *Fundamentals of flight*
        9) *Performance maneuvers*
        10) *Ground reference maneuvers*
        11) *Slow flight, stalls, and spins (single-engine only)*

            a) *Slow flight and stalls (multiengine only)*

        12) *Basic instrument maneuvers*
        13) *Emergency operations*
        14) *Multiengine operations (multiengine only)*
        15) *Postflight procedures*

    b. The flight instruction must be given by a person who has held a flight instructor certificate during the 24 months immediately preceding the date the instruction is given and who has given at least 200 hr. of flight instruction as a CFI.

    c. You must also obtain a logbook endorsement by an appropriately certificated and rated flight instructor who has provided you with spin entry, spin, and spin recovery training in an airplane that is certificated for spins and has found that you are competent and possess instructional proficiency in those training areas.

7. Alternatively, enroll in an FAA-certificated pilot school that has an approved flight instructor certification course (airplane).

    a. These are known as Part 141 schools or Part 142 training centers because they are authorized by Part 141 or Part 142 of the FARs.

        1) All other regulations concerning the certification of pilots are found in Part 61 of the FARs.

    b. The Part 141 course must consist of at least 40 hr. of ground instruction and 25 hr. of flight instructor training.

8. Successfully complete a practical (flight) test which will be given by an FAA inspector or designated pilot examiner. The practical test will be conducted as specified in the FAA's Flight Instructor Practical Test Standards (FAA-S-8081-6A, dated May 1991, with Change 1, dated July 1997).

    a. FAA inspectors are FAA employees and do not charge for their services.

    b. FAA-designated pilot examiners are proficient, experienced flight instructors and pilots who are authorized by the FAA to conduct flight tests. They do charge a fee.

    c. The FAA's Flight Instructor Practical Test Standards are outlined and reprinted in *Flight Instructor Flight Maneuvers and Practical Test Prep.*

1.3 REQUIREMENTS TO OBTAIN A GROUND INSTRUCTOR CERTIFICATE

1. To be eligible for a ground instructor certificate, you must

    a. Be at least 18 years of age.

    b. Be able to read, write, and converse fluently in English (certificates with operating limitations may be available for medically related deficiencies).

    c. Exhibit knowledge by passing the FOI and the appropriate ground instructor pilot knowledge tests.

        1) See item 5.a. on page 2 for information on when the FOI knowledge test is not required.

2. Ground instructor certificates cover three levels of certification:

    a. Basic ground instructor (BGI) may provide

        1) Ground training in the aeronautical knowledge areas required for a recreational or private pilot certificate

        2) Ground training required for a recreational or private pilot flight review

        3) A recommendation for the recreational or private pilot knowledge test

    b. Advanced ground instructor (AGI) may provide

        1) Ground training in the aeronautical knowledge areas required for any certificate or rating

        2) Ground training required for any flight review

        3) A recommendation for a knowledge test required for any certificate or rating

    c. Instrument ground instructor (IGI) may provide

        1) Ground training in the aeronautical knowledge areas required for an instrument rating to a pilot or instructor certificate

        2) Ground training required for an instrument proficiency check

        3) A recommendation for the instrument rating knowledge test for a pilot or instructor certificate

        4) See Gleim's *Instrument Pilot FAA Written Exam* which covers the IGI pilot knowledge test.

1.4 FAA PILOT KNOWLEDGE TEST

This test book is designed to help you prepare for and successfully take the FAA FOI knowledge test for the flight and/or ground instructor certificate. The remainder of this chapter explains the FAA test procedures.

1. All of the 192 questions in the FAA's flight and ground instructor knowledge test bank that are applicable to fundamentals of instructing have been grouped into the following six categories, which are the titles of Chapters 2 through 7:

    Chapter 2 -- The Learning Process
    Chapter 3 -- Barriers to Learning
    Chapter 4 -- Human Behavior and Effective Communication
    Chapter 5 -- Teaching Methods
    Chapter 6 -- Planning Instructional Activity
    Chapter 7 -- Critique and Evaluation

    Note that, in the official FAA flight and ground instructor knowledge test bank containing all of the questions, the FAA's questions are **not** grouped together by topic. We have unscrambled them for you in this book.

2.   In an effort to develop better test questions, the FAA frequently pretests questions on pilot knowledge tests by adding up to 5 "pretest" questions. Thus, rather than the number of questions listed previously, you may be required to answer up to 5 extra pretest questions. The pretest questions will not be graded. You will NOT know which questions are "real" and which are "pretest." Accordingly, you must attempt to answer all questions correctly.

3.   Within each of the chapters listed, questions relating to the same subtopic are grouped together to facilitate your study program. Each subtopic is called a module.

4.   To the right of each question are

   a.   The correct answer,
   b.   The FAA question number, and
   c.   A reference for the answer explanation.

      1)   EXAMPLE: *AIH Chap I* means *Aviation Instructor's Handbook*, Chapter I.

5.   Each chapter begins with an outline of the material tested on the FAA knowledge test. The outlines in this part of the book are somewhat brief and have only one purpose: to help you pass the FAA FOI knowledge test.

   a.   **CAUTION:** The **sole purpose** of this book is to expedite your passing the FAA FOI knowledge test for the flight and/or ground instructor certificate. Accordingly, all extraneous material (i.e., not directly tested on the FAA knowledge test) is omitted even though much more information and knowledge are necessary to be a proficient flight or ground instructor. This additional material is presented in three related books: *Flight/Ground Instructor FAA Written Exam*, *Flight Instructor Flight Maneuvers and Practical Test Prep*, and *Pilot Handbook*.

Follow the suggestions given throughout this chapter and you will have no trouble passing the test the first time you take it.

1.5 HOW TO PREPARE FOR THE FAA PILOT KNOWLEDGE TEST

1.   Begin by carefully reading the rest of this chapter. You need to have a complete understanding of the examination process prior to beginning to study for it. This knowledge will make your studying more efficient.

2.   After you have spent an hour studying this chapter, set up a study schedule, including a target date for taking your pilot knowledge test.

   a.   Do not let the study process drag on because it will be discouraging, i.e., the quicker the better.

   b.   Consider enrolling in an organized ground school course at your local FBO, community college, etc.

   c.   Determine where and when you are going to take your pilot knowledge test.

3.   Work through each of Chapters 2 through 7.

   a.   Each chapter begins with a list of its module titles. The number in parentheses after each title is the number of FAA questions that cover the information in that module. The two numbers following the parentheses are the page numbers on which the outline and the questions for that particular module begin, respectively.

   b.   Begin by studying the outlines slowly and carefully.

   c.   Cover the answer explanations on the right side of each page with your hand or a piece of paper while you answer the multiple-choice questions.

1) Remember, it is very important to the learning (and understanding) process that you honestly commit yourself to an answer. If you are wrong, your memory will be reinforced by having discovered your error. Therefore, it is crucial to cover up the answer and make an honest attempt to answer the question before reading the answer.

2) Study the answer explanation for each question that you answer incorrectly, do not understand, or have difficulty with.

4. Note that this test book (in contrast to most other question and answer books) contains the FAA questions grouped by topic. Thus, some questions may appear repetitive, while others may be duplicates or near-duplicates. Accordingly, do not work question after question (i.e., waste time and effort) if you are already conversant with a topic and the type of questions asked.

5. As you move from module to module and chapter to chapter, you may need further explanation or clarification of certain topics. You may wish to obtain and use *Flight Instructor Flight Maneuvers and Practical Test Prep*, which covers in detail all the information in the FAA Flight Instructor Practical Test Standards, and other information relevant to flight instructors. This book covers the fundamentals of instructing as well as the knowledge and skills required of flight instructors.

6. Keep track of your work!!! As you complete a module in Chapters 2 through 7, grade yourself with an A, B, C, or ? (use a ? if you need help on the subject) next to the module title at the front of the respective chapter.

   a. The A, B, C, or ? is your self-evaluation of your comprehension of the material in that module and your ability to answer the questions.

   A   means a good understanding.
   B   means a fair understanding.
   C   means a shaky understanding.
   ?   means to ask your CFI or others about the material and/or questions, and read the pertinent sections in *Flight Instructor Flight Maneuvers and Practical Test Prep*.

   b. This procedure will provide you with the ability to see quickly (by looking at the first page of Chapters 2 through 7) how much studying you have done (and how much remains) and how well you have done.

   c. This procedure will also facilitate review. You can spend more time on the modules with which you had difficulty.

1.6 WHEN TO TAKE THE FAA PILOT KNOWLEDGE TEST

1. You must be at least 16 years of age to take the FOI knowledge test.

2. Take the FOI knowledge test within the next 30 days.

   a. Get the test behind you.

3. You must obtain your flight or ground instructor certificate within 24 months or you will have to retake your test.

1.7 COMPUTER TESTING CENTERS

The FAA has contracted with several computer testing services to administer FAA pilot knowledge tests. Each of these computer testing services has testing centers throughout the country. You register by calling an 800 number. Call the following testing services for information regarding the location of testing centers most convenient to you and the time allowed and cost to take their fundamentals of instructing (FOI) knowledge test.

CATS   (800) 947-4228

LaserGrade   (800) 211-2754

Also, about twenty Part 141 schools use the AvTEST computer testing system, which is very similar to the computer testing services described above.

1.8 GLEIM'S *FAA TEST PREP* SOFTWARE

Computer testing is consistent with aviation's use of computers (e.g., DUATS, flight simulators, computerized cockpits, etc.). All FAA knowledge tests are administered by computer.

Computer testing is natural after computer study. Computer-assisted instruction is a very efficient and effective method of study. Gleim's *FAA Test Prep* software is designed to prepare you for computer testing. *FAA Test Prep* contains all of the questions in this book, context-sensitive outline material, and on-screen charts and figures. You choose either STUDY MODE or TEST MODE.

In STUDY MODE, the software provides you with an explanation of each answer you choose (correct or incorrect). You design each study session:

Topic(s) you wish to cover

Number of questions

Order of questions -- FAA, Gleim, or random

Order of answers to each question -- FAA or random

Questions marked from last session -- test, study, or both

Questions missed from last session -- test, study, or both

Questions missed from all sessions -- test, study, or both

Questions never answered correctly

In TEST MODE, you decide the format -- CATS, LaserGrade, AvTEST, or Gleim. When you finish your test, you can study the questions missed and access answer explanations. The software imitates the operation of the FAA-approved computer testing companies. Thus, you have a complete understanding of exactly how to take an FAA knowledge test before you go to a computer testing center.

For more information on Gleim's *FAA Test Prep* software, see page 12.

1.9 PART 141 SCHOOLS WITH FAA PILOT KNOWLEDGE TEST EXAMINING AUTHORITY

The FAA permits some FAR Part 141 schools to develop, administer, and grade their own pilot knowledge tests as long as they use the FAA knowledge test bank, i.e., the same questions as in this book. The FAA does not provide the correct answers to the Part 141 schools, and the FAA only reviews the Part 141 school test question selection sheets. Thus, some of the answers used by Part 141 test examiners may not agree with the FAA or those in this book. The latter is not a problem but may explain why you may miss a question on a Part 141 pilot knowledge test using an answer presented in this book.

1.10 AUTHORIZATION TO TAKE THE FAA PILOT KNOWLEDGE TEST

The FAA does not require an instructor endorsement for the FOI or any other instructor knowledge test.

1.11 FORMAT OF THE FAA PILOT KNOWLEDGE TEST

The FAA's fundamentals of instructing knowledge test consists of 50 multiple-choice questions selected from the 192 questions that appear in the next six chapters.

Note that the FAA test will be taken from exactly the same questions that are reproduced in this book. If you study the next six chapters, including all the questions and answers, **you should be assured of passing your test.**

Additionally, all of the FAA figures are contained in a book titled *Computer Testing Supplement for Flight and Ground Instructor*, which will be given to you for your use at the time of your test. Only one FAA figure is used for the FOI knowledge test, and it is reproduced on page 75 of this book.

1.12 WHAT TO TAKE TO THE FAA PILOT KNOWLEDGE TEST

1. Picture identification of yourself
2. Proof of age

1.13 COMPUTER TESTING PROCEDURES

To register to take the FOI knowledge test, you should call one of the testing services listed in Module 1.7, Computer Testing Centers, on page 7, or you may call one of their testing centers. These testing centers and telephone numbers are listed in Gleim's *FAA Test Prep* software under Vendors in the main menu. When you register, you will pay the fee by credit card.

When you arrive at the computer testing center, you will be required to provide positive proof of identification and documentary evidence of your age. The identification presented must include your photograph, signature, and actual residential address. This information may be presented in more than one form of identification. Next, you sign in on the testing center's daily log. Your signature on the logsheet certifies that, if this is a retest, you meet the applicable requirements (see Module 1.16, Failure on the FAA Pilot Knowledge Test, on page 11) and that you have not passed this test in the past 2 years.

Next, you will be taken into the testing room and seated at a computer terminal. A person from the testing center will assist you in logging on the system, and you will be asked to confirm your personal data (e.g., name, Social Security number, etc.). Then you will be prompted and given an online introduction to the computer testing system and you will take a sample test. If you have used our *FAA Test Prep* software, you will be conversant with the computer testing methodology and environment, and you will probably want to skip the sample test and begin the actual test immediately. You will be allowed 1.5 hr. to complete the actual test. This is 1.8 minutes per question. Confirm the time permitted when you call the testing center to register to take the test by computer. When you have completed your test, an Airman Computer Test Report will be printed out, validated (usually with an embossed seal), and given to you by a person from the testing center. Before you leave, you will be required to sign out on the testing center's daily log.

Each computer testing center has certain idiosyncrasies in its paperwork, scheduling, telephone procedures, as well as in its software. It is for this reason that our *FAA Test Prep* software emulates each of these FAA-approved computer testing companies.

1.14 FAA QUESTIONS WITH TYPOGRAPHICAL ERRORS

Occasionally, FAA test questions contain typographical errors such that there is no correct answer. The FAA test development process involves many steps and people, and as you would expect, glitches occur in the system that are beyond the control of any one person. We indicate "best" rather than correct answers for some questions. Use these best answers for the indicated questions.

Note that the FAA corrects (rewrites) defective questions on the computer tests, which it cannot currently do with respect to faulty figures which are printed in the FAA computer testing supplements. Thus, it is important to carefully study questions that are noted to have a best answer in this book.

1.15 YOUR FAA PILOT KNOWLEDGE TEST REPORT

1. You will receive your Airman Computer Test Report upon completion of the test. An example computer test report is reproduced on the next page.

    a. Note that you will receive only one grade as illustrated.

    b. The expiration date is the date by which you must take your FAA practical test.

    c. The report lists the FAA subject matter knowledge codes of the questions you missed, so you can review the topics you missed prior to your practical test.

```
┌─────────────────────────────────────────────────────────┐
│                                                           │
│              Federal Aviation Administration              │
│                Airman Computer Test Report                │
│                                                           │
│   EXAM TITLE:  Fundamentals of Instructing                │
│   NAME:  Jones David John                                 │
│   ID NUMBER:  123456789          TAKE:  1                 │
│   DATE:  08/14/99          SCORE:  82          GRADE: Pass│
│   ------------------------------------------------------- │
│   Knowledge area codes in which questions were answered   │
│   incorrectly.  See appropriate FAA knowledge test study  │
│   guide.  A code may represent more than one incorrect    │
│   response.                                               │
│                                                           │
│   H200 H201 H202 H203                                     │
│                                                           │
│   EXPIRATION DATE:  08/31/01                              │
│                                                           │
│                DO NOT LOSE THIS REPORT                    │
│   ------------------------------------------------------- │
│   Authorized instructor's statement.  (If Applicable)     │
│                                                           │
│   I have given Mr./Ms. _____ additional       │
│   instruction in each subject area shown to be deficient  │
│   and consider the applicant competent to pass the test.  │
│                                                           │
│   Last _____ Initial ____ Cert. No. ____ Type ____   │
│   (Print Clearly)                                         │
│                                                           │
│   Signature _____                               │
│                                    CTD's Embossed Seal    │
└─────────────────────────────────────────────────────────┘
```

2. The following FAA subject matter knowledge codes will appear on your test report to identify the topics from the FAA's *Aviation Instructor's Handbook* (FAA-H-8083-9) with which you had difficulty.

H200 Learning Theory
H201 Definition of Learning
H202 Characteristics of Learning
H203 Principles of Learning
H204 Level of Learning
H205 Learning Physical Skills
H206 Memory
H207 Transfer of Learning
H208 Control of Human Behavior
H209 Control of Human Behavior
H210 Human Needs
H211 Defense Mechanisms
H212 The Flight Instructor as a Practical Psychologist
H213 Basic Elements
H214 Barriers of Effective Communication
H215 Developing Communications Skills
H216 Preparation
H217 Presentation
H218 Application
H219 Review and Evaluation
H220 Organizing Material
H221 Lecture Method
H222 Cooperative or Group Learning Method
H223 Guided Discussion Method
H224 Demonstration-Performance Method
H225 Computer-Based Training Method

H226 The Instructor as a Critic
H227 Evaluation
H228 Instructional Aid Theory
H229 Reasons for Use of Instructional Aids
H230 Guidelines for Use of Instructional Aids
H231 Types of Instructional Aid
H232 Test Preparation Material
H233 Aviation Instructor Responsibilities
H234 Flight Instructor Responsibilities
H235 Professionalism
H236 The Telling-and-Doing Technique
H237 Integrated Flight Instruction
H238 Obstacles to Learning During Flight Instruction
H239 Positive Exchange of Flight Controls
H240 Use of Distractions
H241 Aeronautical Decision Making
H242 Factors Affecting Decision Making
H243 Operational Pitfalls
H244 Evaluating Student Decision Making
H245 Course of Training
H246 Blocks of Learning
H247 Training Syllabus
H248 Lesson Plans
H249 Growth and Development
H250 Sources of Material

a. Look them over and review them with your CFI so (s)he can certify that (s)he reviewed the deficient areas and found you competent in them when you take your flight instructor practical test.

3. Keep your Airman Computer Test Report in a safe place because you must submit it to the FAA examiner when you take your practical test.

1.16 FAILURE ON THE FAA PILOT KNOWLEDGE TEST

1. If you fail (less than 70%) the FOI knowledge test (virtually impossible if you follow the above instructions), you may retake it after your instructor endorses the bottom of your Airman Computer Test Report certifying that you have received the necessary ground training to retake the test.

2. Upon retaking the test, everything is the same except you must also submit your Airman Computer Test Report indicating the previous failure to the examiner.

3. Note that the pass rate on the FOI knowledge test is about 90%; i.e., 1 out of 10 fail the test initially. Reasons for failure include

   a. Failure to study the material tested (contained in the outlines at the beginning of Chapters 2 through 7 of this book);

   b. Failure to practice working the FAA exam questions under test conditions (all of the FAA questions on airplanes appear in Chapters 2 through 7 of this book); and

   c. Poor examination technique, such as misreading questions and not understanding the requirements.

1.17 REORGANIZATION OF FAA QUESTIONS

1. The questions in the FAA's flight and ground instructor knowledge test bank are numbered 6001 to 7230. Note that questions 6001 to 6160 are Fundamentals of Instructing questions and questions 6161 to 7230 are used for the flight and ground instructor test. The FAA questions appear to be presented randomly.

   a. We have reorganized and renumbered the FAA questions into chapters and modules.

   b. The FAA question number is presented in the middle of the first line of the explanation of each answer.

2. Pages 159 and 160 contain a list of the FAA questions numbers 6001 to 6160 with cross-references to the FAA's subject matter knowledge codes and the chapters and question numbers in this book.

   a. For example, the FAA's question 6001 is cross-referenced to the FAA's subject knowledge code H201, Aviation Instructor's Handbook, Chapter I, The Learning Process. The correct answer is A, and the question appears with answer explanations in this book under 2-1, which means it is reproduced in Chapter 2 as question number 1.

With this overview of exam requirements, you are ready to begin the easy-to-study outlines and rearranged questions with answers to build your knowledge and confidence and PASS THE FAA's FUNDAMENTALS OF INSTRUCTING KNOWLEDGE TEST.

The feedback we receive from users indicates that our books and software reduce anxiety, improve FAA test scores, and build knowledge. Studying for each test becomes a useful step toward advanced certificates and ratings.

1.18 SIMULATED FAA PRACTICE TEST

Appendix A, Fundamentals of Instructing Practice Test, beginning on page 95, allows you to practice taking the FAA knowledge test without the answers next to the questions. This test has 50 questions that have been randomly selected from the 192 Fundamentals of Instructing questions in the FAA's flight and ground instructor knowledge test bank. Topical coverage in this practice test is similar to that of the FAA FOI test.

It is very important that you answer all 50 questions at one sitting. You should not consult the answers, especially when being referred to charts or tables in this book where the questions are answered and explained. Analyze your performance based on the answer key which follows the practice test.

Also rely on Gleim's *FAA Test Prep* software to simulate actual computer testing conditions including the screen layouts, instructions, etc., for CATS, LaserGrade, and AvTEST.

1.19 INSTRUCTIONS FOR *FAA TEST PREP* SOFTWARE

To install *FAA Test Prep*, put your CD-ROM in your CD-ROM drive. If an autoplay window appears after you insert the CD, follow the Setup Wizard. If no screen appears after you have inserted the CD, click on the Windows Start button, and select "Run" from a list of options. Type x:\setup.exe (if x is the drive letter of your CD-ROM), and click "OK." Follow the on-screen instructions to finalize the installation.

Gleim Publications requires all *FAA Test Prep* users to register their software for unlimited use, free updates, and technical support. To register, simply use the Personal Registration Number and Library Passkey(s) that were shipped with your CD-ROM, call (800) 87-GLEIM, or register online at (http://www.gleim.com/license.html).

Once you have installed *FAA Test Prep* onto your system, you can begin studying at any time by clicking on the icon placed on your desktop. Use the Tutorial in HELP to go step by step through the Test Prep study process, or start studying right away by clicking on Create Session in the Session menu. *FAA Test Prep* allows you to customize your study process using several different options.

Study Mode

Using Study Mode gives you immediate feedback on why your answer selection for a particular FAA question is correct or incorrect and allows you to access the context-sensitive outline material that helps to explain concepts related to the question. Choose from several different question sources: all questions available for that library, questions from a certain topic (chapters and modules from Gleim books), questions that you missed or marked in the last session you created, questions that you have never answered correctly, questions from certain FAA subject codes, etc. You can mix up the questions by selecting to randomize the question and/or answer order so that you do not memorize answer letters.

You may then grade your study sessions and track your study progress using the performance analysis charts and graphs. The Performance Analysis information helps you to focus on areas where you need the most improvement, saving you time in the overall study process. You may then want to go back and study questions that you missed in a previous session, or you may want to create a study session of questions that you marked in the previous session, and all of these options are made easy with *FAA Test Prep*'s Study Mode.

After studying the outlines and questions in Study Mode, you can switch to Test Mode, which gives you the option of taking your pilot knowledge test under actual testing conditions using one of the emulations of the major testing centers.

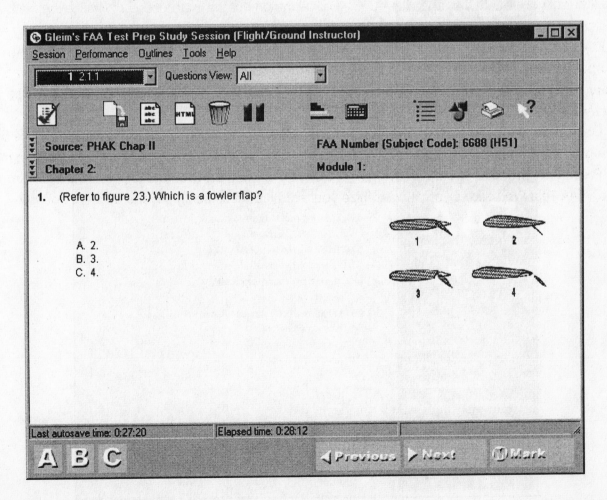

Test Mode

Take an exam in the actual testing environment of any of the major testing centers: CATS, AvTest, or Lasergrade. *FAA Test Prep* emulates the testing formats of these testing centers making it easy for you to study FAA questions under actual exam conditions. After studying with *FAA Test Prep*, you will know exactly what to expect when you go in to take your pilot knowledge test.

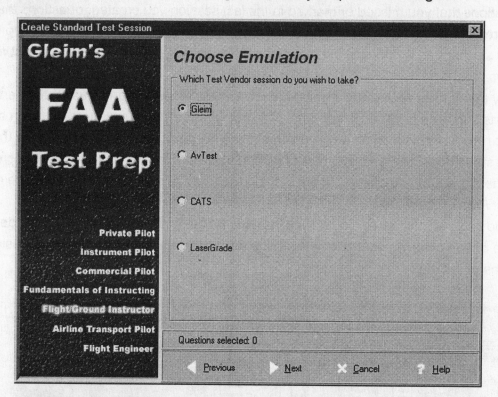

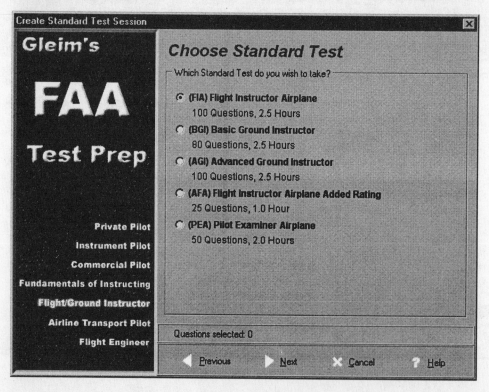

On-Screen Charts and Figures

One of the most convenient features of *FAA Test Prep* is the easily accessible on-screen charts and figures. Several of the FAA questions refer to drawings, maps, charts, and other pictures that provide information to help answer the question. In *FAA Test Prep*, you can pull up any of these figures with the click of a button. You can increase or decrease the size of the images, and you may also use our drawing feature to calculate the true course between two given points (required only on the private pilot knowledge test).

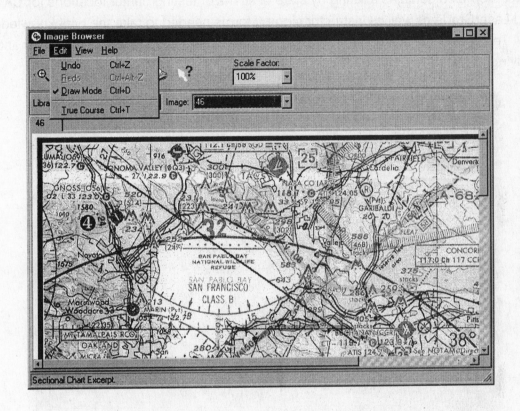

Instructor Print Options

FAA Test Prep is also a useful tool for instructors who want to create quizzes and assignments for their students. An instructor may mark questions in a session and then choose to print marked questions to create a quiz or test. (S)he may select to print an answer sheet, a blank answer sheet, and a renumbered printout of questions marked and any instructions that go along with the quiz or test.

FAA Test Prep also contains a listing by state of all major testing center locations for CATS, AvTest, and LaserGrade as well as instructor sign-off forms needed to take the pilot knowledge tests. Gleim's *FAA Test Prep* is an all-in-one program designed to help anyone with a computer and an interest in flying to pass the pilot knowledge tests.

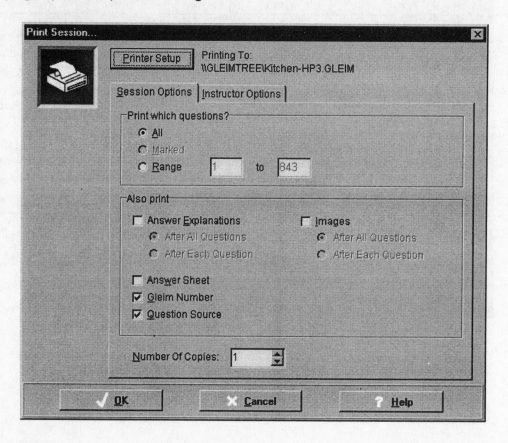

FREE Updates and Technical Support

Gleim offers FREE technical support to all registered users. Call (800) 87-GLEIM, send e-mail to support@gleim.com, or fill out the technical support request form online (www.gleim.com/techform.html). Downloadable library updates will also be available free to registered users of our CD-ROM software. For more information on our update service by e-mail, turn to page 161.

Obtain your copy of *FAA Test Prep* today. Order online at http://www.gleim.com/Aviation/IndivOrderForm.html or call 800 87-GLEIM.

If this Gleim test book saves you time and frustration in preparing for the FAA FOI knowledge test, you should use Gleim's *Flight/Ground Instructor FAA Written Exam* to prepare for those knowledge tests, and Gleim's *Flight Instructor Flight Maneuvers and Practical Test Prep* to prepare for the FAA practical test.

Flight Instructor Flight Maneuvers and Practical Test Prep will assist you in developing the competence and confidence to pass your FAA practical test, just as this book organizes and explains the knowledge needed to pass your FAA knowledge test.

Also, flight maneuvers are quickly perfected when you understand exactly what to expect before you get into an airplane to practice the flight maneuvers. You must be ahead of (not behind) your CFI and your airplane. Gleim's flight maneuvers books explain and illustrate all flight maneuvers so the maneuvers and their execution are intuitively appealing to you.

END OF CHAPTER

18

Gleim Publications, Inc.

(800) 87-GLEIM
(352) 375-0772
FAX # (352) 375-6940
P. O. Box 12848 • University Station
Gainesville, Florida 32604

TO: Users of Our Written Test Books

FROM: Irvin N. Gleim

TOPIC: Our **Flight Maneuvers and Practical Test Prep** Books

Before pilots take their FAA pilot knowledge (written) test, they want to understand the answer to every FAA test question. Our test books are widely used because they help pilots learn and understand exactly what they need to know to do well on their FAA pilot knowledge test.

To help you and all other pilots do well on your FAA practical test(s), we have developed a new series of **Flight Maneuvers and Practical Test Prep** books (a book for each certificate and rating). An easy-to-understand, comprehensive explanation of all knowledge and skill required on your private pilot practical test is essential to you because

1. We outline and illustrate each flight maneuver you will perform during your flight training. You will know what to expect and what to do before your instructor demonstrates the maneuver. You will learn faster because you understand what to do.

2. We have included discussion of common errors made during each flight maneuver. This will help you learn from others' mistakes.

3. Each FAA practical test task is explained in terms of what your FAA-designated examiner may expect you to interpret or demonstrate. You will be thoroughly prepared to complete your practical test confidently and successfully.

4. Finally, we help you focus on gaining *practical test standard* proficiency as quickly as possible to prep you for your FAA practical (flight) test.

Flight Instructor Flight Maneuvers and Practical Test Prep will help you be prepared for the flight instructor practical test. It is also an excellent reference after you earn your certificate.

If your FBO or aviation bookstore does not have **Flight Instructor Flight Maneuvers and Practical Test Prep**, call **(800) 87-GLEIM** to order your copy today. Thank you for recommending both our **FAA Written Exam** books and **Flight Maneuvers and Practical Test Prep** books to your friends and colleagues.

CHAPTER TWO
THE LEARNING PROCESS

2.1 CHARACTERISTICS OF LEARNING (Questions 1-3)

1. Learning can be defined as a change in behavior as a result of experience.

    a. The behavior change can be physical and overt (a better glide path, for instance), or psychological and attitudinal (better motivation, more acute perceptions, insights).

2. The learning process may include any (or all) of the following elements: verbal, conceptual, perceptual, motor skills, emotional, and problem solving.

3. While learning the subject at hand, the student may be learning other useful things as well. This learning is called incidental and can have a significant impact on the student's total development.

2.2 THE PRINCIPLES OF LEARNING (Questions 4-10)

1. Educational psychology professor Edward L. Thorndike has suggested several "principles of learning" that apply to the learning process. While these principles are not absolute, they do give important insight into effective teaching.

2. The **principle of readiness** states that if a student is ready to learn, and has a strong purpose, clear objective, and well-fixed reason for learning, (s)he will make more progress than if (s)he lacks motivation. Readiness implies single-mindedness.

3. The **principle of exercise** states that those things most often repeated are best remembered or performed.

    a. The basis of the principle is to provide opportunities for a student to practice and then direct this process towards a goal.

4. The **principle of effect** relates to the emotional reaction of the learner:

    a. Learning is strengthened when accompanied by a pleasant or satisfying feeling.
    b. Learning is weakened when associated with an unpleasant feeling.

5. The **principle of primacy** states that those things learned first often create a strong, almost unshakable impression.

    a. This principle means that bad habits learned early are hard to break. Instructors must thus insist on correct performance from the outset of maneuvers.

6.   The **principle of intensity** states that a vivid, dramatic, or exciting experience teaches more than a routine or boring experience.

   a.   The principle of intensity thus implies that a student will learn more from the real thing than from a substitute.

7.   The **principle of recency** states that the things most recently learned are best remembered.

   a.   Instructors recognize the principle of recency when they determine the sequence of lectures within a course of instruction.

2.3 PERCEPTION AND INSIGHT (Questions 11-20)

1.   Perceiving involves more than the reception of stimuli from the five senses. Perceptions result when the person gives meaning to sensations being experienced.

   a.   Thus, perceptions are the basis of all learning.

2.   A person's basic need is to maintain, enhance, preserve, and perpetuate the organized self.

   a.   Thus, all perceptions are affected by this basic need.

3.   Self-concept, or self-image, has a great influence on the total perceptual process.

4.   Fear or the element of threat narrows the student's perceptual field.

   a.   The resulting anxiety may limit a person's ability to learn from perceptions.

5.   Insight occurs when associated perceptions are grouped into meaningful wholes, i.e., when one "gets the whole picture."

   a.   Evoking insights is the instructor's major responsibility.

   b.   Instruction speeds the learning process by teaching the relationship of perceptions as they occur, thus promoting the development of insights by students.

   c.   An instructor can help develop student insights by providing a safe environment in which to learn.

2.4 MEMORY (Questions 21-24)

1.   Memory is an integral part of the learning process. It includes three parts: the sensory register, the short-term or working memory, and the long-term memory.

   a.   The **sensory register** receives input from the environment and quickly processes it according to the individual's preconceived concept of what is important. This occurs on a subconscious level.

      1)   **Precoding** is the selective process by which the sensory register recognizes certain stimuli and immediately transmits them to the working memory for action.

         a)   Irrelevant stimuli are discarded by the sensory register

   b.   The **short-term memory** (or working memory) is the receptacle of the information deemed important by the sensory register.

      1)   The information may temporarily remain in the short-term memory, or it may rapidly fade.

         a)   Retention of information by the short-term memory is aided when the information is initially categorized into systematic chunks in a process known as **coding**.

         b)   Retention is also aided by repetition or rehearsal of the information (rote learning).

    2) Information remains in the short-term memory for longer periods when it can be related to an individual's previous knowledge or experiences through a process known as recoding.

        a) **Recoding** may be described as a process of relating incoming information to concepts or knowledge already in memory.

        b) Methods of recoding vary with the subject matter, but they typically involve some type of association, such as rhymes or mnemonics.

            i) The use of associations such as rhymes and mnemonics is best suited to the short-term memory.

    c. The **long-term memory** is where information is stored for future use.

        1) For the stored information to be useful, some special effort must have been expended during the recoding process.

2.5 FORGETTING AND RETENTION (Questions 25-28)

1. The following are three theories of forgetting:

    a. The **theory of disuse** states that a person forgets those things which are not used. Students are saddened by the small amount of actual data retained several years after graduation.

    b. The **theory of interference** holds that people forget because new experiences overshadow the original learning experience. In other words, new or similar subsequent events can displace facts learned previously.

    c. The **theory of repression** states that some forgetting is due to the submerging of ideas or thoughts into the subconscious mind. Unpleasant or anxiety-producing material is forgotten by the individual, although not intentionally. This is a subconscious and protective response.

2. Responses that produce a pleasurable return are called praise.

    a. Praise stimulates remembering because responses that give a pleasurable return tend to be repeated.

2.6 TRANSFER OF LEARNING (Questions 29-31)

1. The student may be either aided or hindered by things learned previously. This process is called transfer of learning.

    a. Positive transfer occurs when the learning of one maneuver aids in learning another.

        1) EXAMPLE: Flying rectangular patterns to aid in flying traffic patterns.

    b. Negative transfer occurs when a performance of a maneuver interferes with the learning of another maneuver.

        1) EXAMPLE: Trying to steer a taxiing plane with the control yoke as one drives a car.

        2) Negative transfer thus agrees with the interference theory of forgetting.

2. By making certain the student understands that what is learned can be applied to other situations, the instructor helps facilitate a positive transfer of learning.

    a. This is the basic reason for the building-block technique of instruction, in which each simple task is performed acceptably and correctly before the next learning task is introduced.

    b. The introduction of instruction in more advanced and complex operations before the initial instruction has been mastered leads to the development of poor habit patterns in the elements of performance.

2.7 LEVELS OF LEARNING (Questions 32-35)

1. Learning may be accomplished at any of four levels.

    a. The lowest level, **rote learning,** is the ability to repeat back what one has been taught without necessarily understanding or being able to apply what has been learned.

        1) EXAMPLE: Being able to cite the maneuvering speed of an airplane.

    b. At the **understanding** level, the student not only can repeat what has been taught but also comprehends the principles and theory behind the knowledge.

        1) EXAMPLE: Being able to explain how gross weight affects maneuvering speed.
        2) Being able to explain (not demonstrate) is the understanding level.

    c. At the **application** level, the student not only understands the theory but also can apply what has been learned and perform in accordance with that knowledge.

        1) This is the level of learning at which most instructors stop teaching.

    d. At the **correlation** level, the student is able to associate various learned elements with other segments or blocks of learning or accomplishment.

        1) EXAMPLE: Know what to do if, during the flight portion of the practical test, the examiner closes the throttle and announces "simulated engine failure."

2.8 DOMAINS OF LEARNING (Questions 36-41)

1. In addition to the four basic levels of learning discussed above, learning can be categorized in other ways.

2. Three **domains of learning** have been identified based on what is learned:

    a. The **cognitive domain** deals with knowledge (e.g., facts, concepts, or relationships).
    b. The **affective domain** relates to attitudes, beliefs, and values.
    c. The **psychomotor domain** concerns physical skills.

3.   Each of the domains of learning has a hierarchy of educational objectives.

    a.   A listing of the hierarchy of objectives is often referred to as a taxonomy.

        1)   A **taxonomy of educational objectives** is a systematic classification scheme for sorting possible learning outcomes into the three domains of learning and ranking them in a developmental hierarchy from least complex to most complex.

            a)   Each of the three domains of learning has several distinct learning outcomes. These outcomes are equivalent to the educational objective levels

        2)   The following are hierarchical taxonomies for the three domains of learning:

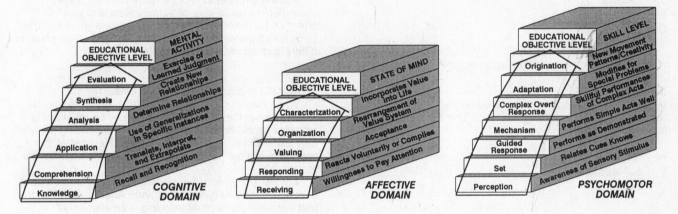

    b.   The educational objectives/learning outcomes become more complex from bottom to top.

2.9 LEARNING SKILLS AND THE LEARNING CURVE (Questions 42-43)

1.   The best way to prepare a student to perform a task is to provide a clear, step-by-step example. Students need a clear picture of what they are to do and how they are to do it.

2.   Learning typically follows a pattern which, if shown on a graph, would be called the learning curve. The first part of the curve indicates rapid early improvement. Then the curve levels off.

    a.   This normal and temporary leveling-off of an individual's learning rate is called a learning plateau.

QUESTIONS AND ANSWER EXPLANATIONS

All of the FAA questions from the Fundamentals of Instructing knowledge test relating to the learning process outlined above are reproduced on the following pages in the same modules as the outlines. To the immediate right of each question are the correct answer and answer explanation. You should cover these answers and answer explanations with your hand or a piece of paper while responding to the questions. Refer to the general discussion in Chapter 1 on how to take the FAA knowledge test.

Remember that the questions from the FAA knowledge test bank have been reordered by topic, and the topics have been organized into a meaningful sequence. Accordingly, the first line of the answer explanation gives the FAA question number and the citation of the authoritative source for the answer.

2.1 Characteristics of Learning

1.
6001. A change in behavior as a result of experience can be defined as

A— learning.
B— knowledge.
C— understanding.

Answer (A) is correct (6001). *(AIH Chap 1)*
Learning can be defined as a change in behavior as a result of experience.
Answer (B) is incorrect because knowledge is awareness as a result of experience, but not necessarily a change in behavior. Answer (C) is incorrect because understanding is only one of the four levels of learning.

2.
6002. The learning process may include some elements such as verbal, conceptual, and

A— habitual.
B— experiential.
C— problem solving.

Answer (C) is correct (6002). *(AIH Chap 1)*
The learning process involves many elements. Verbal, conceptual, perceptual, motor skill, problem solving, and emotional elements may be used at the same time.
Answer (A) is incorrect because habits are the customary or usual way of doing things and can be changed by the learning process. Answer (B) is incorrect because all learning is by experience, but it takes place in different forms in different people.

3.
6003. While learning the material being taught, students may be learning other things as well. This additional learning is called

A— residual.
B— conceptual.
C— incidental.

Answer (C) is correct (6003). *(AIH Chap 1)*
While learning the subject at hand, students may be learning other things as well. They may be developing attitudes (good or bad) about aviation depending on what they experience. This learning is called incidental, but it may have a great impact on the total development of the student.
Answer (A) is incorrect because residual is not a term used to define any type of learning. Answer (B) is incorrect because conceptual learning is an element of learning the subject at hand, not other incidental things.

2.2 The Principles of Learning

4.
6004. Individuals make more progress learning if they have a clear objective. This is one feature of the principle of

A— primacy.
B— readiness.
C— willingness.

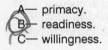

Answer (B) is correct (6004). *(AIH Chap 1)*
One feature of the principle of readiness is that when a student has a strong purpose, a clear objective, and a well-fixed reason to learn something, (s)he will make more progress than if (s)he lacks motivation.
Answer (A) is incorrect because the principle of primacy states that first experiences create a strong, almost unshakable impression. Answer (C) is incorrect because there is no principle of willingness.

5.
6007. Things most often repeated are best remembered because of which principle of learning?

A— Principle of effect.
B— Principle of recency.
C— Principle of exercise.

Answer (C) is correct (6007). *(AIH Chap 1)*
The principle of exercise states that those things most often repeated are best remembered. This is the basis of practice and drill.
Answer (A) is incorrect because the principle of effect relates to the learner's emotional reaction to the learning experience. Answer (B) is incorrect because the principle of recency states that things most recently learned are best remembered.

6.

6005. Providing opportunities for a student to practice and then directing this process towards a goal is the basis of the principle of

A— exercise.
B— learning.
C— readiness.

Answer (A) is correct (6005). *(AIH Chap 1)*
The principle of exercise states that those things most often repeated are best remembered. You must provide opportunities for your student to practice and then direct this process towards a goal.
Answer (B) is incorrect because learning is a change in behavior as a result of experience. The principle of exercise is part of the learning process. Answer (C) is incorrect because the principle of readiness states that individuals learn best when they are ready to learn, not practicing a task.

7.

6006. The principle that is based on the emotional reaction of the learner is the principle of

A— effect.
B— primacy.
C— intensity.

Answer (A) is correct (6006). *(AIH Chap 1)*
The principle of effect is the one which directly relates to the learner's emotional reaction. Pleasant experiences strengthen the learning process whereas unpleasant experiences tend to weaken it.
Answer (B) is incorrect because the principle of primacy states that a strong, almost unshakable impression is created by first experiences. Answer (C) is incorrect because the principle of intensity states that dramatic or exciting experiences teach more than routine experiences.

8.

6010. Which principle of learning often creates a strong impression?

A— Principle of primacy.
B— Principle of intensity.
C— Principle of readiness.

Answer (A) is correct (6010). *(AIH Chap 1)*
Primacy, the state of being first, often creates a strong, almost unshakable, impression. For the instructor, this means that what is taught must be right the first time. The first experience should be positive and functional, and should lay the foundation for all that is to follow.
Answer (B) is incorrect because the principle of intensity means that a student will learn more from the real thing than from a substitute. Answer (C) is incorrect because the principle of readiness means that a student must be willing and eager to learn.

9.

6008. Which principle of learning implies that a student will learn more from the real thing than from a substitute?

A— Principle of effect.
B— Principle of primacy.
C— Principle of intensity.

Answer (C) is correct (6008). *(AIH Chap 1)*
The principle of intensity states that a vivid, dramatic, or exciting learning experience teaches more than a routine or boring experience. Thus, the principle of intensity implies that a student will learn more from a real thing than from a substitute.
Answer (A) is incorrect because the principle of effect is based on the emotional reaction of the student. Thus, pleasant experiences strengthen the learning while unpleasant experiences weaken the learning. These may be experienced by learning from either the real thing or a substitute. Answer (B) is incorrect because the principle of primacy states that a strong, almost unshakable impression is created by first experiences. These experiences may be from either a real thing or a substitute.

10.

6009. Which principle of learning often determines the sequence of lectures within a course of instruction?

A— Principle of primacy.
B— Principle of recency.
C— Principle of intensity.

Answer (B) is correct (6009). *(AIH Chap 1)*
The principle of recency states that the things most recently learned are best remembered. The farther a student is removed time-wise from a new fact or under-standing, the more difficult it is to remember it. The principle of recency often determines the sequence of lectures within a course of instruction.
Answer (A) is incorrect because the principle of primacy means to the instructor that what is taught must be right the first time. Answer (C) is incorrect because the principle of intensity means that a student will learn more from the real experience than a substitute.

2.3 Perception and Insight

11.
6011. What is the basis of all learning?

A— Perception.
B— Motivation.
C— Positive self-concept.

Answer (A) is correct (6011). *(AIH Chap 1)*
Initially, all learning comes from perceptions which are directed to the brain by one or more of the five senses. Perceptions result when a person gives meaning to sensations.
Answer (B) is incorrect because motivation is the dominant force which governs a student's progress and ability to learn, not the basis for all learning. Answer (C) is incorrect because positive self-concept is a factor which affects an individual's ability to learn, not the basis of all learning.

12.
6015. Perceptions result when a person

A— gives meaning to sensations being experienced.
B— is able to discern items of useful information.
C— responds to visual cues first, then aural cues, and relates these cues to ones previously learned.

Answer (A) is correct (6015). *(AIH Chap 1)*
Perceptions occur when a person gives meaning to sensations being experienced. This is the difference between just seeing something and understanding what is seen.
Answer (B) is incorrect because a person who is able to discern items of useful information has learned, not just perceived. Answer (C) is incorrect because it describes the rote level of learning, i.e., memorization without concern for meaning.

13.
6012. A basic need that affects all of a person's perceptions is the need to

A— maintain and enhance the organized self.
B— accomplish a higher level of satisfaction.
C— avoid areas that pose a threat to success.
D

Answer (A) is correct (6012). *(AIH Chap 1)*
A person's basic need is to maintain and enhance the organized self. The self is a person's past, present, and future, and is both physical and psychological. A person's most fundamental need is to preserve and perpetuate this self. Thus, all perceptions are affected by this need.
Answer (B) is incorrect because accomplishing a higher level of satisfaction is a goal, not a basic need. Answer (C) is incorrect because avoiding areas that are a threat to success is a defense mechanism, not a basic need which affects perceptions.

14.
6014. Which factor affecting perception has a great influence on the total perceptual process?

A— Self-concept.
B— Goals and values.
C— Time and opportunity.

Answer (A) is correct (6014). *(AIH Chap 1)*
A student's self-concept (or self-image) has a great influence on the total perceptual process. Negative self-concepts inhibit the perceptual process by introducing psychological barriers which tend to keep a student from perceiving. Positive self-concepts allow the student to be less defensive and more ready to digest experiences by assimilating all of the instructions and demonstrations offered.
Answer (B) is incorrect because perceptions depend on one's goals and values in that every experience is colored by the individual's own beliefs and value structures, but they do not have a great influence on the total perceptual process. Answer (C) is incorrect because it takes time and opportunity to perceive, but it is not a great influence on the total perceptual process.

15.
6019. In the learning process, fear or the element of threat will

A— narrow the student's perceptual field.
B— decrease the rate of associative reactions.
C— cause a student to focus on several areas of perception.

Answer (A) is correct (6019). *(AIH Chap 1)*
Fear or the element of threat will impair the student's perceptual field. This is because one tends to limit attention to the threatening object or condition, rather than to what should be learned.
Answer (B) is incorrect because the element of threat causes stress and anxiety; the mind tends to race, often irrationally, thereby increasing, not decreasing, the rate of associative reactions. Answer (C) is incorrect because fear or the element of threat will cause a student to focus only on the threatening object or condition, not on several areas of perception.

16.
6143. Which is one of the ways in which anxiety will affect a student?

A— Anxiety may limit the student's ability to learn from perceptions.
B— Anxiety will speed up the learning process for the student if properly controlled and directed by the instructor.
C— Anxiety causes dispersal of the student's attention over such a wide range of matters as to interfere with normal reactions.

Answer (A) is correct (6143). *(AIH Chap 9)*
Anxiety is a state of mental uneasiness arising from fear of anything, real or imagined, which threatens the person who experiences it. Anxiety may have a potent effect on actions and on the ability to learn from perceptions.
Answer (B) is incorrect because perceptions blocked by anxiety will tend to slow, not speed up, the learning process. Answer (C) is incorrect because anxiety narrows, not disperses, a student's attention.

17.
6017. The mental grouping of affiliated perceptions is called

A— insights.
B— association.
C— conceptualization.

Answer (A) is correct (6017). *(AIH Chap 1)*
Many principles, theories, and learned tasks can be treated as pieces relating to other pieces in the overall pattern of the task to be learned. This mental relating or grouping of associated perceptions is called insight.
Answer (B) is incorrect because association is not the final, completed mental picture, although it is a necessary process to connect the affiliated perceptions. Answer (C) is incorrect because it refers only to the formation of individual ideas.

18.
6021. Insights, as applied to learning, involve a person's

A— association of learning with change.
B— grouping of associated perceptions into meaningful wholes.
C— ability to recognize the reason for learning a procedure.

Answer (B) is correct (6021). *(AIH Chap 1)*
Insights, as applied to learning, involve a person's grouping of associated perceptions into meaningful wholes. As perceptions increase in number and are grouped to become insights by the student, learning becomes more meaningful and permanent.
Answer (A) is incorrect because insights involve the grouping of perceptions into meaningful wholes, not the association of learning with change. Answer (C) is incorrect because the ability to recognize the reason for learning a procedure is a feature of the principle of readiness, not insight.

19.
6013. Instruction, as opposed to the trial and error method of learning, is desirable because competent instruction speeds the learning process by

A— motivating the student to a better performance.
B— emphasizing only the important points of training.
C— teaching the relationship of perceptions as they occur.

Answer (C) is correct (6013). *(AIH Chap 1)*
Competent instruction speeds the learning process by teaching the relationship of perceptions as they occur, thus promoting the development of insights by the student.
Answer (A) is incorrect because motivating a student to a better performance is just one element of instruction. Answer (B) is incorrect because instructors must emphasize all points of training, not just the major, important points.

20.
6020. Name one way an instructor can help develop student insights.

A— Provide a safe environment in which to learn.
B— Point out various items to avoid during the learning process.
C— Keep learning blocks small so they are easier to understand.

Answer (A) is correct (6020). *(AIH Chap 1)*
Pointing out the relationships of perceptions as they occur, providing a safe and nonthreatening environment in which to learn, and helping the student acquire and maintain a favorable self-concept are most important in fostering the development of insights.
Answer (B) is incorrect because the instructor should point out the relationships of perceptions as they occur, not point out various items to avoid during the learning process. Answer (C) is incorrect because insights develop when a student's perceptions increase in number and are assembled into larger, not smaller, blocks of learning.

2.4 Memory

21.
6039b. Which memory system processes input from the environment?

A— Working.
B— Long-term.
C— Sensory register.

Answer (C) is correct (6039b). *(AIH Chap 1)*
The sensory register receives input from the environment and quickly processes it according to the individual's preconceived concept of what is important (i.e., it recognizes certain stimuli as significant). The sensory register processes inputs or stimuli from the environment within seconds, discards what is considered extraneous, and processes what is considered by the individual to be relevant.
Answer (A) is incorrect because the working, or short-term, memory is the receptacle for the information determined to be relevant by the sensory register. Once in the short-term memory, the information may temporarily remain for immediate use, or it may fade rapidly. Answer (B) is incorrect because the long-term memory is where information is stored for future use.

22.
6039c. The use of some type of association, such as rhymes or mnemonics is best suited to which memory system?

A— Short-term.
B— Sensory.
C— Long-term.

Answer (A) is correct (6039c). *(AIH Chap 1)*
For information to remain in the short term memory for a significant amount of time, it must be categorized in some way. The information is initially grouped into systematic chunks in a process called coding. It must then be related to concepts or knowledge already in memory in a process called recoding. The use of some type of association, such as rhymes or mnemonic devices, is well suited to this task.
Answer (B) is incorrect because the sensory register detects and processes stimuli on a subconscious level. They are then discarded or transferred to the short-term memory according the individual's preconceived concept of what is important. Answer (C) is incorrect because, in order for information stored in long-term memory to be useful, some special effort must have been expended during the recoding process while the information was in short-term memory.

23.
6039d. How can recoding be described?

A— The relating of incoming information to concepts or knowledge already in memory.
B— The initial storage of information in short-term memory.
C— The selective process where the sensory register is set to recognize certain stimuli.

Answer (A) is correct (6039d). *(AIH Chap 1)*
Recoding takes place in the short-term memory, when new information is adjusted to individual experiences. Recoding may be described as a process of relating incoming information to concepts or knowledge already in memory.
Answer (B) is incorrect because the initial storage of information in short-term memory is coding, not recoding. Answer (C) is incorrect because the selective process where the sensory register is set to recognize certain stimuli is precoding, not recoding.

24.
6039e. Where is information for future use stored?

A— Short-term memory.
B— Sensory register.
C— Long-term memory.

Answer (C) is correct (6039e). *(AIH Chap 1)*
Information for future use is stored in the long-term memory.
Answer (A) is incorrect because short-term memory is where information is temporarily stored, not stored for future use, after the sensory register deems it to be significant. Answer (B) is incorrect because the sensory register processes stimuli from the environment according to the individual's preconception of what is important. Significant information is sent to the short term memory for immediate, not future, use.

2.5 Forgetting and Retention

25.
6036. When a person has difficulty recalling facts after several years, this is known as

A— disuse.
B— repression.
C— poor retention.

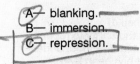

Answer (A) is correct (6036). *(AIH Chap 1)*
The theory of disuse states that a person forgets those things that are not used or, at least, not used frequently.
Answer (B) is incorrect because repression is the practice of submerging an unpleasant experience into the subconscious. Answer (C) is incorrect because poor retention results in forgetting due to disuse, interference, or repression.

26.
6035. When the learning of similar things overshadows other learning experiences, it is called

A— suppression.
B— correlation.
C— interference.

Answer (C) is correct (6035). *(AIH Chap 1)*
The theory of interference states that new or similar events can often replace previously learned facts. Most susceptible to this replacement by interference are closely similar materials and materials not well learned to begin with.
Answer (A) is incorrect because suppression is not a consideration (or theory) as to why a person forgets. Answer (B) is incorrect because correlation is the highest level of learning, which means that it is resistant to forgetting.

27.
6034. According to one theory, some forgetting is due to the practice of submerging an unpleasant experience into the subconscious. This is called

A— blanking.
B— immersion.
C— repression.

Answer (C) is correct (6034). *(AIH Chap 1)*
The theory of repression states that some forgetting is due to the submersion of ideas or thoughts into the subconscious mind. For instance, information learned during an unpleasant experience may be buried out of reach of memory.
Answer (A) is incorrect because blanking refers to a temporary inability to remember, not to a theory of forgetting. Answer (B) is incorrect because immersion is not a theory of forgetting.

28.
6037. Responses that produce a pleasurable return are called

A— reward.
B— praise.
C— positive feedback.

Answer (B) is correct (6037). *(AIH Chap 1)*
Responses which give a pleasurable return, called praise, tend to be repeated, thus stimulating and encouraging retention.
Answer (A) is incorrect because rewards are motivators, and are not usually responses (i.e., praise); that is, they are normally financial, self-interest, or public recognition. Answer (C) is incorrect because positive feedback (i.e., constructive criticism) is part of the learning, not retention, process. Positive feedback teaches a student how to capitalize on things done well and to use them to compensate for lesser accomplishments.

2.6 Transfer of Learning

29.
6039a. The performance of rectangular patterns helps a student fly traffic patterns. What type transfer of learning is this?

A— Lateral.
B— Positive.
C— Deliberate.

Answer (B) is correct (6039a). *(AIH Chap 1)*
Transfers of learning can be negative or positive. Since the learning of Task A (flying rectangular patterns) helps in the learning of Task B (flying traffic patterns), it is advantageous and, therefore, a positive transfer of learning.
Answer (A) is incorrect because there is no lateral transfer of learning, only positive or negative. Answer (C) is incorrect because there is no deliberate transfer of learning, only positive or negative.

30.
6038. Which transfer of learning occurs when the performance of a maneuver interferes with the learning of another maneuver?

A— Adverse.
B— Positive.
C— Negative.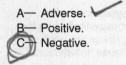

Answer (C) is correct (6038). *(AIH Chap 1)*
Transfers of learning can be negative or positive. If the learning of Task A helps in the learning of Task B, the transfer of learning is deemed to be positive. If, on the other hand, Task A interferes with Task B, the transfer is a hindrance to learning and is thus negative.
Answer (A) is incorrect because there is no adverse transfer of learning, only positive or negative. Answer (B) is incorrect because the transfer of learning is a hindrance and is thus negative.

31.
6040a. To ensure proper habits and correct techniques during training, an instructor should

A— use the building block technique of instruction.
B— repeat subject matter the student has already learned.
C— introduce challenging material to continually motivate the student.

Answer (A) is correct (6040a). *(AIH Chap 1)*
The building-block technique of teaching insists that each simple task be performed correctly before the next is introduced. This technique fosters thorough and meaningful performance and good habits, which will be carried over into future learning.
Answer (B) is incorrect because too much repetition can lead to boredom. The instructor must mix teaching methods to sustain interest and promote learning. Answer (C) is incorrect because complex or difficult tasks introduced before simpler ones are mastered can be frustrating, not motivating, for the student. This approach will not ensure proper habits; the student will likely develop bad habits from trying to perform tasks not completely understood.

2.7 Levels of Learning

32.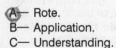
6027. What level of knowledge is being tested if asked, "What is the maneuvering speed of the aircraft listed in the owner's manual?"

A— Rote.
B— Application.
C— Understanding.

Answer (A) is correct (6027). *(AIH Chap 1)*
The lowest level, rote learning, is the ability to repeat something back that one has been taught, without understanding or being able to apply what has been learned. An example of rote learning is to be able to cite the maneuvering speed of the aircraft listed in the owner's manual.
Answer (B) is incorrect because application is the ability of a student to apply what has been taught. This is the third level of learning and is achieved after the student understands, has practiced, and can consistently perform a task. Answer (C) is incorrect because the second level of learning is understanding, which has been achieved when a student can put together a block of learning and develop an insight into the performance of a task.

33.
6028. During the flight portion of a practical test, the examiner simulates complete loss of engine power by closing the throttle and announcing "simulated engine failure." What level of learning is being tested?

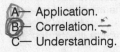

A— Application.
B— Correlation.
C— Understanding.

Answer (B) is correct (6028). *(AIH Chap 1)*
When the examiner simulates complete loss of engine power by closing the throttle and announcing "simulated engine failure," the examiner is testing at the correlation level of learning. The applicant must be able to correlate (associate) the engine failure with the requirements to perform the elements of an emergency approach and landing; i.e., establish best-glide speed, select a field, perform restart checklist, plan a flight pattern to the selected field, complete all appropriate checklists, etc.
Answer (A) is incorrect because the application level of learning is tested when the examiner closes the throttle and tells the applicant to perform an emergency approach and landing. Answer (C) is incorrect because the understanding level of learning is tested when the examiner asks the applicant to explain the elements of an emergency approach and landing.

34.
6030. At which level of learning do most instructors stop teaching?

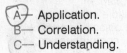

A— Application.
B— Correlation.
C— Understanding.

Answer (A) is correct (6030). *(AIH Chap 1)*
Most instructors stop teaching at the application level of learning. Discontinuing instruction on an element at this point and directing subsequent instruction exclusively to other elements is characteristic of piecemeal instruction, which is usually inefficient. It violates the building block concept of instruction by failing to apply what has been learned to future learning tasks.
Answer (B) is incorrect because correlation is the highest level of learning and should be the goal of each instructor. Instructions all too often stop at the application level. Answer (C) is incorrect because understanding is the second level of learning, and at this point, a student understands a task but may not be able to do it. Instructors will usually continue teaching to the next level, which is application.

35.
6029. When asking a student to explain how gross weight affects maneuvering speed, what level of learning is being tested?

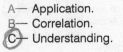

A— Application.
B— Correlation.
C— Understanding.

Answer (C) is correct (6029). *(AIH Chap 1)*
At the understanding level of learning, a student will be able to explain how gross weight affects maneuvering speed (V_A). Understanding is the next level after rote memorization and the level before acquiring the skill to apply knowledge, which is application (correlation is the fourth and highest level of learning). Being able to explain (not demonstrate) is the understanding level of learning, not the application or correlation level.
Answer (A) is incorrect because, at the application level, a student will be able to apply the knowledge that gross weight affects maneuvering speed when determining the appropriate airspeed for entering turbulent air or maneuvers that require an airspeed at or below V_A. Answer (B) is incorrect because, at the correlation level, a student has developed the ability to correlate the elements of maneuvering speed with other concepts such as gust loads, accelerated stalls, load factors, acceleration forces in the aircraft, etc.

2.8 Domains of Learning

36.
6040b. Which domain of learning deals with knowledge?

A— Affective.
B— Cognitive.
C— Psychomotor.

Answer (B) is correct (6040b). *(AIH Chap 1)*
    Domains of learning are classified based on what is to be learned. The cognitive domain of learning deals with knowledge (e.g., facts, concepts, or relationships).
    Answer (A) is incorrect because the affective domain deals with attitudes, beliefs, and values, not knowledge. Answer (C) is incorrect because the psychomotor domain deals with physical skills, not knowledge.

37.
6040c. Affective domain relates to

A— physical skills.
B— knowledge.
C— attitudes, beliefs, and values.

Answer (C) is correct (6040c). *(AIH Chap 1)*
    Domains of learning are classified based on what is to be learned. The affective domain relates to attitudes, beliefs, and values.
    Answer (A) is incorrect because the psychomotor domain, not the affective domain, relates to physical skills. Answer (B) is incorrect because the cognitive domain, not the affective domain, relates to knowledge.

38.
6040d. The educational objective levels for the cognitive domain are

A— receiving, responding, valuing, organization, and characterization.
B— perception, set, guided response mechanism, complex overt response, adaptation, and origination.
C— knowledge, comprehension, application, analysis, synthesis, and evaluation.

Answer (C) is correct (6040d). *(AIH Chap 1)*
    Each domain of learning has multiple educational objective levels. The six educational objective levels of the cognitive domain are knowledge, comprehension, application, analysis, synthesis, and evaluation.
    Answer (A) is incorrect because receiving, responding, valuing, organization, and characterization are the five educational objective levels of the affective, not cognitive, domain. Answer (B) is incorrect because perception, set, guided response mechanism, complex overt response, adaptation, and origination are the seven educational objective levels of the psychomotor, not cognitive, domain.

39.
6040e. The listing of the hierarchy of objectives is often referred to as a

A— taxonomy.
B— skill.
C— domain.

Answer (A) is correct (6040e). *(AIH Chap 1)*
    Each of the domains of learning has a hierarchy of educational objectives. The listing of the hierarchy of objectives is often called a taxonomy.
    Answer (B) is incorrect because a skill is what is learned in the psychomotor domain of learning. It is not a hierarchy of educational objectives. Answer (C) is incorrect because domains of learning contain, but are not, hierarchies of educational objectives.

40.
6040f. The most complex outcome in the affective domain is

A— organization.
B— characterization.
C— valuing.

Answer (B) is correct (6040f). *(AIH Chap 1)*
    A taxonomy of educational objectives is a systematic classification scheme for sorting learning outcomes into the three domains of learning (cognitive, affective, and psychomotor) and ranking the desired outcomes in a developmental hierarchy from least complex to most complex. The most complex learning outcome in the affective domain is characterization, in which the learner incorporates a value or attitude into his/her life.
    Answer (A) is incorrect because organization (in which the learner rearranges his/her value system to accommodate a new value or attitude) is the second-most-complex, not the most complex, learning outcome in the affective domain. Answer (C) is incorrect because valuing (in which the learner accepts a new value or attitude) is the third-most-complex, not the most complex, learning outcome in the affective domain.

41.

6040g. The least complex outcome in the psychomotor domain is

A— adaptation.
B— mechanism.
C— perception.

Answer (C) is correct (6040g). *(AIH Chap 1)*

A taxonomy of educational objectives is a systematic classification scheme for sorting learning outcomes into the three domains of learning (cognitive, affective, and psychomotor) and ranking the desired outcomes in a developmental hierarchy from least complex to most complex. The least complex learning outcome in the psychomotor domain is perception, in which the learner has awareness of sensory stimuli.

Answer (A) is incorrect because adaptation (in which the learner modifies his/her performance of a skill for special problems) is the second-most-complex, not the least complex, learning outcome in the psychomotor domain. Answer (B) is incorrect because mechanism (in which the learner performs simple acts well) is the fourth-least-complex, not the least complex, learning outcome in the psychomotor domain.

2.9 Learning Skills and the Learning Curve

42.

6031. The best way to prepare a student to perform a task is to

A— explain the purpose of the task.
B— provide a clear, step-by-step example.
C— give the student an outline of the task.

Answer (B) is correct (6031). *(AIH Chap 1)*

The best way to prepare a student to perform a task is to provide a clear, step-by-step example. Having a model to follow permits a student to get a clear picture of each step in the sequence (i.e., what it is, how to do it).

Answer (A) is incorrect because, while a student should know the purpose of a task, (s)he must be provided with a clear, step-by-step example showing how to perform the task. Answer (C) is incorrect because an outline is not as useful as a clear, step-by-step example.

43.

6033. A learning plateau may be defined as the

A— point in the learning curve at which skill proficiency retrogresses.
B— normal and temporary leveling-off of an individual's learning rate.
C— achievement of the highest possible level of competence for a particular individual.

Answer (B) is correct (6033). *(AIH Chap 1)*

A learning plateau may be defined as the normal and temporary leveling-off of an individual's learning rate. This is normal and should be expected by you and your student after an initial period of rapid improvement.

Answer (A) is incorrect because a learning plateau is a temporary leveling-off or slower rate of learning, not retrogression. Answer (C) is incorrect because a learning plateau is a temporary leveling-off of an individual's learning rate, not achievement of the highest possible level of competence.

END OF CHAPTER

CHAPTER THREE
BARRIERS TO LEARNING

3.1 SELF-CONCEPT (Questions 1-2)

1.   Self-concept is how one pictures oneself.

   a.   This is the most powerful determinant in learning.

   b.   Self-concept has a great influence on the total perceptual process.

2.   Negative self-concept contributes most to a student's failure to remain receptive to new experiences and creates a tendency to reject additional training.

3.   Thus, an instructor can foster the development of insights by helping the student acquire and maintain a favorable self-concept.

3.2 DEFENSE MECHANISMS (Questions 3-10)

1.   Certain behavior patterns are called defense mechanisms because they are subconscious defenses against the reality of unpleasant situations. People use these defenses to soften feelings of failure, alleviate feelings of guilt, and protect feelings of personal worth and adequacy.

2.   Although defense mechanisms can serve a useful purpose, they can involve some degree of self-deception and distortion of reality.

   a.   They alleviate symptoms, not causes.

3.   Common defense mechanisms:

   a.   **Rationalization** -- When a person cannot accept the real reasons for his/her own behavior, this device permits the substitution of excuses for reasons. Rationalization is a subconscious technique for justifying actions that otherwise would be unacceptable.

   b.   **Flight** -- Students escape from frustration by taking physical or mental flight.

     1)   To flee physically, students may develop symptoms or ailments that give them excuses for removing themselves from the frustration.

     2)   More frequent than physical flight is mental flight or daydreaming.

   c.   **Aggression** -- A person can avoid a frustrating situation by means of aggressive behavior. Shouting and accusing others are typical defense mechanisms. Social pressure usually forces student aggressiveness into more subtle forms. Typically, students may

     1)   Ask irrelevant questions,
     2)   Refuse to participate in class activities, or
     3)   Disrupt activities.

   d.   **Resignation** -- Students become so frustrated that they lose interest and give up.

     1)   They may no longer believe it profitable or even possible to work further.

     2)   Resignation usually occurs when the student has completed early lessons without grasping the fundamentals and then becomes bewildered and lost in the advanced phase.

3.3 STRESS AND ANXIETY (Questions 11-14)

1. Normal individuals react to stress by responding rapidly and exactly, often automatically, within their experience and training.

    a. This underlines the need for proper training prior to emergency situations.

    b. The effective individual thinks rapidly, acts rapidly, and is extremely sensitive to his/her surroundings.

2. Some abnormal reactions to stress include:

    a. Inappropriate reactions such as extreme overcooperation, painstaking self-control, inappropriate laughter or singing, and very rapid changes in emotion.

    b. Marked changes in mood (e.g., high spirits followed by deep depression).

    c. Severe, unreasonable anger toward the flight instructor, service personnel, or others.

3. Anxiety is probably the most significant psychological barrier affecting flight instruction. It is the extreme worry brought on by stressful situations (e.g., an emergency, an exam, etc.). Anxiety can be countered by

    a. Treating fears as a normal reaction rather than ignoring them,
    b. Reinforcing the student's enjoyment of flying, and
    c. Teaching students to cope with fears.

3.4 THE OVERCONFIDENT OR IMPATIENT STUDENT (Questions 15-18)

1. Impatience is a greater deterrent to learning pilot skills than is generally recognized.

    a. The impatient student fails to understand the need for preliminary training. (S)he seeks only the final objective without considering the means necessary to reach it.

    b. Impatience can be corrected by the instructor by presenting the necessary preliminary training one step at a time, with clearly stated goals for each step.

2. Because they make few mistakes, apt students may assume that the correction of those errors is unimportant.

    a. This overconfidence soon results in faulty performance.

    b. For apt students a good instructor will constantly raise the standard of performance for each lesson, demanding greater effort.

QUESTIONS AND ANSWER EXPLANATIONS

All of the FAA questions from the Fundamentals of Instructing knowledge test relating to the barriers to learning material outlined above are reproduced on the following pages in the same modules as the outlines. To the immediate right of each question are the correct answer and answer explanation. You should cover these answers and answer explanations with your hand or a piece of paper while responding to the questions. Refer to the general discussion in Chapter 1 on how to take the FAA pilot knowledge test.

Remember that the questions from the FAA pilot knowledge test bank have been reordered by topic, and the topics have been organized into a meaningful sequence. Accordingly, the first line of the answer explanation gives the FAA question number and the citation of the authoritative source for the answer.

3.1 Self-Concept

1.
6016. The factor which contributes most to a student's failure to remain receptive to new experiences and which creates a tendency to reject additional training is

A— basic needs.
B— element of threat.
C— negative self-concept.

Answer (C) is correct (6016). (AIH Chap 1)
A student with a negative self-concept is resistant to new experiences and may reject additional training. People tend to avoid experiences which contradict their self-concept.
Answer (A) is incorrect because a student's basic needs can be used by the instructor to promote learning. For instance, personal safety is one of the most important basic needs, and aviation training heavily emphasizes this need. Answer (B) is incorrect because an element of threat will cause a student to limit his/her attention to the threatening object or condition. Once this is removed, the student will be able to learn.

2.
6018. An instructor may foster the development of insights by

A— helping the student acquire and maintain a favorable self-concept.
B— pointing out the attractive features of the activity to be learned.
C— keeping the rate of learning consistent so that it is predictable.

Answer (A) is correct (6018). (AIH Chap 1)
Especially in a field such as aviation training, the instructor can foster the development of insights by helping the student acquire and maintain a favorable self-concept. The student who feels sure of his/her knowledge, skills, and judgments learned in class will also feel better about actual performance and his/her own ability to fly.
Answer (B) is incorrect because the attractive features in a learning situation tend to increase motivation rather than insight. Answer (C) is incorrect because learning rates will vary, not stay constant, with each training lesson.

3.2 Defense Mechanisms

3.
6045. Although defense mechanisms can serve a useful purpose, they can

A— provide feelings of adequacy.
B— alleviate the cause of problems.
C— involve some degree of self-deception and distortion of reality.

Answer (C) is correct (6045). (AIH Chap 2)
Although defense mechanisms can serve a useful purpose, they can also be hindrances. Because they involve some self-deception and distortion of reality, defense mechanisms do not solve problems.
Answer (A) is incorrect because defense mechanisms mask and protect feelings of adequacy rather than provide them. Answer (B) is incorrect because defense mechanisms alleviate symptoms, not causes, of problems.

4.
6044. When a student uses excuses to justify inadequate performance, it is an indication of the defense mechanism known as

A— flight.
B— aggression.
C— rationalization.

Answer (C) is correct (6044). (AIH Chap 2)
Rationalization is a subconscious technique for justifying unacceptable actions or performance. This allows a student to substitute excuses for reasons, and to make those excuses plausible and acceptable to themselves.
Answer (A) is incorrect because flight is the defense mechanism in which the student escapes (either physically or mentally) from a frustrating experience. Answer (B) is incorrect because aggression is the defense mechanism in which the student uses aggressive behavior to deal with feelings of frustration.

5.

6047. Taking physical or mental flight is a defense mechanism students use when they

A— want to escape from frustrating situations. ✓
B— cannot accept the real reasons for their behavior.
C— lose interest during the advanced stages of training.

Answer (A) is correct (6047). *(AIH Chap 2)*
    The defense mechanism of flight allows a student to escape from a frustrating situation. This escape can be physical flight (absenteeism, illness, etc.) or mental flight (daydreaming).
    Answer (B) is incorrect because, if a student cannot accept the real reasons for his/her behavior, (s)he may rationalize, not take flight. Answer (C) is incorrect because a student who loses interest during the advanced stages of training may resign, not take flight, and give up. This is common if a student has not understood the fundamentals.

6.

6048. When students subconsciously use the defense mechanism called rationalization, they

A— use excuses to justify acceptable behavior.
B— cannot accept the real reasons for their behavior.
C— develop symptoms that give them excuses for removing themselves from frustration.

Answer (B) is correct (6048). *(AIH Chap 2)*
    Rationalization is a subconscious technique for justifying unacceptable actions or performance. This allows a student to substitute excuses for reasons, and to make those excuses plausible and acceptable to themselves.
    Answer (A) is incorrect because, in rationalization, excuses are used to justify unacceptable, not acceptable, behavior. Answer (C) is incorrect because, when students develop symptoms that give them excuses for removing themselves from frustration, they are using the defense mechanism of physical flight.

7.

6050. When a student engages in daydreaming, it is the defense mechanism of

A— flight.
B— fantasy.
C— avoidance.

Answer (A) is correct (6050). *(AIH Chap 2)*
    A student engaging in daydreaming is an example of flight or mental escape.
    Answer (B) is incorrect because fantasy is not a defense mechanism in and of itself, yet it is involved in the defense mechanism of flight: fantasy in mental flight (daydreaming). Answer (C) is incorrect because avoidance is not a defense mechanism in and of itself, yet it is involved in the defense mechanism of flight: avoidance in physical flight.

8.

6049. When students display the defense mechanism called aggression, they

A— become visibly angry, upset, and childish.
B— may refuse to participate in class activities.
C— attempt to justify actions by asking numerous questions.

Answer (B) is correct (6049). *(AIH Chap 2)*
    Examples of subtle aggression include students who ask irrelevant questions, refuse to participate in class activities, or disrupt activities within the group. Aggressive behavior is used to avoid facing failure.
    Answer (A) is incorrect because, although such behavior is characteristic of aggression, it is relatively uncommon in a classroom due to social pressure. Student aggressiveness is usually more subtle in nature and will thus be expressed less obviously. Answer (C) is incorrect because attempting to justify actions is an example of rationalization.

9.

6046. When a student asks irrelevant questions or refuses to participate in class activities, it usually is an indication of the defense mechanism known as

A— flight.
B— aggression.
C— resignation.

Answer (B) is correct (6046). *(AIH Chap 2)*
    Examples of subtle aggression include students who ask irrelevant questions, refuse to participate in class activities, or disrupt activities within the group. Aggressive behavior is used to avoid facing failure.
    Answer (A) is incorrect because flight is the defense mechanism when a person removes him/herself, physically or mentally, from a frustrating situation. Answer (C) is incorrect because resignation is a process of becoming frustrated and not believing that continuing will be worthwhile, i.e., the person is resigned to failure and gives up.

10.
6051. When a student becomes bewildered and lost in the advanced phase of training after completing the early phase without grasping the fundamentals, the defense mechanism is usually in the form of

A— submission.
B— resignation.
C— rationalization.

3.3 Stress and Anxiety

11.
6130. When under stress, normal individuals usually react

A— by showing excellent morale followed by deep depression.
B— by responding rapidly and exactly, often automatically, within the limits of their experience and training.
C— inappropriately such as extreme overcooperation, painstaking self-control, and inappropriate laughing or singing.

12.
6133. Which would most likely be an indication that a student is reacting abnormally to stress?

A— Slow learning.
B— Inappropriate laughter or singing.
C— Automatic response to a given situation.

13.
6131. One possible indication of a student's abnormal reaction to stress would be

A— a hesitancy to act.
B— extreme overcooperation.
C— a noticeable lack of self-control.

14.
6132. The instructor can counteract anxiety in a student by

A— treating the student's fears as a normal reaction.
B— discontinuing instruction in tasks that cause anxiety.
C— allowing the student to decide when he/she is ready for a new maneuver to be introduced.

Answer (B) is correct (6051). *(AIH Chap 2)*
When a student has become frustrated, lost interest, given up, and no longer believes it profitable or possible to work further, resignation has taken place. A student in this frame of mind accepts defeat. Typically, such a student has not grasped the fundamentals and is bewildered by later lessons.
Answer (A) is incorrect because submission is not a defense mechanism, but may be characteristic of resignation. Answer (C) is incorrect because rationalization is a process of making excuses for unacceptable behavior.

Answer (B) is correct (6130). *(AIH Chap 2)*
When under stress, normal individuals begin to respond rapidly and exactly, within the limits of their experience and training. Many responses are automatic, which indicates the need for proper training in emergency operations prior to an actual emergency.
Answer (A) is incorrect because marked changes in mood, e.g., excellent morale followed by deep depression is an abnormal, not a normal, reaction to stress. Answer (C) is incorrect because inappropriate reactions such as extreme overcooperation, painstaking self-control, and inappropriate laughter or singing are abnormal, not normal, reactions to stress.

Answer (B) is correct (6133). *(AIH Chap 2)*
Inappropriate laughter or singing is an abnormal reaction to stress. The instructor should be alert for other inappropriate (and possibly dangerous) reactions.
Answer (A) is incorrect because slow learning is a normal, not an abnormal, reaction to stress. Answer (C) is incorrect because automatic response to a given situation is a normal, not an abnormal, reaction to stress.

Answer (B) is correct (6131). *(AIH Chap 2)*
Extreme overcooperation is an indication that a student is reacting abnormally to stress. The abnormally tense or anxious student may be noticeably over-agreeable.
Answer (A) is incorrect because a hesitancy to act is an indication of anxiety, not an abnormal reaction to stress. Answer (C) is incorrect because painstaking self-control, not a lack thereof, is an indication of an abnormal reaction to stress.

Answer (A) is correct (6132). *(AIH Chap 2)*
Psychologists tell us that a student's fear is a normal reaction and should be treated as such by an instructor. Treating fear as normal will help in counteracting anxiety.
Answer (B) is incorrect because discontinuing instruction in stressful tasks will not help the student to overcome the anxiety. Perhaps a different approach to the task is necessary. Answer (C) is incorrect because it describes an example of negative motivation which would tend to contribute to the student's anxiety.

3.4 The Overconfident or Impatient Student

15.

6140. Which obstacle to learning is a greater deterrent to learning pilot skills than is generally recognized?

A— Anxiety.
B— Impatience.
C— Physical discomfort.

Answer (B) is correct (6140). (AIH Chap 9)
Failing to understand the need for preliminary training, the impatient student can only see the ultimate objective of flying an airplane. (S)he may desire to make an early solo or cross-country flight before certain basic elements of flight have been learned. This impatience can be detrimental to the usual, careful acquisition of pilot skills.
Answer (A) is incorrect because, although anxiety may be detrimental to the learning process, it is generally recognized as such, whereas impatience has an equal effect and is not widely recognized. Answer (C) is incorrect because, although physical discomfort may be detrimental to the learning process, it is generally recognized as such, whereas impatience has an equal effect and is not widely recognized.

16.

6139. Students who grow impatient when learning the basic elements of a task are those who

A— are less easily discouraged than the unaggressive students.
B— should have the preliminary training presented one step at a time with clearly stated goals for each step.
C— should be advanced to the next higher level of learning and not held back by insisting that the immediate goal be reached before they proceed to the next level.

Answer (B) is correct (6139). (AIH Chap 9)
Impatient students fail to see why they must learn one step thoroughly before they move to the next. Presenting the preliminary training with clearly stated goals for each step will minimize student impatience.
Answer (A) is incorrect because impatient students are often aggressive and more easily discouraged than unaggressive students. Answer (C) is incorrect because it is necessary to hold a student until (s)he masters the basics if the whole task is to be performed competently and safely. This is the basis of the building block technique of instruction.

17.

6126. What should an instructor do with a student who assumes that correction of errors is unimportant?

A— Divide complex flight maneuvers into elements.
B— Try to reduce the student's overconfidence to reduce the chance of an accident.
C— Raise the standard of performance for each lesson, demanding greater effort.

Answer (C) is correct (6126). (AIH Chap 8)
Because apt students make few mistakes, they may assume that the correction of errors is not important. Such overconfidence soon results in faulty performance. For such students, a good instructor will constantly raise the standard of performance for each lesson, demanding greater effort.
Answer (A) is incorrect because dividing complex tasks into simpler elements should be done with students whose slow progress is due to a lack of confidence, not apt students. Answer (B) is incorrect because reducing students' overconfidence would be inefficient for properly motivating the apt student. After realizing the impatience of such students comes only from improperly paced instruction, instructors should give them challenges fitting their abilities.

18.

6125. Faulty performance due to student overconfidence should be corrected by

A— increasing the standard of performance for each lesson.
B— praising the student only when the performance is perfect.
C— providing strong, negative evaluation at the end of each lesson.

Answer (A) is correct (6125). (AIH Chap 8)
Because apt students make few mistakes, they may assume that the correction of errors is not important. Such overconfidence soon results in faulty performance. For such students, a good instructor will constantly raise the standard of performance for each lesson, demanding greater effort.
Answer (B) is incorrect because students need consistent, fair critique of every performance, perfect or not. Overly high standards also frustrate students by making them work too hard without reward (and for an unrealistic goal). Answer (C) is incorrect because the principle of effect states that learning is weakened when associated with an unpleasant feeling. Aside from being unfair, the continual negative evaluations will also increasingly frustrate students.

END OF CHAPTER

CHAPTER FOUR
HUMAN BEHAVIOR AND EFFECTIVE COMMUNICATION

4.1 HUMAN NEEDS (Questions 1-3)

1. Human needs can be organized into a series of levels. The "pyramid of human needs" has been suggested by Abraham Maslow. For instance, physical needs must be satisfied before so-called "higher" needs can be used as motivators. He suggests that needs must be satisfied in the following ascending order:

    a. **Physical needs** pertain to food, rest, exercise, sex, etc. Until these needs are satisfied to a reasonable degree, a student cannot concentrate on learning.

    b. **Safety needs** include shelter and protection against danger, threat, and deprivation.

    c. **Social needs** are the needs to belong and to associate with other people.

    d. **Egoistic needs** will usually have a direct influence on the student-instructor relationship. Egoistic needs are of two kinds:

        1) Relating to one's self-esteem: needs for self-confidence, independence, achievement, and knowledge.

        2) Relating to one's reputation: needs for status, appreciation, and the deserved respect of one's fellow beings.

    e. **Self-fulfillment needs** are at the top of the hierarchy of human needs. These are the needs for realizing one's own potentialities, for continued development, and for being creative.

        1) This need of a student should offer the greatest challenge to an instructor.

        2) Helping students realize self-fulfillment is perhaps the most worthwhile accomplishment an instructor can achieve.

4.2 MOTIVATION (Questions 4-11)

1. Motivation is probably the dominant force governing the student's progress and ability to learn.

    a. Slumps in learning very often go hand-in-hand with slumps in motivation.

2. Positive motivations are provided by the promise or achievement of rewards.

3. Negative motivations are those which cause a student to react with fear and anxiety.

    a. Negative motivations in the form of reproof and threats should be avoided with all but the most overconfident and impulsive students.

4. It is important for an instructor to make the student aware that a particular lesson can help him/her reach an important goal.

    a. When students are unable to see the benefits or purpose of a lesson, they will be less motivated.

    b. Confusion, disinterest, and uneasiness on the part of the student could happen as a result of not knowing the objective of each period of instruction.

5. Motivations may be

    a. Positive or negative,
    b. Tangible or intangible,
    c. Obvious or subtle and difficult to identify.

6. Students are like any worker in wanting tangible returns for his/her efforts. If such motivation is to be effective, students must believe that their efforts will be suitably rewarded. Instructors should remember always to tailor individual lessons to the objective.

7. An instructor can most effectively maintain a high level of student motivation by making each lesson a pleasurable experience.

4.3 EFFECTIVE COMMUNICATION (Questions 12-17)

1. The process of communication is composed of three dynamically interrelated elements:

    a. A source (instructor)
    b. The symbols used in composing and transmitting the message (e.g., words)
    c. The receiver (student)

2. Communication takes place when one person transmits ideas or feelings to another person or to a group of people.

    a. The effectiveness of communication is measured by the similarity between the idea transmitted and the idea received.

    b. Effective communication has taken place when, and only when, the receivers react with understanding and change their behavior accordingly.

    c. Instruction has taken place when a procedure has been explained and the desired student response has occurred.

3. The effectiveness of persons acting in the role of communicators is related to at least three basic factors.

    a. First, their ability to select symbols that are meaningful to the listener.

    b. Second, communicators consciously or unconsciously reveal attitudes toward themselves, toward the ideas they are trying to transmit, and toward their receivers.

        1) Thus, to communicate effectively, instructors must reveal a positive attitude while delivering their message.

    c. Third, to be more likely to communicate effectively, communicators should speak or write from a broad background of accurate, up-to-date, stimulating material.

4. To understand the process of communication, at least three characteristics of receivers must be understood.

    a. First, they exercise their ability to question and comprehend the ideas that have been transmitted.

  b. Second, the receiver's attitude may be one of resistance, willingness, or of passive neutrality. Communicators must gain the receiver's attention and then retain it.

  1) The communicator will be more successful in this area by using a varied communicative approach.

  c. Third, the receiver's background, experience, and education frame the target at which communicators must aim.

4.4 BARRIERS TO EFFECTIVE COMMUNICATION (Questions 18-21)

1. Probably the greatest single barrier to effective communication is the lack of a common core of experience between communicator and receiver.

  a. A communicator's words cannot communicate the desired meaning to another person unless the listener or reader has had some experience with the objects or concepts to which these words refer.

2. Overuse of abstractions should be avoided.

  a. Concrete words refer to objects that human beings can experience directly.

  b. Abstract words stand for ideas that cannot be directly experienced or things that do not call forth specific mental images.

  1) Abstractions thus serve as shorthand symbols that sum up large areas of experience.

  c. The danger with using abstract words is that they may not evoke in the listener's mind the specific items of experience the communicator intends.

  d. By using concrete words, the communicator narrows (and gains better control of) the image produced in the minds of the listeners and readers.

4.5 INSTRUCTOR RESPONSIBILITIES (Questions 22-27)

1. Evaluation of demonstrated ability during flight instruction must be based upon established standards of performance, suitably modified to apply to the student's experience and stage of development as a pilot.

  a. In evaluating student demonstrations of piloting ability, it is important for the flight instructor to keep the student informed of his/her progress.

  1) This may be done as each procedure/maneuver is completed, or summarized during post-flight critiques.

2. Flight instructors have the responsibility and authority to make logbook endorsements for student pilots and other pilots.

  a. Examples of all common endorsements can be found in the current issue of AC 61-65, Appendix 1.

3. Flight instructors have a particular responsibility to provide guidance and restraint regarding the solo operations of their students.

  a. Before receiving an instructor endorsement for solo flight, a student should be required to demonstrate the consistent ability to perform all of the fundamental maneuvers.

  b. The student should also be capable of handling ordinary problems that might occur, such as traffic pattern congestion, a change in the active runway, or unexpected crosswinds.

4.6 INSTRUCTOR PROFESSIONALISM (Questions 28-33)

1. Although the term professionalism is widely used, it is rarely defined. In fact, no single definition can encompass all of the qualifications and considerations of true professionalism. The following are some of the major considerations.

2. Professionals must be able to reason logically and accurately.

3. Professionalism requires good decision-making ability.

    a. Professionals cannot limit their actions and decisions to standard patterns and practice.

4. Professionalism demands a code of ethics.

5. The professional flight instructor should be straightforward and honest.

    a. Anything less than a sincere performance is quickly detected and immediately destroys instructor effectiveness.

    b. Student confidence tends to be destroyed if instructors bluff when in doubt about some point.

    c. The well-prepared instructor instills not only confidence but good habits, since preparing well for a flight is a basic requirement for safe flying. Students quickly become apathetic when they recognize that the flight instructor is inadequately prepared.

6. The attitude, movements, and general demeanor of the flight instructor contribute a great deal to his/her professional image.

    a. The instructor should avoid erratic movements, distracting speech habits, and capricious changes in mood. The professional image requires development of a calm, thoughtful, and disciplined, but not somber, demeanor.

7. The professional relationship between the instructor and the student should be based on a mutual acknowledgment that both the student and the instructor are important to each other and that both are working toward the same objective.

    a. Accepting lower-than-normal standards to please a student will **NOT** help the student/instructor relationship.

    b. Reasonable standards strictly enforced are not resented by an earnest student.

8. The professional flight instructor should accept students as they are with all of their faults and problems.

    a. However, (s)he should also build student self-confidence, set challenges, and generally create an atmosphere for learning.

9. A flight instructor who is not completely familiar with current pilot certification and rating requirements cannot do a competent job of flight instruction.

    a. For a professional performance as a flight instructor, it is essential that the instructor maintain current copies of:

        1) The *Federal Aviation Regulations*, especially Parts 1, 61, and 91.
        2) An *Airman's Information Manual*,
        3) *Practical Test Standards*, and
        4) Appropriate pilot training manuals.

    b. True performance as a professional is based on study and research.

10. Flight instructors fail to provide competent instruction when they permit students to partially learn an important item of knowledge or skill.

    a. More importantly, such deficiencies may in themselves allow hazardous inadequacies to develop in the student's ongoing piloting performance.

11. Aviation instructors should be constantly alert for ways to improve the services they provide to their students, their effectiveness, and their qualifications.

4.1 Human Needs

1.
6041. Before a student can concentrate on learning, which human needs must be satisfied?

A— Safety.
B— Physical.
C— Security.

Answer (B) is correct (6041). *(AIH Chap 2)*
Physical needs are the most basic of the human needs. Thus, they must be met before any learning can take place. Until the needs of food, water, rest, etc., are satisfied, the student cannot concentrate on learning.
Answer (A) is incorrect because physical, not safety, needs must be satisfied before a student can concentrate on learning. Safety needs are protection from danger, threat, and deprivation. Answer (C) is incorrect because physical, not security, needs must be satisfied before a student can concentrate on learning. Security (or safety) needs are protection from danger, threat, and deprivation.

2.
6042. After individuals are physically comfortable and have no fear for their safety, which human needs become the prime influence on their behavior?

A— Social.
B— Physical.
C— Egoistic.

Answer (A) is correct (6042). *(AIH Chap 2)*
The order of human needs according to Abraham Maslow are (1) physical, (2) safety, (3) social, (4) egoistic, and (5) self-fulfillment. In this hierarchy, social needs come after physical and safety needs are satisfied.
Answer (B) is incorrect because the question states that the individuals are physically comfortable. Answer (C) is incorrect because egoistic needs have the fourth priority, not the third priority as the question asks.

3.
6043. Which of the student's human needs offer the greatest challenge to an instructor?

A— Social.
B— Egoistic.
C— Self-fulfillment.

Answer (C) is correct (6043). *(AIH Chap 2)*
The greatest challenge for an instructor is to help the student realize his/her potentialities for continued development. This is helping the student meet the need for self-fulfillment.
Answer (A) is incorrect because social needs are not a challenge to the instructor. Social needs are those to belong and to give and receive friendship, which the student must satisfy on his/her own. Answer (B) is incorrect because, although making a student feel self-confident and deserving of respect (egoism) is important and usually has a direct influence on the instructor-student relationship, it is not the instructor's greatest challenge.

4.2 Motivation

4.
6025. Which is generally the more effective way for an instructor to properly motivate students?

A— Maintain pleasant personal relationships with students.
B— Provide positive motivations by the promise or achievement of rewards.
C— Reinforce their self-confidence by requiring no tasks beyond their ability to perform.

Answer (B) is correct (6025). *(AIH Chap 1)*
Providing positive motivation is generally considered the most effective way to properly motivate people. Positive motivations are provided by the promise or achievement of rewards.
Answer (A) is incorrect because maintaining pleasant personal relationships with students (while desirable) is not the more effective way for an instructor to properly motivate students. Answer (C) is incorrect because a student who is not required to perform a task beyond present abilities will neither be motivated nor make any progress.

5.
6023. Motivations that cause a student to react with fear and anxiety are

A— tangible.
B— negative.
C— difficult to identify.

Answer (B) is correct (6023). *(AIH Chap 1)*
Negative motivations may produce fears and may thus be seen by the student as threats. Negative motivation generally intimidates students and should be avoided.
Answer (A) is incorrect because motivations, whether tangible or intangible, can be either positive or negative. Answer (C) is incorrect because motivations, whether very subtle or difficult to identify, can be either positive or negative.

6.
6026. Motivations in the form of reproof and threats should be avoided with all but the student who is

A— overconfident and impulsive.
B— avidly seeking group approval.
C— experiencing a learning plateau.

Answer (A) is correct (6026). *(AIH Chap 1)*
Educational experts have shown that negative motivation is useful only for a student who is overconfident and impulsive. Otherwise, negative motivation in the form of reproof and threats tends to discourage student behavior.
Answer (B) is incorrect because group approval is a strong motivating force. Use of reproofs and threats with a student seeking group approval would only alienate him/her from the group. Answer (C) is incorrect because one of the reasons a student has reached a learning plateau is due to a lack of motivation. Use of reproofs and threats would only cause a student to remain at the plateau longer.

7.
6053. When students are unable to see the benefits or purpose of a lesson, they will

A— be less motivated.
B— not learn as quickly.
C— be expected to increase their efforts.

Answer (A) is correct (6053). *(AIH Chap 1)*
Students will be less motivated if they are unable to see the benefits or purpose of a lesson. It is important for the instructor to make the student aware that a particular lesson can help him/her reach an important goal.
Answer (B) is incorrect because, while a student may not learn as quickly when (s)he is unable to see the benefits or purpose of a lesson, (s)he will become less motivated. Answer (C) is incorrect because the frustration of working without a known goal will likely decrease, not increase, their efforts.

8.
6124b. Confusion, disinterest, and uneasiness on the part of the student could happen as a result of not knowing the

A— importance of each period of instruction.
B— objective of each period of instruction.
C— subject of each period of instruction.

Answer (B) is correct (6124b). *(AIH Chap 8)*
Knowing the objective of each period of instruction gives meaning and interest to the student as well as the instructor. Not knowing the objective of the lesson often leads to confusion, disinterest, and uneasiness on the part of the student.
Answer (A) is incorrect because confusion, disinterest, and uneasiness on the part of the student could happen as a result of not knowing the objective of each period of instruction, not its importance. Answer (C) is incorrect because confusion, disinterest, and uneasiness on the part of the student could happen as a result of not knowing the objective of each period of instruction, not its subject. The subject of the instructional period will be obvious if it has been planned appropriately.

9.
6022. Which statement is true concerning motivations?

A— Motivations must be tangible to be effective.
B— Motivations may be very subtle and difficult to identify.
C— Negative motivations often are as effective as positive motivations.

Answer (B) is correct (6022). *(AIH Chap 1)*
Motivations may be subtle, subconscious, and difficult to identify. A student may be motivated without even being aware (s)he is being influenced.
Answer (A) is incorrect because intangible motivations can be as effective (or even more effective) than tangible motivations. Rewards such as accomplishment, fame, and peer acceptance are intangible, but they are among the best positive motivators. Answer (C) is incorrect because negative motivation tends to discourage the student.

10.
6024. For a motivation to be effective, students must believe their efforts will be rewarded in a definite manner. This type of motivation is

A— subtle.
B— negative.
C— tangible.

Answer (C) is correct (6024). *(AIH Chap 1)*
Students, like any worker, need and want tangible returns for their efforts. These rewards must be constantly apparent to the student during instruction.
Answer (A) is incorrect because the student is often unaware of the application of subtle motivation and thus feels unrewarded for his/her effort. Answer (B) is incorrect because negative motivations are not as effective as positive motivations, as they tend to intimidate students and cause unpleasant experiences.

11.
6124a. An instructor can most effectively maintain a high level of student motivation by

A— making each lesson a pleasurable experience.
B— relaxing the standards of performance required during the early phase of training.
C— continually challenging the student to meet the highest objectives of training that can be established.

Answer (A) is correct (6124a). *(AIH Chap 1)*
An instructor can most effectively maintain a high level of motivation by making each lesson a pleasant experience for a student. People avoid negative experiences, but they will seek out and want to repeat positive experiences.
Answer (B) is incorrect because relaxing the standards of performance required during the early phase of training may actually reduce a student's motivation. Reasonable standards strictly enforced are not resented by an earnest student. Answer (C) is incorrect because performance standards should be set to the student's potential and not his/her current ability or to unrealistically high objectives. Improvement must be fostered.

4.3 Effective Communication

12.
6056. The effectiveness of communication between instructor and student is measured by the

A— degree of dynamic, interrelated elements.
B— similarity between the idea transmitted and the idea received.
C— relationship between communicative and dynamic elements.

Answer (B) is correct (6056). *(AIH Chap 3)*
Communication takes place when one person transmits ideas or feelings to another person or group of people. Its effectiveness is measured by the similarity between the idea transmitted and the idea received.
Answer (A) is incorrect because the process, not the effectiveness, of communication is composed of three dynamic, interrelated elements -- the source, the symbols, and the receiver. Answer (C) is incorrect because the relationship between the communicative elements (source, symbols, and receiver) is dynamic. There are no dynamic elements.

13.
6059. Effective communication has taken place when, and only when, the

A— information is transmitted and received.
B— receivers react with understanding and change their behavior accordingly.
C— receivers have the ability to question and comprehend ideas that have been transmitted.

Answer (B) is correct (6059). *(AIH Chap 3)*
The rule of thumb among communicators is that communication succeeds only in relation to the reaction of the receiver. Effective communication has taken place only when the receivers react with understanding and change their behavior.
Answer (A) is incorrect because information may be transmitted and received without effective communication. Only when the receiver reacts to the information being transmitted and received with understanding, and changes his/her behavior accordingly, has effective communication taken place. Answer (C) is incorrect because the ability to question and comprehend ideas that have been transmitted is only one characteristic of a receiver.

14.
6039f. When has instruction taken place?

A— When a procedure has been explained, and the desired student response has occurred.✓
B— When the student hears what is presented.
C— When all the required material has been presented.

Answer (A) is correct (6039f). *(AIH Chap 3)*
Instruction has taken place when the instructor has explained a particular procedure and subsequently determined that the desired student response has occurred.
Answer (B) is incorrect because instruction has taken place when the instructor has explained a particular procedure and subsequently determined that the desired student response has occurred, not only when the student hears what is presented. Answer (C) is incorrect because instruction has taken place when the instructor has explained a particular procedure and subsequently determined that the desired student response has occurred, not only when all the required material has been presented.

15.
6058. To communicate effectively, instructors must

A— recognize the level of comprehension.
B— provide an atmosphere which encourages questioning.
C— reveal a positive attitude while delivering their message.

Answer (C) is correct (6058). *(AIH Chap 3)*
Communicators consciously or unconsciously reveal attitudes toward themselves, the ideas they are trying to transmit, and their receivers. These attitudes must be positive if the communicators are to communicate effectively.
Answer (A) is incorrect because an instructor can recognize the level of a student's comprehension in the application step of the teaching process, not during the communication process. Answer (B) is incorrect because, while an instructor should provide an atmosphere which encourages questioning, the student must exercise his/her ability to ask questions to communicate effectively.

16.
6057. To be more likely to communicate effectively, an instructor should speak or write from a background of

A— technical expertise.
B— knowing the ideas presented.
C— up-to-date, stimulating material.

Answer (C) is correct (6057). *(AIH Chap 3)*
A basic factor of a communicator's effectiveness is the ability to speak or write from a broad background of accurate, up-to-date, and stimulating material.
Answer (A) is incorrect because a speaker or writer with technical expertise may depend on technical jargon. Reliance on technical language can impede effective communication, especially when the receiver lacks a similar background. Answer (B) is incorrect because just knowing the ideas presented does not ensure that effective communication will take place. A communicator must be able to make the receiver react with understanding and change his/her behavior accordingly.

17.
6060. In the communication process, the communicator will be more successful in gaining and retaining the receiver's attention by

A— being friendly and informative.
B— using a varied communicative approach.
C— using a variety of audiovisual aids in class.

Answer (B) is correct (6060). *(AIH Chap 3)*
The most successful communicator will use the variety of channels that best communicates the necessary ideas and techniques, i.e., a varied communicative approach.
Answer (A) is incorrect because effective, engaging communication is more complex than merely being friendly. The source, the symbols, and the receiver are all interrelated in the communication process. Answer (C) is incorrect because audio-visual aids can often further the learning, not the communication, process by supporting, supplementing, or reinforcing important ideas. By presenting the material in a new manner, instructional aids can even improve communication between instructor and student.

4.4 Barriers to Effective Communication

18.
6063. Probably the greatest single barrier to effective communication in the teaching process is a lack of

A— respect for the instructor.
B— personality harmony between instructor and student.
C— a common experience level between instructor and student.

19.
6064. A communicator's words cannot communicate the desired meaning to another person unless the

A— words have meaningful referents.
B— words give the meaning that is in the mind of the receiver.
C— listener or reader has had some experience with the objects or concepts to which these words refer.

20.
6062. The danger in using abstract words is that they

A— sum up vast areas of experience.
B— call forth different mental images in the minds of the receivers.
C— will not evoke the specific items of experience in the listener's mind that the communicator intends.

21.
6061. By using abstractions in the communication process, the communicator will

A— bring forth specific items of experience in the minds of the receivers.
B— be using words which refer to objects or ideas that human beings can experience directly.
C— not evoke in the listener's or reader's mind the specific items of experience the communicator intends.

Answer (C) is correct (6063). *(AIH Chap 3)*
The greatest single barrier to effective communication is the lack of common experience between the communicator and the receiver. Those with the least in common usually find it difficult to communicate.
Answer (A) is incorrect because, while lack of respect for the instructor is a barrier to communication, it is not as great and as prevalent as a lack of common experience between the communicator and the receiver. Answer (B) is incorrect because, while lack of personality harmony is a barrier to communication, it is not as great and as prevalent as a lack of common experience between the communicator and the receiver.

Answer (C) is correct (6064). *(AIH Chap 3)*
Since a common core of experience is basic to effective communication, a communicator's words cannot communicate the desired meaning to another person unless the listener or the reader has had some experience with the objects or concepts to which these words refer.
Answer (A) is incorrect because the words must have not only meaningful referents, but the exact same meaningful referents in order for the communicator and the receiver to share a desired meaning. Answer (B) is incorrect because words only arouse desired meanings if the communicator generates the desired response in the mind of the receiver. The nature of this response is determined by the receiver's past experiences with the words and the concepts to which they refer.

Answer (C) is correct (6062). *(AIH Chap 3)*
The purpose of abstract words is not to bring forth specific ideas in the mind of the receiver but to serve as shorthand symbols that sum up vast areas of experience. The danger in using abstract words is that they will not evoke the specific items in the listener's mind that the communicator intends.
Answer (A) is incorrect because the purpose, not the danger, of using abstract words is to use them as shorthand symbols that sum up vast areas of experience. Answer (B) is incorrect because abstract words do not call forth mental images; on the contrary, they stand for ideas that cannot be directly experienced.

Answer (C) is correct (6061). *(AIH Chap 3)*
Abstract words are necessary and useful. Their purpose is not to bring forth specific items of experience in the minds of receivers but to serve as shorthand symbols that refer to thoughts or ideas. The danger is that an abstract term might not evoke in the listener's mind the specific item of experience the communicator intended.
Answer (A) is incorrect because abstract words are not used to bring forth specific items of experience in the minds of the receivers. Answer (B) is incorrect because concrete, not abstract, words refer to objects or ideas that human beings can experience directly.

4.5 Instructor Responsibilities

22.
6129c. Evaluation of demonstrated ability during flight instruction must be based upon

A— the progress of the student.
B— the instructor's opinion concerning the maneuver(s).
C— established standards of performance.

Answer (C) is correct (6129c). *(AIH Chap 8)*
Evaluation of demonstrated student ability during flight instruction must be based upon established standards of performance, suitably modified to apply to the student's experience and stage of development as a pilot.
Answer (A) is incorrect because evaluation must be based on established standards of performance, not the progress of the student. Answer (B) is incorrect because evaluation must be based upon established standards of performance, not on the instructor's opinion.

23.
6129b. Evaluation of demonstrated ability during flight instruction must be based upon

A— the instructor's background and experience relating to student pilots at this stage of training.
B— the progress of the student, considering the time and experience attained since beginning training.
C— established standards of performance, suitably modified to apply to the student's experience.

Answer (C) is correct (6129b). *(AIH Chap 8)*
Evaluation of demonstrated student ability during flight instruction must be based upon established standards of performance, suitably modified to apply to the student's experience and stage of development as a pilot.
Answer (A) is incorrect because evaluation should be based on established standards of performance and modified based on the student's experience, not the instructor's experience. Answer (B) is incorrect because evaluation should be based on established standards of performance, not the student's progress since beginning training, modified based on the student's experience.

24.
6129d. In evaluating student demonstrations of piloting ability, it is important for the flight instructor to

A— remain silent and observe.
B— keep the student informed of progress.
C— explain errors in performance immediately.

Answer (B) is correct (6129d). *(AIH Chap 8)*
In evaluating student demonstrations of piloting ability, it is important for the flight instructor to keep the student informed of his/her progress. This may be done as each procedure/maneuver is completed, or summarized during post-flight critiques.
Answer (A) is incorrect because, in evaluating student demonstrations of piloting ability, it is important for the flight instructor to keep the student informed of his/her progress, not remain silent and observe. Answer (C) is incorrect because students should be allowed to make mistakes and correct them on their own; errors should not be pointed out immediately because students learn by correcting their mistakes. The error can be explained at the completion of the procedure/maneuver or during a post-flight critique.

25.
6129g. Examples of all common endorsements can be found in the current issue of

A— AC 61-67, Appendix 1.
B— AC 91-67, Appendix 1.
C— AC 61-65, Appendix 1.

Answer (C) is correct (6129g). *(AIH Chap 8)*
Examples of all common endorsements can be found in the current issue of AC 61-65, Appendix 1.
Answer (A) is incorrect because examples of all common endorsements can be found in the current issue of AC 61-65, not AC 61-67, Appendix 1. Answer (B) is incorrect because examples of all common endorsements can be found in the current issue of AC 61-65, not AC 91-67, Appendix 1.

26.
6129f. Before endorsing a student for solo flight, the instructor should require the student to demonstrate consistent ability to perform

A— all maneuvers specified in the Student Pilot Guide.
B— all of the fundamental maneuvers.
C— slow flight, stalls, emergency landings, takeoffs and landings, and go-arounds.

Answer (B) is correct (6129f). *(AIH Chap 8)*
Before endorsing a student for solo flight, the instructor should require the student to demonstrate the consistent ability to perform all of the fundamental maneuvers.
Answer (A) is incorrect because, before endorsing a student for solo flight, the instructor should require the student to demonstrate the consistent ability to perform all of the fundamental maneuvers, not all maneuvers specified in the Student Pilot Guide (which contains no maneuvers). Answer (C) is incorrect because, before endorsing a student for solo flight, the instructor should require the student to demonstrate the consistent ability to perform all of the fundamental maneuvers, not just slow flight, stalls, emergency landings, takeoffs, landings, and go-arounds.

27.
6129e. The student should be capable of handling problems that might occur, such as traffic pattern congestion, change in active runway, or unexpected crosswinds prior to

A— the first solo cross-country flight.
B— initial solo.
C— being recommended for a Recreational or Private Pilot Certificate.

Answer (B) is correct (6129e). *(AIH Chap 8)*
Flight instructors have a responsibility to provide guidance and restraint regarding the solo operations of their students. Before receiving an instructor endorsement for solo flight, a student should be required to demonstrate the consistent ability to perform all of the fundamental maneuvers, and should be capable of handling ordinary problems that might occur, such as traffic pattern congestion a change in the active runway, or unexpected crosswinds.
Answer (A) is incorrect because the student should be capable of handling problems that might occur prior to initial solo, not the first solo cross-country flight. Answer (C) is incorrect because the student should be capable of handling problems that might occur prior to initial solo, not being recommended for a recreational or private pilot certificate.

4.6 Instructor Professionalism

28.
6123a. Which statement is true regarding true professionalism as an instructor?

A— Anything less than sincere performance destroys the effectiveness of the professional instructor.
B— To achieve professionalism, actions and decisions must be limited to standard patterns and practices.
C— A single definition of professionalism would encompass all of the qualifications and considerations which must be present.

Answer (A) is correct (6123a). *(AIH Chap 8)*
Professionalism demands a code of ethics. Professionals must be true to themselves and to those they serve. Anything less than a sincere performance will be detected by students and immediately destroy instructor effectiveness.
Answer (B) is incorrect because professionalism requires good judgment. Professionals cannot limit their actions and decisions to standard patterns and practice. Answer (C) is incorrect because professionalism is so multi-dimensional that no single definition can encompass all of the qualifications and considerations.

29.
6123b. Aviation instructors should be constantly alert for ways to improve the services they provide to their students, their effectiveness, and their

A— appearance.
B— qualifications.
C— demeanor.

Answer (B) is correct (6123b). *(AIH Chap 8)*
Professional aviation instructors must never become complacent or satisfied with their own qualifications and abilities. Aviation instructors should be constantly alert for ways to improve the services they provide to their students, their effectiveness, and their qualifications.
Answer (A) is incorrect because, while an instructor's personal appearance is important to maintaining a professional image, aviation instructors should be constantly alert for ways to improve the services they provide to their students, their effectiveness, and their qualifications. Answer (C) is incorrect because, while an instructor's demeanor is important to maintaining a professional image, aviation instructors should be constantly alert for ways to improve the services they provide to their students, their effectiveness, and their qualifications.

30.
6055. Student confidence tends to be destroyed if instructors

A— bluff whenever in doubt about some point.
B— continually identify student errors and failures.
C— direct and control the student's actions and behavior.

Answer (A) is correct (6055). *(AIH Chap 8)*
No one, including students, expects an instructor to be perfect. An instructor can gain the respect of students by honestly acknowledging mistakes. If the instructor tries to cover up or bluff, students will be quick to sense it and lose their confidence in the instructor.
Answer (B) is incorrect because identifying the student's errors and failures helps the student to progress and gain confidence. Answer (C) is incorrect because directing the student's actions and behavior is a basic responsibility of the flight instructor.

31.
6142. Students quickly become apathetic when they

A— realize material is being withheld by the instructor.
B— understand the objectives toward which they are working.
C— recognize that the instructor is not adequately prepared.

Answer (C) is correct (6142). *(AIH Chap 9)*
Students become apathetic when they recognize that the instructor has made inadequate preparations for the instruction being given, or when the instruction appears to be deficient, contradictory, or insincere.
Answer (A) is incorrect because students will lose respect for the instructor (not become apathetic) when they realize material is being withheld by the instructor. Answer (B) is incorrect because it is optimal that both the student and instructor understand the objectives so that they may work cooperatively toward them.

32.
6127. Which statement is true regarding the achievement of an adequate standard of performance?

A— A flight instructor should devote major effort and attention to the continuous evaluation of student performance.
B— Flight instructors can affect a genuine improvement in the student/instructor relationship by not strictly enforcing standards.
C— Flight instructors fail to provide competent instruction when they permit students to partially learn an important item of knowledge or skill.

Answer (C) is correct (6127). *(AIH Chap 8)*
Flight instructors fail to provide competent instruction when they permit their students to partially learn an important item of knowledge or skill. More importantly, such deficiencies may in themselves allow hazardous inadequacies in the student's later piloting performance.
Answer (A) is incorrect because a flight instructor should devote major effort and attention to all areas of the teaching process, not only to the evaluation of student performance. Answer (B) is incorrect because it is a fallacy to believe that a flight instructor can affect a genuine improvement in the student/instructor relationship by not strictly enforcing standards. Reasonable standards strictly enforced are not resented by an earnest student.

33.
6123c. True performance as a professional is based on study and

A— perseverance.
B— research.
C— attitude.

Answer (B) is correct (6123c). *(AIH Chap 8)*
True performance as a professional is based on study and research.
Answer (A) is incorrect because true performance as a professional is based on study and research, not perseverance. Answer (C) is incorrect because true performance as a professional is based on study and research, not attitude.

END OF CHAPTER

CHAPTER FIVE
TEACHING METHODS

5.1 LECTURE METHOD (Questions 1-8)

1. The lecture is used primarily for

    a. Introducing students to new subject material,
    b. Summarizing ideas,
    c. Showing relationships between theory and practice, and
    d. Reemphasizing main points.

2. There are four types of lectures:

    a. The illustrated talk in which the speaker relies heavily on visual aids to convey his ideas to the listeners;

    b. The briefing in which the speaker presents a concise array of facts to the listeners who do not expect elaboration or supporting material;

    c. The formal speech in which the speaker's purpose is to inform, persuade, or entertain; and

    d. The teaching lecture for which the instructor must plan and deliver an oral presentation in a manner that helps the students reach the desired learning outcomes.

3. One advantage of a teaching lecture is that the instructor can present many ideas in a relatively short time. Facts and ideas that have been logically organized can be concisely presented in rapid sequence.

    a. Thus, a teaching lecture is the most economical of all teaching methods in terms of the time required to present a given amount of material.

4. One disadvantage of a teaching lecture is that the instructor does not receive direct reaction (either words or actions) from the students when using the teaching lecture.

    a. Thus, the instructor must develop a keen perception for subtle response from the class and must be able to interpret the meaning of these reactions and adjust the lesson accordingly.

        1) These reactions could be in the form of facial expressions, manner of taking notes, and apparent interest or lack of interest in the lesson.

    b. The instructor must recognize that the lecture method is least useful for evaluating student performance.

5. The following four steps should be followed in preparing a lecture:

    a. Establish the objective and desired outcomes,
    b. Research the subject,
    c. Organize the material, and
    d. Plan productive classroom activities.

6. The teaching lecture is probably best delivered extemporaneously but from a written outline.

    a. Because the exact words which express an idea are chosen at the moment of delivery, the lecture can be personalized or suited to the moment more easily than one that is read or spoken from memory.

7. In the teaching lecture, use simple rather than complex words whenever possible.

    a. Picturesque slang and free-and-easy colloquialisms, if they suit the subject, can add variety and vividness to a teaching lecture.

    b. Errors in grammar and use of vulgarisms detract from an instructor's dignity and reflect upon the intelligence of the students.

8. The lecture can be formal or informal.

    a. A formal lecture provides no active student participation.

    b. The distinguishing characteristic of an informal lecture is the active student participation.

        1) The instructor can inspire active student participation during informal lectures through the use of questions.

5.2 COOPERATIVE OR GROUP LEARNING METHOD (Questions 9-12)

1. Cooperative group learning is an instructional strategy which organizes students into small groups so that they can work together to maximize their own and each other's learning.

    a. The most significant characteristic of group learning is that it continually requires active participation of the student.

    b. The main reason that students are put in cooperative learning groups is so they can individually achieve greater success than if they were to study alone.

2. Instructors should organize small heterogeneous groups of students who have different academic abilities, ethnic backgrounds, race, and gender.

    a. Heterogeneous groups lead students to learn to work together, to seek more support for opinions, and to tolerate each other's viewpoints.

        1) The main advantage of heterogeneous groups is that students tend to interact and achieve in ways and at levels that are rarely found with other instructional strategies.

5.3 GUIDED DISCUSSION METHOD (Questions 13-18)

1. Fundamentally, the guided discussion method of teaching is the reverse of the lecture method. The instructor uses questions to guide and stimulate discussion among students. The instructor does not present new ideas.

2. In the guided discussion, learning is achieved through the skillful use of questions.

    a. Questions facilitate discussion, which in turn develops an understanding of the subject.

3. Questions used in a guided discussion can be broken into several types, each with its usefulness in the guided discussion:

    a. **Overhead** -- directed to the entire group to stimulate thought and response from each group member.

    b. **Rhetorical** -- also stimulates thought, but instructor will answer it him/herself. This is normally used in a lecture, not a guided discussion.

    c.   **Direct** -- question addressed to an individual for a response.

    d.   **Reverse** -- The instructor answers a student's question by redirecting the question for that student to provide the answer.

    e.   **Relay** -- The reverse question is addressed to the entire group, not the individual.

4.   In preparing questions, the instructor should remember that the purpose is to bring about discussion, not merely to get answers.

    a.   Leadoff questions should be open-ended, i.e., they should start with "how" or "why."

    b.   Avoid questions that begin with "what," "when," or "does" because they only require short, categorical answers such as "yes," "no," "green," "one," etc.

5.   Each question, in order to be effective, should

    a.   Have a specific purpose,
    b.   Be clear in meaning,
    c.   Contain a single idea,
    d.   Stimulate thought,
    e.   Require definite answers, and
    f.   Relate to previously taught information.

6.   When it appears the students have adequately discussed the ideas that support a particular part of the lesson, the instructor should summarize what they have accomplished.

    a.   This interim summary is one of the most effective tools available to the instructor.

        1)   This summary can be made immediately after the discussion of each learning outcome.

        2)   It consolidates what students learned, emphasizes how much they know already, and points out any aspects they missed.

7.   Unless the students have some knowledge to exchange with each other, they cannot reach the desired learning outcomes.

    a.   Students without some background in a subject should not be asked to discuss that subject.

5.4 DEMONSTRATION/PERFORMANCE METHOD (Questions 19-23)

1.   The demonstration/performance method is based on the principle that we learn by doing.

    a.   It is the most commonly used teaching method of flight instructors.
    b.   This is the ideal method for teaching a skill such as using a flight computer.

2.   The demonstration/performance method of instruction has five essential steps:

    a.   Explanation -- the instructor must explain the objectives of the particular lesson to the student.

    b.   Demonstration -- the instructor must show the student how to perform a skill.

    c.   Student performance -- the student must act and do, i.e., practice.

    d.   Instructor supervision -- this is done concurrently with student performance. The instructor coaches, as necessary, the student's practice.

    e.   Evaluation -- the instructor judges the student performance.

3. The telling and doing technique of flight instruction is basically the demonstration/ performance method of instruction. This consists of performing several steps in proper order.

    a. Instructor tells -- instructor does
    b. Student tells -- instructor does
    c. Student tells -- student does
    d. Student does -- instructor evaluates

5.5 COMPUTER-BASED TRAINING (CBT) METHOD (Questions 24-26)

1. The computer-based training (CBT) method takes advantage of the abilities of computers to organize and present information.

2. CBT can take different forms:

    a. An instructor can use software to present a lesson using graphics or text projected on a screen

    b. Interactive software can be used by individuals or small groups to supplement traditional forms of instruction. The software can be used to learn, review, and practice new material.

        1) This type of CBT is directed by the instructor, who is available for questions and guides student activity.

        2) With interactive CBT software, the student is frequently able to control the pace of instruction, review previous material, jump forward, and receive instant feedback.

            a) One of the major advantages of interactive CBT is that students can progress at a rate which is comfortable for them.

        3) With interactive CBT, the presentation varies (i.e., the computer responds in different ways) based on the student's responses (input) to the interactive segments.

5.6 INTEGRATED METHOD OF FLIGHT INSTRUCTION (Questions 27-30)

1. Integrated flight instruction is flight instruction during which students are taught to perform flight maneuvers both by outside visual references and by reference to flight instruments, from the first time each maneuver is introduced.

    a. In a student's first instruction on the function of flight controls you would include the instrument indication to be expected, as well as the outside references used in attitude control.

2. The primary objective of integrated flight instruction is to form the habit patterns for the observance of and reliance on flight instruments.

    a. Such habits have been proved to produce more capable and safer pilots.

    b. The ability to fly in instrument meteorological conditions (IMC) is not the objective of this type of primary training.

3. During the conduct of integrated flight instruction, you are responsible for collision avoidance while your student is flying by simulated instruments, i.e., under the hood.

    a. You must guard against diverting your attention to the student's performance for extended periods.

4. At the same time, you must be sure that your student develops, from the first lesson, the habit of looking for other traffic when (s)he is not operating under simulated instrument conditions.

    a. Any observed tendency of a student to enter a maneuver without clearing the area must be corrected immediately.

5.7 THE POSITIVE APPROACH IN FLIGHT INSTRUCTION (Questions 31-32)

1. In flight instruction, an effective positive approach will point out the pleasurable features of flying before the unpleasant possibilities are discussed.

2. EXAMPLE: A positive first flight lesson:

    a. A preflight inspection familiarizing the student with the airplane and its components.
    b. A perfectly normal flight to a nearby airport and back.

        1) The instructor calls the student's attention to how easy the trip was in comparison with other ways to travel and the fact that no critical incidents were encountered or expected.

3. EXAMPLE: A negative first flight lesson:

    a. An exhaustive indoctrination on preflight procedures with emphasis on the potential for disastrous mechanical failures in flight.

    b. Instructions on the dangers of taxiing an airplane too fast.

    c. A series of stalls with emphasis on the difficulties in recovering from them. (The side effect of this performance is likely to be airsickness.)

    d. A series of simulated forced landings, stating that every pilot should always be prepared to cope with an engine failure.

QUESTIONS AND ANSWER EXPLANATIONS

All of the FAA questions from the Fundamentals of Instructing knowledge test relating to the teaching methods outlined above are reproduced below in the same modules as the outlines. To the immediate right of each question are the correct answer and answer explanation. You should cover these answers and answer explanations with your hand or a piece of paper while responding to the questions. Refer to the general discussion in Chapter 1 on how to take the FAA pilot knowledge test.

Remember that the questions from the FAA pilot knowledge test bank have been reordered by topic, and the topics have been organized into a meaningful sequence. Accordingly, the first line of the answer explanation gives the FAA question number and the citation of the authoritative source for the answer.

5.1 Lecture Method

1.

6068. In the teaching process, which method of presentation is suitable for presenting new material, for summarizing ideas, and for showing relationships between theory and practice?

A— Lecture method.
B— Integrated instruction method.
C— Demonstration/performance method.

Answer (A) is correct (6068). *(AIH Chap 5)*

The lecture is used primarily to introduce students to new material. It is also valuable for summarizing ideas, showing relationships between theory and practice, and reemphasizing main points. The lecture is the most efficient teaching method in terms of time and student numbers, if not in other ways.

Answer (B) is incorrect because the integrated method of flight instruction means that, from the first time a maneuver is introduced, students are taught to perform it both by outside visual references and by reference to flight instruments. Answer (C) is incorrect because the demonstration/performance method is better suited to teaching a skill (i.e., flight instruction).

2.

6079. What is one advantage of a lecture?

A— Uses time economically.
B— Excellent when additional research is required.
C— Allows for maximum attainment of certain types of learning outcomes.

Answer (A) is correct (6079). *(AIH Chap 5)*

In a lecture, the instructor can present many ideas in a relatively short time. Facts and ideas that have been logically organized can be concisely presented in rapid sequence. Lecturing is unquestionably the most economical of all teaching methods in terms of time required to present a given amount of material.

Answer (B) is incorrect because one advantage of the lecture is that it can be used to present information without requiring students to do additional research. Answer (C) is incorrect because a disadvantage, not an advantage, of a lecture is that the lecture does not enable the instructor to estimate the student's progress, thus learning may not be maximized.

3.

6082a. Which teaching method is most economical in terms of the time required to present a given amount of material?

A— Briefing.
B— Teaching lecture.
C— Demonstration/performance.

Answer (B) is correct (6082a). *(AIH Chap 5)*

The teaching lecture is unquestionably the most economical of all teaching methods in terms of the time required to present a given amount of material. The instructor can concisely present many ideas that have been logically organized in rapid sequence.

Answer (A) is incorrect because, although a briefing is a type of lecture, it is used to present a concise array of facts to the listeners who do not expect elaboration or supporting material. Answer (C) is incorrect because the demonstration/performance method is the least, not the most, economical in terms of time required to present a given amount of material.

4.

6077. Which is a true statement regarding the teaching lecture?

A— Delivering the lecture in an extemporaneous manner is not recommended.
B— Instructor receives direct feedback from students which is easy to interpret.
C— Instructor must develop a keen perception for subtle responses and be able to interpret the meaning of these reactions.

Answer (C) is correct (6077). *(AIH Chap 5)*

In the teaching lecture, the instructor must develop a keen perception for subtle responses from the class (e.g., facial expressions, manner of taking notes, and apparent interest or lack of interest in the lesson), and must be able to interpret the meaning of these reactions and adjust the lesson accordingly.

Answer (A) is incorrect because the lecture is best delivered extemporaneously, but from a written outline. The lecture can thus be personalized to suit different audience moods. Answer (B) is incorrect because, in the teaching lecture, the instructor's feedback is not as direct as other teaching methods and therefore is harder, not easier, to interpret.

5.

6076. The first step in preparing a lecture is to

A— research the subject.
B— develop the main ideas or key points.
C— establish the objective and desired outcome.

6.

6078. During a teaching lecture, what would detract from an instructor's dignity and reflect upon the student's intelligence?

A— Use of figurative language.
B— Errors in grammar and use of vulgarisms.
C— Using picturesque slang and colloquialisms.

7.

6081. The distinguishing characteristic of an informal lecture is the

A— use of visual aids.
B— student's participation.
C— requirement for informal notes.

8.

6080. An instructor can inspire active student participation during informal lectures through the use of

A— questions.
B— visual aids.
C— encouragement.

Answer (C) is correct (6076). *(AIH Chap 5)*
The following four steps, in order, should be used in preparing a lecture.

1. Establish the objectives and desired outcomes
2. Research the subject
3. Organize the material
4. Plan productive classroom activities

Answer (A) is incorrect because researching the subject is the second, not the first, step in preparing a lecture. Answer (B) is incorrect because developing the main ideas or key points is the third, not the first, step in preparing a lecture.

Answer (B) is correct (6078). *(AIH Chap 5)*
During a teaching lecture, errors in grammar and the use of vulgarisms detract from an instructor's dignity and reflect upon the student's intelligence.
Answer (A) is incorrect because figurative language, when used properly, can add interest and color to a lecture. Answer (C) is incorrect because picturesque slang and colloquialisms, if they suit the subject, can add variety and vividness to a lecture.

Answer (B) is correct (6081). *(AIH Chap 5)*
The distinguishing characteristic of an informal lecture is the active student participation. A formal lecture does not include student participation.
Answer (A) is incorrect because visual aids can be used in either the formal or informal lecture. Answer (C) is incorrect because the requirement for informal notes is not the distinguishing characteristic of an informal lecture. Notes may or may not be used in the formal or informal lecture.

Answer (A) is correct (6080). *(AIH Chap 5)*
An instructor can inspire student participation during informal lectures through the use of questions. In this way, the students are encouraged to make contributions that supplement the lecture.
Answer (B) is incorrect because visual aids emphasize and enhance the lecture but do not help get the students actively involved. Answer (C) is incorrect because encouragement aids learning in all situations, not just participation during lectures.

5.2 Cooperative or Group Learning Method

9.
6082e. An instructional strategy which organizes students into small groups so that they can work together to maximize their own and each other's learning is called

A— workshop learning.
B— heterogeneous group learning.
C— cooperative or group learning.

Answer (C) is correct (6082e). (AIH Chap 5)
    Cooperative group learning is an instructional strategy which organizes students into small groups so that they can work together to maximize their own and each other's learning.
    Answer (A) is incorrect because workshop learning may take place individually; it does not necessarily involve groups. Answer (B) is incorrect because cooperative group learning is an instructional strategy which organizes students into small groups so that they can work together to maximize their own and each other's learning. Heterogeneous groups are recommended for effective cooperative group learning.

10.
6082b. The most significant characteristic of group learning is that it

A— continually requires active participation of the student.
B— continually requires active participation of both the student and the instructor.
C— usually requires passive participation of the student.

Answer (A) is correct (6082b). (AIH Chap 5)
    Many positive characteristics have been attributed to group learning, the most significant of which is that it continually requires active participation of the student.
    Answer (B) is incorrect because the most significant characteristic of group learning is that it continually requires active participation of the student, not the instructor. The instructor must allow groups to work by themselves if the students are to maximize each other's learning. Answer (C) is incorrect because group learning requires active, not passive, participation of the student.

11.
6082d. The main reason that students are put in cooperative learning groups is so they

A— learn and help each other.
B— can individually achieve greater success than if they were to study alone.
C— learn that teamwork is essential if all members are to learn equally well.

Answer (B) is correct (6082d). (AIH Chap 5)
    The main reason that students are put in cooperative learning groups is so they can individually achieve greater success than if they were to study alone.
    Answer (A) is incorrect because, while students do learn and help each other, the main reason that students are put in cooperative learning groups is so they can individually achieve greater success than if they were to study alone. Answer (C) is incorrect because, while teamwork is essential to group learning, it is unlikely that all members will learn equally well. Students are put in cooperative learning groups so they can individually achieve greater success than if they were to study alone.

12.
6082c. The main advantage(s) with heterogeneous groups are that students tend to

A— think for themselves since they are in a group of dissimilar students.
B— interact and achieve in ways and at levels that are rarely found with other instructional strategies.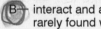
C— interact and achieve since they are in a group of similar students.

Answer (B) is correct (6082c). (AIH Chap 5)
    Instructors should organize small heterogeneous groups of students who have different academic abilities, ethnic backgrounds, race, and gender. The main advantage of heterogeneous groups is that students tend to interact and achieve in ways and at levels that are rarely found with other instructional strategies.
    Answer (A) is incorrect because heterogeneous groups lead students to learn to work together, to seek more support for opinions, and to tolerate each other's viewpoints, not to think for themselves. Answer (C) is incorrect because heterogeneous groups contain dissimilar, not similar, students.

5.3 Guided Discussion Method

13.
6085. In a guided discussion, learning is achieved through the

A— skillful use of questions.
B— use of questions, each of which contains several ideas.
C— use of reverse questions directed to the class as a whole.

14.
6083. A question directed to an entire group to stimulate thought and response from each group member is identified as

A— Relay.
B— Overhead.
C— Rhetorical.

15.
6087. In a guided discussion, leadoff questions should usually begin with

A— why.
B— what.
C— when.

16.
6086. Which question would be best as a leadoff question for a guided discussion on the subject of torque?

A— Does torque affect an airplane?
B— How does torque affect an airplane?
C— What effect does torque have on an airplane in a turn?

Answer (A) is correct (6085). *(AIH Chap 5)*
The guided discussion method relies on the students to provide ideas, experiences, opinions, and information. The instructor guides the discussion by use of questions which are aimed to draw out what the students know. Thus, learning is achieved through the skillful use of questions.
Answer (B) is incorrect because, in a guided discussion, each question used should contain only one, not several, ideas. Answer (C) is incorrect because a relay, not reverse, question is redirected to the class as a whole.

Answer (B) is correct (6083). *(AIH Chap 5)*
In the guided discussion, learning is produced through skillful use of questions. To begin a guided discussion, the instructor should use an overhead question. This type of question is directed to the entire group to stimulate thought and response from each student.
Answer (A) is incorrect because a relay question responds to a student's question by redirecting it back to the rest of the group. Answer (C) is incorrect because a rhetorical question is similar in nature to an overhead question, but the instructor answers the question. This is more commonly used in lecturing than in guided discussion.

Answer (A) is correct (6087). *(AIH Chap 5)*
In preparing questions, the instructor should remember that the purpose is to bring about discussion, not merely to get only short categorical answers (i.e., yes, no, one, etc.). Thus, lead-off questions should usually begin with "how" or "why."
Answer (B) is incorrect because a question beginning with "what" usually requires only a short categorical answer and will not encourage a discussion. Answer (C) is incorrect because a question beginning with "when" usually requires a short answer and will not encourage a discussion.

Answer (B) is correct (6086). *(AIH Chap 5)*
In preparing questions to lead off a guided discussion, the instructor should remember that the purpose is to bring about discussion, not merely answers. Avoid questions that require only short, categorical (i.e., yes or no) answers. Lead-off questions should usually begin with "how" or "why."
Answer (A) is incorrect because a question beginning with "does" only requires a yes or no answer and will not encourage a discussion. Answer (C) is incorrect because a question beginning with "what" only requires a short, categorical answer and will not encourage a discussion.

17.

6088. When it appears students have adequately discussed the ideas presented during a guided discussion, one of the most valuable tools an instructor can use is

A— a session of verbal testing.

B— a written test on the subject discussed.

C— an interim summary of what the students accomplished.

Answer (C) is correct (6088). *(AIH Chap 5)*

When it appears the students have discussed the ideas that support a particular part of the lesson, the instructor should summarize what the students have accomplished. This interim summary is one of the most effective tools available to the instructor in a guided discussion. To bring ideas together and help in transition, an interim summary should be made after the discussion of each desired learning outcome.

Answer (A) is incorrect because a session of verbal testing goes against the intention of the guided discussion, where the instructor aims to "draw out" what the students know in a structured but personable manner. Answer (B) is incorrect because a written test on the subject without an instructor summary would be testing student opinions and experiences rather than facts.

18.

6084. Which statement about the guided discussion method of teaching is true?

A— The lesson objective becomes apparent at the application level of learning.

B— Students without a background in the subject can also be included in the discussion.

C— Unless the students have some knowledge to exchange with each other, they cannot reach the desired learning outcomes.

Answer (C) is correct (6084). *(AIH Chap 5)*

Throughout the time the instructor prepares the students for their discussion (e.g., early lectures, homework assignments), the students should be made aware of the lesson objectives. This gives them the background for a fruitful guided discussion. Students without some background in a subject should not be asked to discuss that subject.

Answer (A) is incorrect because the lesson objective should be known while the students are preparing for the guided discussion, or at least during the introduction, not afterward at the application level of learning. Answer (B) is incorrect because students with no background in the subject will not be able to contribute to an effective discussion.

5.4 Demonstration/Performance Method

19.

6066. Which method of presentation is desirable for teaching a skill such as ground school lesson on the flight computer?

A— Lecture/application.

B— Presentation/practice.

C— Demonstration/performance.

Answer (C) is correct (6066). *(AIH Chap 5)*

The demonstration/performance method of teaching is based on the principle that you learn by doing. Students learn physical or mental skills best by actually performing them under supervision. Learning to use a flight computer is an ideal application of this teaching method.

Answer (A) is incorrect because the lecture method is not suitable to teach flight computer use because the lecture does not provide for student participation and, as a consequence, lets the instructor do all the work. Answer (B) is incorrect because presentation/practice is not a method of presentation.

20.
6089. What are the essential steps in the demonstration/
performance method of teaching?

A— Demonstration, practice, and evaluation.
B— Demonstration, student performance, and evaluation.
C— Explanation, demonstration, student performance,
     instructor supervision, and evaluation.

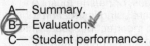

Answer (C) is correct (6089). *(AIH Chap 5)*
     The demonstration/performance method of teaching
is based on the principle that we learn by doing. Thus, it
is used by flight instructors in teaching procedures and
maneuvers. The five essential steps are:

1. Explanation
2. Demonstration
3. Student performance
4. Instructor supervision
5. Evaluation

     Answer (A) is incorrect because the five, not three,
essential steps in the demonstration/performance method
of teaching are explanation, demonstration, student
performance, not practice, instructor supervision, and
evaluation. Answer (B) is incorrect because the five, not
three, essential steps in the demonstration/performance
method of teaching are explanation, demonstration,
student performance, instructor supervision, and
evaluation.

21.
6091a. What is the last step in the demonstration/
performance method?

A— Summary.
B— Evaluation.
C— Student performance.

Answer (B) is correct (6091a). *(AIH Chap 5)*
     The demonstration/performance method of teaching
is based on the principle that we learn by doing. Thus, it
is used by flight instructors in teaching procedures and
maneuvers. The five essential steps are:

1. Explanation
2. Demonstration
3. Student performance
4. Instructor supervision
5. Evaluation

     Answer (A) is incorrect because summary is not a step
in the demonstration/performance method. Answer (C) is
incorrect because student performance is the third, not
last, step in the demonstration/performance method.

22.
6090. In the demonstration/performance method of
instruction, which two separate actions are performed
concurrently?

A— Instructor explanation and demonstration.
B— Student performance and instructor supervision.
C— Instructor explanation and student demonstration.

Answer (B) is correct (6090). *(AIH Chap 5)*
     In the demonstration/performance method of instruc-
tion, student performance and instructor supervision are
performed concurrently. As the student practices to
learn, the instructor supervises and coaches as
necessary.
     Answer (A) is incorrect because, during the explana-
tion phase, the instructor explains to the student the
actions they are to perform. This is accomplished during
the preflight discussion. The demonstration is done in
the airplane as the instructor shows the student how to
perform a maneuver. Answer (C) is incorrect because
instructor supervision, not explanation, and student
performance, not demonstration, are performed
concurrently.

23.

6134. The basic demonstration/performance method of instruction consists of several steps in proper order. They are

A— instructor tells--student does; student tells--student does; student does--instructor evaluates.

B— instructor tells--instructor does; student tells--instructor does; student does--instructor evaluates.

C— instructor tells--instructor does; student tells--instructor does; student tells--student does; student does--instructor evaluates.

Answer (C) is correct (6134). *(AIH Chap 9)*

The telling and doing technique of flight instruction (basically the demonstration/performance method) is very effective and valuable in teaching procedures and maneuvers. First, the instructor explains, then demonstrates. Then the student performs, first by explaining as the instructor does, then by explaining and doing it him/herself while the instructor supervises. Finally, the instructor evaluates how the student performs.

Answer (A) is incorrect because it omits the first step, which is instructor tells--instructor does. The second step is student tells--instructor does, not vice versa. Answer (B) is incorrect because it omits the third step of student tells--student does.

5.5 Computer-Based Training (CBT) Method

24.

6091b. Which statement is true concerning computer-based training (CBT)?

A— The instructor need not be actively involved with the students when using instructional aids.

B— CBT may be used by the instructor as stand-alone training.

C— One of the major advantages of CBT is that students can progress at a rate which is comfortable for them.

Answer (C) is correct (6091b). *(AIH Chap 5)*

With computer-based training software, the student is frequently able to control the pace of instruction, review previous material, jump forward, and receive instant feedback.

Answer (A) is incorrect because the instructor does need to be involved with the students when using instructional aids. The instructor must either use those aids to present an idea to the class, or he/she must be available to assist students that are using instructional aids on their own. Answer (B) is incorrect because, while CBT can take a major role in some training programs, those programs must still be guided and enhanced by the instructor.

25.

6091c. Some of the more advanced computer-based training (CBT) applications allow students to progress through a series of interactive segments where the presentation varies as a result of their

A— training.

B— responses.

C— needs.

Answer (B) is correct (6091c). *(AIH Chap 5)*

Interactive software varies the presentation based on the responses of the user to the interactive segments.

Answer (A) is incorrect because the presentation of more advanced CBT applications varies as a result of the student's responses to the interactive segments, not his/her training. The choice of CBT applications depends on the training that is being conducted. Answer (C) is incorrect because the presentation of more advanced CBT applications varies as a result of the student's responses to the interactive segments, not his/her needs. The choice of CBT applications may vary depending on an individual student's needs.

26.

6091d. The major advantage of computer-based training (CBT) over other forms of instruction is that it is interactive - the computer responds in different ways, depending on the student's

A— background.

B— input.

C— training.

Answer (B) is correct (6091d). *(AIH Chap 5)*

The major advantage of CBT is that it is interactive. The software responds based on choices made by the user (input). This approach keeps the student involved in the learning process.

Answer (A) is incorrect because the computer responds based on the student's input, not background. The choice of CBT software may depend on the student's academic or experiential background. Answer (C) is incorrect because the computer responds based on the student's input, not training. The choice of CBT software depends on the type of training to be conducted.

5.6 Integrated Method of Flight Instruction

27.
6136. The primary objective of integrated flight instruction is the

A— formation of firm habit patterns for observing and relying on flight instruments.
B— difference in the pilot's operation of the flight controls during both VMC and IMC.
C— developing of the habit of occasionally monitoring their own and the aircraft's performance.

28.
6135. Integrated flight instruction has many benefits, but the main objective is to

A— develop the student's ability to fly the aircraft during inadvertent IMC.
B— ensure the student is not overly dependent on instruments during VFR flight.
C— help the student develop habit patterns for observance of and reliance on flight instruments.

29.
6137. Which is an acceptable procedure when using the integrated method of flight instruction?

A— Use alternate and distinct periods devoted entirely to instrument flight or to visual flight.
B— Prior to the first flight, clearly explain the differences in the manipulation of flight controls for maintaining aircraft control when under simulated instrument conditions and when using references outside the aircraft.
C— Include in the student's first instruction on the function of flight controls the instrument indication to be expected, as well as the outside references used in attitude control.

Answer (A) is correct (6136). *(AIH Chap 9)*
The primary objective of the integrated flight training method is the formation of firm habit patterns for observing and relying on flight instruments from the student's first piloting experience. The goal is to teach proper use of flight instruments in VFR flight.
Answer (B) is incorrect because there should be no difference in the pilot's operation of the flight controls in either VMC or IMC. The manipulation of the flight controls is identical, regardless of which references are used to determine the attitude of the airplane. Answer (C) is incorrect because the pilot's habit of occasionally monitoring his/her own performance along with the aircraft's is an objective of basic flight instruction, not integrated flight instruction.

Answer (C) is correct (6135). *(AIH Chap 9)*
The primary objective of the integrated method of flight training is to develop firm habit patterns for observance of and reliance on flight instruments as well as outside references from the student's first piloting experience. The goal is to teach proper use of flight instruments in VFR flight.
Answer (A) is incorrect because the ability to fly the aircraft in IMC is not an objective of integrated flight instruction. Answer (B) is incorrect because the objective of integrated flight instruction is to ensure that the student is not overly dependent on outside visual references, not flight instruments.

Answer (C) is correct (6137). *(AIH Chap 9)*
When using the integrated method of flight instruction, you should include in the student's first instruction on the function of flight controls the instrument indications to be expected, as well as the outside references used in attitude control.
Answer (A) is incorrect because integrated flight instruction means simultaneous, not alternate, instruction in instrument and visual references. Answer (B) is incorrect because there is no distinction in the student's operation of the flight controls, regardless of whether outside references or instrument indications are used for the performance of a maneuver.

30.
6138. During integrated flight instruction, the instructor must be sure the student

A— develops the habit of looking for other traffic.
B— is able to control the aircraft for extended periods under IMC.
C— can depend on the flight instruments when maneuvering by outside references.

Answer (A) is correct (6138). *(AIH Chap 9)*
If students are allowed to believe that the instructor assumes all responsibility for avoiding other traffic, they cannot develop the habit of keeping a constant watch, which is essential to safety. Any observed tendency of a student to enter flight maneuvers without first making a careful check for other possible air traffic must be corrected immediately.
Answer (B) is incorrect because the ability to control the aircraft for extended periods under IMC is not the objective of integrated flight instruction. Answer (C) is incorrect because the instructor must be sure not to let the student focus his attention on the instruments at the expense of looking for other traffic.

5.7 The Positive Approach in Flight Instruction

31.
6129a. Which is an example of a positive approach in the first flight lesson of a student with no previous aviation experience?

A— Conducting a thorough preflight.
B— A normal flight to a nearby airport and return.
C— Instruction in the care which must be taken when taxiing an airplane.

Answer (B) is correct (6129a). *(AIH Chap 8)*
A normal flight to a nearby airport and back shows the student some of the pleasant aspects of aviation. Such an introductory lesson leaves a positive impression in the new student's mind. Positive teaching results in positive learning.
Answer (A) is incorrect because, in the first flight lesson of a student with no aviation experience, conducting a thorough, exhausting preflight is an example of a negative, not a positive, approach. The student may question whether learning to fly is a good idea or not. Answer (C) is incorrect because, in the first flight lesson of a student with no aviation experience, instruction in the care which must be taken when taxiing an airplane is an example of a negative, not a positive, approach. The student may question whether learning to fly is a good idea or not.

32.
6128. Which statement is true regarding positive or negative approaches in aviation instructional techniques?

A— A student with normal abilities should not be affected by an instructor who emphasizes emergency procedures early in training.
B— A positive approach, to be effective, will point out the pleasurable features of aviation before the unpleasant possibilities are discussed.
C— The introduction of emergency procedures before the student is acquainted with normal operations is likely to be neither discouraging nor affect learning.

Answer (B) is correct (6128). *(AIH Chap 8)*
Flight instructor success depends, in large measure, on the ability to frame instructions so that students develop a positive image of flying. A positive approach, to be effective, will point out the pleasurable features of aviation before the unpleasant possibilities are discussed. A negative approach generally results in negative learning because the student's perceptual process would be adversely affected by fear.
Answer (A) is incorrect because an instructor who emphasizes emergency procedures early in training will most likely have a negative effect on the learning process regardless of a student's abilities. The student new to aviation is still quite impressionable. Answer (C) is incorrect because the introduction of emergency procedures before the student is acquainted with normal operations most likely will be discouraging, threatening, and will adversely affect learning.

END OF CHAPTER

CHAPTER SIX
PLANNING INSTRUCTIONAL ACTIVITY

6.1 COURSE DEVELOPMENT (Questions 1-5)

1. Any instructional activity must be competently planned and organized if it is to achieve the desired learning outcomes.

   a. First, you must determine the overall objectives and standards of the course.

   b. Then, you must identify the blocks of learning which constitute the necessary parts of the total objective.

      1) You must ensure that each block of learning identified is truly an integral part of the overall objective.

         a) Extraneous blocks of instruction are expensive frills, especially in flight instruction, and detract from the completion of the final objective.

      2) The blocks of learning must be developed and arranged in their proper sequence.

         a) In this way, a student can master the segments of the overall pilot performance requirements individually and can progressively combine these with other related segments until their sum meets the final objective.

2. A training syllabus is an abstract or digest of the course of training. It consists of the blocks of learning to be completed in the most efficient order.

   a. The order of training can and should be altered, when necessary, to suit the progress of the student and the demands of special circumstances.

      1) However, it is often preferable to skip to a completely different part of the syllabus when the conduct of a scheduled lesson is impossible, rather than proceeding to the next lesson, which may be predicated completely on skills to be developed during the lesson which is being postponed.

6.2 ORGANIZATION OF MATERIAL (Questions 6-12)

1. The teaching process can be divided into four basic steps: preparation, presentation, application, and review/evaluation.

   a. Every lesson, when developed adequately, falls logically into these four steps.

2. Regardless of the teaching method used (lecture, guided discussion or demonstration-performance), an instructor must properly organize the material. One effective way to organize a lesson is -- introduction, development, and conclusion.

   a. The **introduction** sets the stage for everything to come. The introduction can be divided into three subparts.

      1) **Attention** -- The instructor must gain the students' attention and focus it on the subject.

2)   **Motivation** -- The instructor should offer specific reasons why they need to learn the material. This motivation should appeal to each student personally and accentuate the desire to learn.

3)   **Overview** -- Each lesson introduction should contain an overview that tells the group what is to be covered during the period.

b.   The **development** is the main part of the lesson during which the instructor organizes the explanations and demonstrations in a manner that helps the students achieve the desired learning outcomes.

1)   The instructor must logically organize the material to show the relationships of the main points to each other. This is done by developing the main points in one of the following ways:

a)   From past to present

b)   From simple to complex

c)   From known to unknown (i.e., using a student's previous experiences and knowledge to acquire new concepts)

d)   From most frequently used (most familiar) to least frequently used

c.   The **conclusion** retraces the important elements of the lesson and relates them to the objective.

1)   This reinforces the student's learning and improves retention of what has been learned.

2)   New ideas should not be introduced in the conclusion because doing so at this point in the lesson will only confuse the student.

6.3 LESSON PLAN (Questions 13-28)

1.   Each lesson of the training syllabus includes an objective, content, and completion standards.

2.   A lesson plan is an organized outline that is developed for a single instructional period.

a.   A properly constructed lesson plan will provide an outline that tells the instructor what to do, in what order to do it, and what teaching procedure to use.

b.   The lesson plan must be appropriate for the particular student.

1)   Standard lesson plans may not be effective for students requiring a different approach.

2)   Therefore, the main concern in developing a lesson plan is the student.

3.   A lesson plan should be prepared in writing for each instructional period, regardless of the instructor's experience.

a.   A so-called mental outline is not a lesson plan.

b.   Another instructor should be able to take the lesson plan and know what to do in conducting the same period of instruction.

4.   Lesson plans help instructors keep a constant check on their own activity, as well as that of their students.

5.   A characteristic of a well-planned lesson is that it should contain new material that is related to the lesson previously presented.

a.   In flight training, a short review of earlier lessons is usually necessary.

6. Each lesson plan should contain the following items: lesson objective, elements, schedule, equipment, instructor's actions, student's actions, and completion standards. See the illustration below.

LESSON ___GROUND REFERENCE MANEUVERS___ **STUDENT** _____ **DATE** _____

OBJECTIVE
- TO DEVELOP THE STUDENT'S SKILL IN PLANNING AND FOLLOWING A PATTERN OVER THE GROUND COMPENSATING FOR WIND DRIFT AT VARYING ANGLES.

ELEMENTS
- USE OF GROUND REFERENCES TO CONTROL PATH.
- OBSERVATION AND CONTROL OF WIND EFFECT.
- CONTROL OF AIRPLANE ATTITUDE, ALTITUDE, AND HEADING.

SCHEDULE
- PREFLIGHT DISCUSSION.   : 10
- INSTRUCTOR DEMONSTRATIONS.   : 25
- STUDENT PRACTICE.   : 45
- POSTFLIGHT CRITIQUE.   : 10

EQUIPMENT
- CHALKBOARD FOR PREFLIGHT DISCUSSION.
- IFR VISOR FOR MANEUVERS REVIEWED.

INSTRUCTOR'S ACTIONS
- PREFLIGHT – DISCUSS LESSON OBJECTIVE. DIAGRAM "S" TURNS, EIGHTS ALONG A ROAD, AND RECTANGULAR COURSE ON A CHALKBOARD.

- INFLIGHT – DEMONSTRATE ELEMENTS. DEMONSTRATE FOLLOWING A ROAD, "S" TURNS, EIGHTS ALONG A ROAD, AND RECTANGULAR COURSE. COACH STUDENT PRACTICE.

- POSTFLIGHT – CRITIQUE STUDENT PERFORMANCE AND MAKE STUDY ASSIGNMENT.

- PREFLIGHT – DISCUSS LESSON OBJECTIVE AND RESOLVE QUESTIONS.

STUDENT'S ACTIONS
- INFLIGHT – REVIEW PREVIOUS MANEUVERS INCLUDING POWER-OFF STALLS AND FLIGHT AT MINIMUM CONTROLLABLE AIRSPEED. PERFORM EACH NEW MANEUVER AS DIRECTED.

- POSTFLIGHT – ASK PERTINENT QUESTIONS.

COMPLETION STANDARDS
- STUDENT SHOULD DEMONSTRATE COMPETENCY IN MAINTAINING ORIENTATION, AIRSPEED WITHIN 10 KNOTS, ALTITUDE WITHIN 100 FEET, AND HEADINGS WITHIN 10 DEGREES, AND IN MAKING PROPER CORRECTION FOR WIND DRIFT.

---

7. Also see Figure 1A on page 80 for an example of a ground lesson plan.

7.   The objectives of each lesson should be clearly stated.

    a.   The objective is the reason for the lesson--what the student is expected to know or be able to do at the end of the lesson.

    b.   Keeping the student informed of lesson objectives and completion standards minimizes the student's insecurity.

8.   Fatigue is the primary consideration in determining the length and frequency of flight instruction periods.

    a.   Fatigue, resulting from excessive or lengthy instruction, reduces a student's learning ability.

9.   When planning time for student performance, a primary consideration is the length of the practice session.

    a.   A beginning student reaches a point where additional practice is not only unproductive but may be harmful.

    b.   As a student gains experience, longer periods of practice are profitable.

10.   A blank lesson plan is provided on page 162 so you may make copies for your use.

6.4 INSTRUCTIONAL AIDS (Questions 29-32)

1.   Instructional aids are useful tools to emphasize, support, and supplement the key points in a lesson.

    a.   Instructional aids include models, chalkboards, charts, and projected material (i.e., videotapes, movies, slides, etc.).

2.   The following four-step procedure should be used to determine if and when instructional aids are necessary.

    a.   Clearly establish the lesson objective, being certain what must be communicated.

    b.   Gather the necessary data by researching for support material.

    c.   Organize the material into an outline or lesson plan. The outline should include all key points to be presented.

    d.   Finally, determine what ideas should be supported with instructional aids.

        1)   They should be compatible with the learning outcomes to be achieved.
        2)   They should be designed to cover the key points in a lesson.

3.   Instructional aids used in the teaching/learning process should not be used as a crutch by the instructor.

QUESTIONS AND ANSWER EXPLANATIONS

All of the FAA questions from the Fundamentals of Instructing knowledge test relating to planning instructional activity outlined above are reproduced on the following pages in the same modules as the outlines. To the immediate right of each question are the correct answer and answer explanation. You should cover these answers and answer explanations with your hand or a piece of paper while responding to the questions. Refer to the general discussion in Chapter 1 on how to take the FAA knowledge test.

Remember that the questions from the FAA knowledge test bank have been reordered by topic, and the topics have been organized into a meaningful sequence. Accordingly, the first line of the answer explanation gives the FAA question number and the citation of the authoritative source for the answer.

6.1 Course Development

1.
6144. In planning any instructional activity, the first consideration should be to

A— determine the overall objectives and standards. ✓
B— establish common ground between the instructor and student.
C— identify the blocks of learning which make up the overall objective.

Answer (A) is correct (6144). *(AIH Chap 10)*
The first step in planning any instructional activity is to determine the overall objectives and standards. If the instructor does not have a logical view of what is to be achieved, then the students will not.

Answer (B) is incorrect because establishing a common ground between the instructor and student is the purpose of a lesson introduction, not the first step in planning instructional activity. Answer (C) is incorrect because the second, not the first, consideration in planning for any instructional activity is to identify the blocks of learning which make up the overall objective.

2.
6147. In planning instructional activity, the second step is to

A— develop lesson plans for each period or unit of instruction.
B— identify blocks of learning which constitute the necessary parts of the total objective.
C— develop a training syllabus that will serve as a guide for conducting training at each level of learning.

Answer (B) is correct (6147). *(AIH Chap 10)*
In planning instructional activity, the second step (after the overall training objectives have been established) is the identification of the blocks of learning which constitute the necessary parts of the total objective.

Answer (A) is incorrect because, to develop lesson plans for each period or unit of instruction, an instructor must first determine the overall objectives, then identify the blocks of learning necessary to meet those objectives. Answer (C) is incorrect because a training syllabus is an abstract of the course of training. It consists of the blocks of learning to be completed in the most efficient order, and thus, must be developed after the blocks have been identified.

3.
6146. Development and assembly of blocks of learning in their proper relationship will provide a means for

A— both the instructor and student to easily correct faulty habit patterns.
B— challenging the student by progressively increasing the units of learning.
C— allowing the student to master the segments of the overall pilot performance requirements individually and combining these with other related segments.

Answer (C) is correct (6146). *(AIH Chap 10)*
Training for a skill as complicated and involved as piloting an aircraft requires the development and assembly, in their appropriate sequence, of many segments or blocks of learning. In this way, a student can master the segments of the overall pilot performance requirements individually and can progressively combine these with other related segments until (s)he learns to fly, which is the final objective.

Answer (A) is incorrect because organizing the appropriate blocks of learning in their proper relationship should prevent the formation of bad habits. This is the basic reason for the building block technique of instruction. Answer (B) is incorrect because the challenge presented to the student is one way to test for a useful size of a minimum block of learning, but progressively increasing the blocks of learning may deter the student's progress.

4.
6145. Which statement is true concerning extraneous blocks of instruction during a course of training?

A— They are usually necessary parts of the total objective.
B— They detract from the completion of the final objective.
C— They assist in the attainment of the lesson's objective.

Answer (B) is correct (6145). *(AIH Chap 10)*
While identifying the blocks of learning to be used in the course, the instructor must examine each carefully to see that it is truly an integral part of the structure. Extraneous blocks of instruction can detract from, rather than assist, in the completion of the final objective.

Answer (A) is incorrect because extraneous blocks of instruction are unnecessary, not necessary, parts of the total objective. Answer (C) is incorrect because extraneous blocks of instruction detract, not assist, in the attainment of the lesson's objective.

5.

6149. When it is impossible to conduct a scheduled lesson, it is preferable for the instructor to

A— review and possibly revise the training syllabus

B— proceed to the next scheduled lesson, or if this is not practical, cancel the lesson.

C— conduct a lesson that is not predicated completely on skills to be developed during the lesson which was postponed.

Answer (C) is correct (6149). *(AIH Chap 10)*
It is preferable for the instructor to skip to a completely different part of the syllabus when it is impossible to conduct a scheduled lesson, rather than proceeding to the next lesson, which may be predicated completely on skills to be developed during the lesson which was postponed.
Answer (A) is incorrect because an instructor should review and possibly revise the training syllabus when there is an applicable change to the FARs or PTSs, not because a lesson had to be postponed. Answer (B) is incorrect because the next lesson may need skills that were to be learned in the postponed lesson.

6.2 Organization of Material

6.

6065. When teaching new material, the teaching process can be divided into which steps?

A— Preparation, presentation, application, and review and evaluation.

B— Preparation, demonstration, practice, and review.

C— Explanation, demonstration, practice, and evaluation.

Answer (A) is correct (6065). *(AIH Chap 4)*
The four basic steps in the teaching process are preparation, presentation, application, and review and evaluation.
Answer (B) is incorrect because demonstration and practice are examples of teaching methods, not basic steps in the teaching process. Answer (C) is incorrect because explanation, demonstration, and practice are examples of teaching methods, not basic steps in the teaching process.

7.

6150b. Every lesson, when adequately developed, falls logically into the four steps of the teaching process -

A— preparation, introduction, presentation, and review and evaluation.

B— preparation, introduction, presentation, and review and application.

C— preparation, presentation, application, and review and evaluation.

Answer (C) is correct (6150b). *(AIH Chap 10)*
Every lesson, when developed adequately, falls logically into the four steps of the teaching process: preparation, presentation, application, and review/ evaluation.
Answer (A) is incorrect because the second basic step in the teaching process is presentation, not introduction, and the third basic step is application, not presentation. Answer (B) is incorrect because the second basic step in the teaching process is presentation, not introduction, the third basic step is application, not presentation, and the fourth basic step is review and evaluation, not review and application.

8.

6073. The method of arranging lesson material from the simple to complex, past to present, and known to unknown, is one that

A— creates student thought pattern departures.

B— shows the relationships of the main points of the lesson.

C— requires students to actively participate in the lesson.

Answer (B) is correct (6073). *(AIH Chap 5)*
An instructor must logically organize the lesson material to show the relationships of the main points. This can be done by arranging the material from the simple to the complex, past to present, known to unknown, and from the most frequently used to the least frequently used.
Answer (A) is incorrect because, by arranging lesson material from the simple to complex, past to present, and known to unknown, the instructor will make meaningful transitions from one point to another and thus keep the students oriented, not creating thought pattern departures. Answer (C) is incorrect because the objective of each lesson, not the method of arranging material, should require students to actively participate (either directly or indirectly) in the lesson in order to achieve the desired learning outcomes.

9.
6072. In organizing lesson material, which step sets the stage for everything to come?

A— Overview.
B— Conclusion.
C— Introduction.

Answer (C) is correct (6072). *(AIH Chap 5)*
The introduction to a lesson should set the stage for everything to come. The introduction is made up of three elements: attention, motivation, and overview.
Answer (A) is incorrect because the overview is included in the introduction and tells the group what is to be covered during the period of instruction, not how it relates to the entire course. Answer (B) is incorrect because the conclusion retraces the important elements of the lesson and relates them to the lesson objective. It does not set the stage for everything to come because it is at the end of a lesson.

10.
6071. The proper sequence for the subparts of an introduction is

A— attention, motivation, and overview.
B— attention, development, and overview.
C— overview, motivation, and conclusion.

Answer (A) is correct (6071). *(AIH Chap 5)*
The proper sequence for the subparts of an introduction is attention, motivation, and overview. First, the instructor must gain the student's attention and focus it on the subject at hand. Second, the introduction should offer the students specific reasons for needing to be familiar with, to know, to understand, to apply, or to be able to perform whatever they are about to learn. This motivation should appeal to each student personally and accentuate the desire to learn. Third, every lesson introduction should contain an overview that tells the group what is to be covered during the period.
Answer (B) is incorrect because development is the main part of the lesson, not a subpart of the introduction. Answer (C) is incorrect because conclusion is the review portion of the lesson, not a subpart of the introduction.

11.
6075. In developing a lesson, the instructor should organize explanations and demonstrations to help the student

A— achieve the desired learning outcome.
B— acquire a thorough understanding of the material presented.
C— acquire new concepts, generally progressing from the known to the unknown.

Answer (A) is correct (6075). *(AIH Chap 5)*
In developing a lesson, the instructor should organize the subject matter (explanations and demonstrations) in a manner that helps the student achieve the desired learning outcome.
Answer (B) is incorrect because the student's ability to acquire a thorough understanding of the material is dependent on more than an instructor's organized presentation, e.g., motivation, needs, etc. Answer (C) is incorrect because progressing from the known to the unknown is a way of logically organizing the lesson material to show the relationships of the main points, not the intent of developing a lesson, which is to help the student achieve the desired learning outcome.

12.
6074. When teaching from the known to the unknown, an instructor is using the student's

A— current knowledge of the subject.
B— previous experiences and knowledge.
C— previously held opinions, both valid and invalid.

Answer (B) is correct (6074). *(AIH Chap 5)*
Teaching from the known to the unknown allows the instructor to use the student's previous experience and knowledge as the point of departure from which to lead into new ideas and concepts.
Answer (A) is incorrect because, when teaching from the known to the unknown, an instructor is using a student's knowledge of related subjects, not the subject at hand. Answer (C) is incorrect because organizing lessons using the known to the unknown pattern requires students' previous knowledge, not their previously held opinions.

6.3 Lesson Plan

13.
6153. A lesson plan, if constructed properly, will provide an outline for

A— proceeding from the unknown to the known.
B— the teaching procedure to be used in a single instructional period.
C— establishing blocks of learning that become progressively larger in scope.

Answer (B) is correct (6153). *(AIH Chap 10)*
   A properly constructed lesson plan is an organized outline or blueprint for a single instructional period. It is a necessary guide for the instructor in that it tells what to do, in what order to do it, and what procedure to use in teaching the material of the lesson.
   Answer (A) is incorrect because the lesson plan will usually proceed from the known to the unknown, not unknown to known. Answer (C) is incorrect because a syllabus, not a lesson plan, will provide an outline for establishing blocks of learning that become progressively larger in scope.

14.
6148. Each lesson of a training syllabus includes

A— attention, motivation, and overview.
B— introduction, development, and conclusion.
C— objective, content, and completion standards.

Answer (C) is correct (6148). *(AIH Chap 10)*
   Each lesson of a written training syllabus includes an objective, content, and completion standards.
   Answer (A) is incorrect because attention, motivation, and overview are the parts of an introduction to a lesson. Answer (B) is incorrect because the structure of every lesson as it is being presented to a student, not as found in a written syllabus, should be based on an introduction, a development, and a conclusion.

15.
6154. (Refer to figure 1 on page 75.) Section A is titled:

A— Overview.
B— Objective.
C— Introduction.

Answer (B) is correct (6154). *(AIH Chap 10)*
   Section A of Fig. 1 is titled: Objective. The objective of the lesson is the reason for the lesson and should clearly state what the instructor expects the student to know or do at the completion of the lesson.
   Answer (A) is incorrect because overview is a subpart of an introduction to a lesson, not a titled section of a lesson plan. Answer (C) is incorrect because an introduction is part of an effective way to organize a lesson, not a titled section of a lesson plan.

16.
6155. (Refer to figure 1 on page 75.) Section B is titled:

A— Elements.
B— Blocks of Learning.
C— Course of Training.

Answer (A) is correct (6155). *(AIH Chap 10)*
   Section B of Fig. 1 is titled: Elements. This is a statement of the elements of knowledge and skill necessary for the fulfillment of the lesson objective. This may include both elements previously learned and those to be introduced during this lesson.
   Answer (B) is incorrect because blocks of learning are identified and used in preparing lesson plans, not a titled section of a lesson plan. Answer (C) is incorrect because the course of training is the overall objective of the instruction and is comprised of many different lesson plans, not a titled section of a lesson plan.

LESSON GROUND REFERENCE MANEUVERS   STUDENT _____ DATE _____

A _____   TO DEVELOP THE STUDENT'S SKILL IN PLANNING
AND FOLLOWING A PATTERN OVER THE GROUND
COMPENSATING FOR WIND DRIFT AT VARYING ANGLES.

B _____   USE OF GROUND REFERENCES TO CONTROL PATH.
OBSERVATION AND CONTROL OF WIND EFFECT.
CONTROL OF AIRPLANE ATTITUDE, ALTITUDE, AND
HEADING.

C _____   PREFLIGHT DISCUSSION.   : 10
INSTRUCTOR DEMONSTRATIONS.   : 25
STUDENT PRACTICE.   : 45
POSTFLIGHT CRITIQUE.   : 10

D _____   CHALKBOARD FOR PREFLIGHT DISCUSSION.
IFR VISOR FOR MANEUVERS REVIEWED.

E _____   PREFLIGHT – DISCUSS LESSON OBJECTIVE. DIAGRAM
"S" TURNS, EIGHTS ALONG A ROAD, AND RECTANGULAR
COURSE ON A CHALKBOARD.

INFLIGHT – DEMONSTRATE ELEMENTS.
DEMONSTRATE FOLLOWING A ROAD, "S" TURNS, EIGHTS
ALONG A ROAD, AND RECTANGULAR COURSE. COACH
STUDENT PRACTICE.

POSTFLIGHT – CRITIQUE STUDENT PERFORMANCE AND
MAKE STUDY ASSIGNMENT.

F _____   PREFLIGHT – DISCUSS LESSON OBJECTIVE AND
RESOLVE QUESTIONS.

INFLIGHT – REVIEW PREVIOUS MANEUVERS INCLUDING
POWER-OFF STALLS AND FLIGHT AT MINIMUM CONTROLLABLE
AIRSPEED. PERFORM EACH NEW MANEUVER AS DIRECTED.

POSTFLIGHT – ASK PERTINENT QUESTIONS.

G _____   STUDENT SHOULD DEMONSTRATE COMPETENCY
IN MAINTAINING ORIENTATION, AIRSPEED WITHIN
10 KNOTS, ALTITUDE WITHIN 100 FEET, AND HEADINGS
WITHIN 10 DEGREES, AND IN MAKING PROPER
CORRECTION FOR WIND DRIFT.

FIGURE 1.—Lesson Plan.

17.
6158. (Refer to figure 1 on page 75.) Section C is titled:

A— Schedule.
B— Overview.
C— Training Schedule:

Answer (A) is correct (6158). *(AIH Chap 10)*
Section C of Fig. 1 is titled: Schedule. The instructor should estimate the amount of time to be devoted to the presentation of the elements of that lesson.
Answer (B) is incorrect because overview is a subpart of an introduction to a lesson, not a titled section of a lesson plan. Answer (C) is incorrect because the correct title is schedule, not training schedule.

18.
6159. (Refer to figure 1 on page 75.) Section D is titled:

A— Apparatus.
B— Equipment.
C— Preparation.

Answer (B) is correct (6159). *(AIH Chap 10)*
Section D of Fig. 1 is titled: Equipment. This includes all instructional materials and training aids required to teach the lesson.
Answer (A) is incorrect because the correct title is equipment, not apparatus. Answer (C) is incorrect because preparation is something both the student and instructor should do before a lesson, not a titled section of a lesson plan.

19.
6157. (Refer to figure 1 on page 75.) Section E is titled:

A— Content.
B— Discussion.
C— Instructor's Actions.

Answer (C) is correct (6157). *(AIH Chap 10)*
Section E of Fig. 1 is titled: Instructor's Actions. This is a statement of the instructor's proposed procedures for presenting the elements of knowledge and performance involved in the lesson.
Answer (A) is incorrect because content is not a titled section of a lesson plan. Answer (B) is incorrect because, while this section states that a discussion will take place, it is specifically those actions taken by the instructor and not the student.

20.
6160. (Refer to figure 1 on page 75.) Section F is titled:

A— Application.
B— Understanding.
C— Student's Actions.

Answer (C) is correct (6160). *(AIH Chap 10)*
Section F of Fig. 1 is titled: Student's Actions. This is a statement of desired student responses to instruction.
Answer (A) is incorrect because, while this involves application of what the instructor has presented to the student, this section is the instructor's desired student's action during the lesson. Answer (B) is incorrect because understanding is a level of learning, not a titled section of a lesson plan.

21.
6156. (Refer to figure 1 on page 75.) Section G is titled:

A— Summary.
B— Evaluation.
C— Completion Standards.

Answer (C) is correct (6156). *(AIH Chap 10)*
Section G of Fig. 1 is titled: Completion Standards. This is the evaluation basis for determining how well the student has met the objective of the lesson in terms of knowledge and skill.
Answer (A) is incorrect because a summary of a lesson would take place during the postflight discussion. Answer (B) is incorrect because evaluation is part of the teaching process and would be used by the instructor to compare the student's performance to the completion standards.

22.
6150a. Which statement is true regarding lesson plans?

A— Lesson plans should not be directed toward the course objective; only to the lesson objective.
B— A well-thought-out mental outline of a lesson may be used any time as long as the instructor is well prepared.
C— Lesson plans help instructors keep a constant check on their own activity as well as that of their students.

Answer (C) is correct (6150a). *(AIH Chap 10)*
Lesson plans help instructors keep a constant check on their own activity, as well as that of their students. The development of lesson plans by instructors signifies, in effect, that they have taught the lesson to themselves prior to attempting to teach the lesson to students.
Answer (A) is incorrect because a lesson plan should serve as a means of relating the lesson to the objectives of the course, as well as the lesson. Answer (B) is incorrect because a mental outline of a lesson is not a lesson plan. A lesson plan should be in written form regardless of an instructor's preparation.

23.
6054. When the instructor keeps the student informed of lesson objectives and completion standards, it minimizes the student's feelings of

A— insecurity.
B— resignation.
C— aggressiveness.

Answer (A) is correct (6054). *(AIH Chap 8)*
Students feel insecure when they do not know the lesson objectives and the completion standards to which they will be held. Instructors can minimize such feelings of insecurity by telling students what is expected of them and what to anticipate.
Answer (B) is incorrect because resignation occurs when a student completes the early phase of training without understanding the fundamentals, not the objectives or completion standards, and becomes lost in the advanced phase. Answer (C) is incorrect because aggression occurs when a student becomes angry at something or someone. Aggression (or any other defense mechanism) may be used to defend a feeling of insecurity when a student is not kept informed.

24.
6152. Which statement is true about lesson plans?

A— Lesson plans should follow a prescribed format.
B— Standard prepared lesson plans are effective for teaching all students.
C— The use of standard lesson plans may not be effective for students requiring a different approach.

Answer (C) is correct (6152). *(AIH Chap 10)*
A lesson plan for an instructional period should be appropriate to the background, experience, and ability of the particular student(s). If the procedures outlined in the lesson plan are not leading to the desired results, the instructor should change the approach. Thus, the use of standard lesson plans may not be effective for students requiring a different approach.
Answer (A) is incorrect because, although lesson plans should all contain certain items, the format to be followed should be tailored to the particular student(s). Answer (B) is incorrect because lesson plans are only an outline of the lesson. An instructor may have to adapt the procedures in a standard prepared lesson plan so it will be effective with different students.

25.
6150c. The main concern in developing a lesson plan is the

A— format.
B— content.
C— student.

Answer (C) is correct (6150c). *(AIH Chap 10)*
The lesson plan must be appropriate for the particular student. Because standard lesson plans may not be effective for students who require a different approach, the main concern in developing a lesson plan is the student.
Answer (A) is incorrect because the format of the lesson plan will be developed based on the needs of the student and the subject being taught. One lesson plan format does not work well for all students; therefore, the format of a lesson plan is an ending point, not a starting point, in lesson plan development. Answer (B) is incorrect because, while the content of a lesson plan is a concern in its development (e.g., how much time should be devoted to which subjects), the main concern in developing a lesson plan is the student.

26.

6151. With regard to the characteristics of a well-planned lesson, each lesson should contain

A— new material that is related to the lesson previously presented.

B— one basic element of the principle, procedure, or skill appropriate to that lesson.

C— every bit of information needed to reach the objective of the training syllabus.

Answer (A) is correct (6151). *(AIH Chap 10)*

One characteristic of a well-planned lesson is content, which means each lesson should contain new material. However, the new facts, principles, or skills should be related to the lesson previously presented. A short review of earlier lessons is usually necessary, especially in flight training.

Answer (B) is incorrect because all of the elements, not only one, necessary to learn a simple procedure, principle, or skill should be presented. Answer (C) is incorrect because each lesson should include all of the information needed to reach the objective of a particular lesson, but not everything needed for the entire syllabus.

27.

6141. What is the primary consideration in determining the length and frequency of flight instruction periods?

A— Fatigue.

B— Mental acuity.

C— Instructor preparation.

Answer (A) is correct (6141). *(AIH Chap 9)*

Fatigue is the primary consideration in determining the length and frequency of flight instruction periods. Flight instruction should be continued only so long as the student is alert, receptive to instruction, and is performing at a level consistent with experience.

Answer (B) is incorrect because fatigue, not mental acuity, is the primary consideration in determining the length and frequency of flight instruction periods. Fatigue may be either physical or mental, or both. Answer (C) is incorrect because fatigue, not instructor preparation, is the primary consideration in determining the length and frequency of flight instruction periods. Poor instructor preparation will make students become apathetic, not fatigued.

28.

6032. A primary consideration in planning for student performance is the

A— student's motivational level.

B— student's intellectual level.

C— length of the practice session.

Answer (C) is correct (6032). *(AIH Chap 1)*

In planning for student performance, a primary consideration is the length of time devoted to practice. A beginning student reaches a point where additional practice is not only unproductive but may even be harmful. When that point is reached, errors increase and motivation declines. As a student gains experience, longer periods of practice are profitable.

Answer (A) is incorrect because a student's motivational level is important to an instructor since it directly relates to the student's progress and ability to learn, not as a primary consideration in planning for student performance. Answer (B) is incorrect because a primary consideration in student performance is the length of time devoted to practice, not the student's intellectual level.

6.4 Instructional Aids

29.
6119. Which is a true statement concerning the use of instructional aids?

A— Instructional aids ensure getting and holding the student's attention.

B— Instructional aids should be designed to cover the key points in a lesson.

C— Instructional aids should not be used simply to cover a subject in less time.

Answer (B) is correct (6119). (AIH Chap 7)
Instructional aids are a good way to improve communication between the instructor and the students. Instructional aids should be designed to cover the key points in a lesson.
Answer (A) is incorrect because appropriate instructional aids will help to get the student's attention, but they cannot ensure that it will hold the student's attention. Answer (C) is incorrect because instructional aids can help get a point across quickly and clearly, thus reducing the time spent on some subjects.

30.
6122. The use of instructional aids should be based on their ability to support a specific point in the lesson. What is the first step in determining if and where instructional aids are necessary?

A— Organize subject material into an outline or a lesson plan.

B— Determine what ideas should be supported with instructional aids.

C— Clearly establish the lesson objective, being certain what must be communicated.

Answer (C) is correct (6122). (AIH Chap 7)
The first step in developing a lesson plan using instructional aids is, as in any lesson plan, to establish the lesson objective. Visual or other aids must help achieve the overall lesson objective. They should be strategically placed to recapture interest, shift to a new topic, or provide emphasis.
Answer (A) is incorrect because organizing the outline or lesson plan is the third, not first, step in the process. Answer (B) is incorrect because the final, not first, step in determining if and where instructional aids are necessary is to determine what ideas in the lesson should be supported with instructional aids.

31.
6120. Instructional aids used in the teaching/learning process should be

A— self-supporting and require no explanation.

B— compatible with the learning outcomes to be achieved.

C— selected prior to developing and organizing the lesson plan.

Answer (B) is correct (6120). (AIH Chap 7)
After establishing lesson objectives, researching the subject, and organizing the material into a lesson plan, the instructor should determine what needs to be supported by visual or other instructional aids. The aids should be compatible with the learning outcomes to be achieved.
Answer (A) is incorrect because instructional aids are not self-supporting and will require explanation.
Answer (C) is incorrect because instructional aids should be compatible with the desired learning outcomes, which can best be done after, not prior to, developing and organizing the lesson plan.

32.
6121. Instructional aids used in the teaching/learning process should not be used

A— as a crutch by the instructor.

B— for teaching more in less time.

C— to visualize relationships between abstracts.

Answer (A) is correct (6121). (AIH Chap 7)
Aids used in conjunction with oral presentation should emphasize, not distract from, the oral message. Also, the instructor should realize that such aids do not take the place of a sound lesson plan or instructor's input.
Answer (B) is incorrect because aids do help teach more in less time because they clarify and emphasize the lecture. The class can move to new material sooner.
Answer (C) is incorrect because instructional aids should be used to help students to visualize relationships between abstracts.

LESSON PLAN

Introduction (3 minutes)

A _____   Relates aircraft accident in which a multi-engine airplane ran off the end of the runway. This could have been avoided by correctly computing the landing distance. Relate similar personal experience of the same type of mishap.

B _____   Tell students how landing distance can affect them (any aircraft, plus future application).

C _____   Explain what will be learned. Explain how the lesson will proceed. Define landing distance and explain the normal landing distance chart. Then, demonstrate how to solve for landing distance. The students will practice theprocedure: at least once with supervision and at least once with as little help as possible. Next, the students will be evaluated according to the standards. Finally, the lesson will conclude with questions and answers, followed by a brief summary.

Body (29 minutes)

D _____   Define landing distance. Explain the normal landing distance chart to include the scale and interpolation. Ensure students can see demonstration and encourage questions. Demonstrate the pocedure using °C with a headwind and °F with a tailwind. Show the normal landing distance chart with given data in the following order:
1. temperature
2. pressure altitude
3. gross weight
4. headwind-tailwind component
5. read ground roll distance from graph

E _____   Review standards. Hand out chart and practice problems. Remind students to use a pencil, to make small tick marks, and to work as accurately as possible. Explain that they should follow the procedure on the chart to work the practice problems. Encourage students to ask questions. Check progress of each student continually so they develop skill proficiency within acceptable standards. Reteach any area(s) of difficulty to the class as they go along.

F _____   Review procedure again from the chart. Reemphasize standards of acceptable performance including time available. Prepare area for evaluation by removing the task step chart and practice problem sheets, and by handing out the evaluation problems. Ask students to work the three problems according to conditions and standards specified. Terminate evaluation after 6 minutes. Evaluate each student's performance and tactfully reveal results. Record results for use in reteaching any area(s) of difficulty in the summary.

Conclusion (3 minutes)

G _____   Review lessons with emphasis on any weak areas(s).

H _____   Remind students that landing distance will be an important consideration in any aircraft they fly.

I _____   Advise students that this lesson will be used as a starting point fro the next lesson. Assign study materials for the next lesson.

FIGURE 1A.—Lesson Plan.

Figure 1A is a sample ground lesson plan in contrast to the sample flight lesson plan illustrated in Figure 1 (on page 75). Lesson plans are discussed on pages 138 through 148. Use the lesson plan on page 143 to write in the section titles in Figure 1A above so you will be able to answer any FAA questions about Figure 1A.

CHAPTER SEVEN
CRITIQUE AND EVALUATION

7.1 THE INSTRUCTOR'S CRITIQUE (Questions 1-8)

1. No instructor skill is more important than the ability to analyze, appraise, and judge student performance.

    a. A student looks to the instructor for guidance, suggestions for improvement, and encouragement.

    b. To enhance a student's acceptance of further instruction, the instructor should keep the student informed of the progress made.

        1) This will help to minimize student frustrations, which will keep the student motivated to learn.

2. A critique should always be conducted immediately after the student's performance, while the details are easy to recall.

    a. The instructor may critique any activity which a student performs or practices to improve skill, proficiency, and learning.

3. A critique is a step in the learning process, not the grading process.

4. A critique is not necessarily negative in content. It considers the good along with the bad, the whole in terms of its parts, and the parts in relation to each other.

5. The purpose of a critique is to improve the student's performance and to provide him/her with something constructive with which to work and on which to build.

    a. The critique should provide direction and guidance to improve performance.

6. A critique should be **objective**.

    a. The effective critique is focused on student performance, and should not reflect the personal opinions, likes, dislikes, and biases of the instructor.

    b. The critique must be based on the performance as it was, not as it could have been.

7. A critique should be **flexible**.

    a. The instructor must fit the tone, technique, and content of the critique to the occasion and the student.

    b. An effective critique is flexible enough to satisfy the requirements of the moment.

8. A critique should be **acceptable**.

    a. Before students willingly accept their instructor's criticism they must first accept the instructor.

    b. The students must have confidence in the instructor's qualifications, teaching ability, sincerity, competence, and authority.

    c. Instructors cannot rely solely on their position to make a critique acceptable to their students.

9.   A critique should be **comprehensive**.

   a.   A comprehensive critique is not necessarily long, nor must it treat every aspect of the performance in detail.

   b.   The instructor must decide whether the greater benefit will come from a discussion of a few major points or a number of minor points.

   c.   An effective critique covers strengths as well as weaknesses.

10.   A critique should be **constructive**.

   a.   A critique is pointless unless a student profits from it.

   b.   Praise for praise's sake is of no value if a student is not taught how to capitalize on things which are done well and to use them to compensate for lesser accomplishments.

   c.   Also, it is not enough to identify a fault or weakness.

      1)   To tell students that their work is unsatisfactory with no explanation will most likely result in the students becoming frustrated.

      2)   The students must be briefed on the errors made and told how to correct them so progress and accomplishment can be made.

11.   A critique should be **thoughtful**.

   a.   An effective critique reflects an instructor's thoughtfulness toward the student's need for self-esteem, recognition, and approval from others.

      1)   The critique should never minimize the inherent dignity and importance of the individual.

   b.   Ridicule, anger, or fun at the expense of the student has no place in the critique.

12.   A critique should be **specific**.

   a.   The instructor's comments and recommendations should be specific, not so general that the student can find nothing to hold onto.

   b.   Express ideas with firmness and authority in terms that cannot be misunderstood.

      1)   Students should have no doubt what they did well and what they did poorly, and specifically how they can improve.

7.2 TYPES OF TESTING (Questions 9-11)

1.   **Norm-referenced testing** measures a student's performance against the performance of other students.

2.   **Criterion-referenced testing** measures a student's performance against a carefully written, measurable standard or criterion.

   a.   Practical tests for pilot certification are an example of criterion-referenced testing.

      1)   The objective of the Practical Test Standards (PTS) is to ensure the certification of pilots at a high level of performance and proficiency, consistent with safety.

   b.   A pretest constructed to measure knowledge and skills necessary to begin a course is a criterion-referenced test.

7.3 ORAL QUIZZING (Questions 12-18)

1. The most practical means of evaluation is oral quizzing of students by the instructor. Questions may be loosely classified as fact and thought questions.

    a. The answer to a fact question is based on memory or recall.

    b. Thought questions require the student to combine a knowledge of facts with an ability to analyze situations, solve problems, and arrive at conclusions.

2. Proper quizzing by the instructor can have a number of desirable results. It can

    a. Reveal the effectiveness of training procedures,
    b. Check student retention and comprehension of what has been learned,
    c. Review material already covered,
    d. Help retain student interest and stimulate thinking,
    e. Emphasize the important points of training,
    f. Identify points that need more emphasis, and
    g. Promote active student participation.

3. Characteristics of effective questions:

    a. Each question must have only one correct answer.

        1) This is a characteristic of good objective-type (fact) questions and generally true of all good questions.

        2) Each question should call for a specific answer which can be readily evaluated by the instructor.

    b. Each question must apply to the subject being taught.

    c. Each question should be brief and concise, but must be clear and definite.

    d. Each question should center on only one idea which is limited to who, what, where, when, how, or why, not a combination.

    e. Each question should present a challenge.

        1) A question must be of suitable difficulty for the students at that particular stage of training.

4. When answering student questions, the instructor needs to clearly understand the question before attempting an answer.

    a. The instructor should display interest in the student's questions and give as direct and accurate an answer as possible.

    b. If a student's question is too advanced for the particular lesson and confusion may result from a complete answer, the instructor may

        1) Carefully explain that the question was good and pertinent;

        2) Explain that to answer would unnecessarily complicate the learning task at hand; and

        3) Advise the student to reintroduce the question later at the appropriate point in training, or meet outside class for a more complete discussion.

5. Occasionally, a student will ask a question the instructor cannot answer. The best course is to freely admit not knowing the answer.

    a. The instructor should then promise to find out or offer to help the student look it up in appropriate references.

7.4 TYPES OF WRITTEN TEST QUESTIONS (Questions 19-26)

1.   Written test questions fall into two general categories:

   a.   Supply-type and
   b.   Selection-type.

2.   Supply-type questions require the student to furnish a response in the form of a word, sentence, or paragraph.

   a.   Supply-type test items

      1)   Require students to organize their thoughts and ideas,

      2)   Demand the ability to express ideas, and

      3)   Are subjective.

         a)   Thus, their main disadvantage is that they cannot be graded uniformly.

         b)   The same test graded by different instructors probably would be assigned different scores.

      4)   Take longer for students to answer and for instructors to grade, which is another disadvantage.

3.   Selection-type questions include items for which two or more alternative responses are provided.

   a.   Selection-type test items

      1)   Are highly objective.

         a)   Thus, they are graded uniformly regardless of the student or grader.

      2)   Allow direct comparison of students' accomplishments. For example, it is possible to compare student performance

         a)   Within the same class,
         b)   Between classes, and
         c)   Under different instructors.

   b.   True-false, multiple-choice, and matching type questions are prime examples of selection-type questions.

4.   The true-false test item is well adapted to the testing of knowledge of facts and detail, especially when there are only two possible answers.

   a.   The chief disadvantage of the true-false test item is that it creates the greatest probability of guessing since the student always has a 50% chance of guessing correctly.

5.   Multiple-choice test items may be used to determine student achievement, ranging from acquisition of facts to understanding, reasoning, and ability to apply what has been learned.

   a.   One of the major difficulties encountered in the construction of multiple test items is inventing plausible sounding incorrect choices (distractors) which will be attractive to students lacking knowledge or understanding.

   b.   When multiple-choice items are intended to measure achievement at a higher level of learning, some or all of the alternatives should be acceptable, but one should be clearly better than the others.

   c.   Multiple-choice test items should have all alternatives of approximately equal length.

      1)   The common error made by instructors is to make the correct alternative longer than the incorrect ones.

6. Matching test items are particularly good for measuring the student's ability to recognize relationships and to make associations between terms, parts, words, phrases, or symbols listed in one column with related items in another column.

    a. Matching reduces the probability of guessing correct responses compared to a series of multiple-choice items covering the same material.

7.5 CHARACTERISTICS OF A GOOD TEST (Questions 27-31)

1. Reliability

    a. A written test that has reliability yields consistent results.

2. Validity

    a. A written test has validity when it measures what it is supposed to measure and nothing else.

3. Usability

    a. A written test is usable when it is easy to give, easy to read, the wording is clear and concise, figures are appropriate to the test items and clearly drawn, and the test is easily graded.

4. Comprehensiveness

    a. A written test is said to be comprehensive when it samples liberally whatever is being measured.

5. Discrimination

    a. A written test having the characteristic of discrimination will measure small differences in achievement between students.

        1) It will also distinguish between students both low and high in achievement of the course objectives.

7.6 REVIEW AND EVALUATION (Questions 32-34)

1. Review and evaluation of the student's learning should be an integral part of each lesson.

    a. Evaluation of student performance and accomplishment should be based on the objectives and goals established in the lesson plan.

2. Performance testing is desirable for evaluating training that involves an operation, procedure, or process.

    a. This method of evaluation is particularly suited to the measurement of a student's ability in performing a task, either mental or physical.

QUESTIONS AND ANSWER EXPLANATIONS

All of the FAA questions from the Fundamentals of Instructing knowledge test relating to the learning process and the material outlined above are reproduced below in the same modules as the outlines. To the immediate right of each question are the correct answer and answer explanation. You should cover these answers and answer explanations with your hand or a piece of paper while responding to the questions. Refer to the general discussion in Chapter 1 on how to take the FAA pilot knowledge test.

Remember that the questions from the FAA pilot knowledge test bank have been reordered by topic, and the topics have been organized into a meaningful sequence. Accordingly, the first line of the answer explanation gives the FAA question number and the citation of the authoritative source for the answer.

7.1 The Instructor's Critique

1.

6070. To enhance a student's acceptance of further instruction, the instructor should

A— keep the student informed of the progress made.
B— continually prod the student to maintain motivational levels.
C— establish performance standards a little above the student's actual ability.

Answer (A) is correct (6070). *(AIH Chap 8)*
Keeping the student informed of progress will tend to enhance a student's acceptance of further instruction. A student who is unaware of progress may lose interest, which decreases motivation and hinders learning.
Answer (B) is incorrect because, if an instructor continually prods a student, the student's motivational level will decrease, not remain the same, due to his/her becoming frustrated. This will then lead to a decrease, not increase, in the student's desire to learn. Answer (C) is incorrect because the student will become frustrated by his/her inability to reach standards above his/her actual level of skill. This will lead to a decrease, not increase, in the desire to learn.

2.

6094. When an instructor critiques a student, it should always be

A— done in private.
B— subjective rather than objective.
C— conducted immediately after the student's performance.

Answer (C) is correct (6094). *(AIH Chap 6)*
The critique should always be conducted immediately after the student's performance, while the performance is still fresh in the student's mind. Specific comments on "your third turn," for instance, would have little value a week after the maneuver was performed.
Answer (A) is incorrect because a critique may be conducted in private or before the entire class. A critique presented before the entire class can be beneficial to every student in the classroom as well as to the student who performed the exercise. Answer (B) is incorrect because the critique should be objective rather than subjective.

3.

6092. Which statement is true about an instructor's critique of a student's performance?

A— The critique should always be conducted in private.
B— It is a step in the learning process, not in the grading process.
C— Instructor comments and recommendations should be based on the performance the way it should have been.

Answer (B) is correct (6092). *(AIH Chap 6)*
A critique is a step in the learning process, not the grading process. A critique should be used to guide students to better performance.
Answer (A) is incorrect because a critique may be conducted in private or before the entire class. A critique presented before the entire class can be beneficial to every student in the classroom as well as to the student who performed the exercise. Answer (C) is incorrect because a critique must be based on the performance as it was, not as it should have been.

4.

6095. An instructor's critique of a student's performance should

A— treat every aspect of the performance in detail.
B— be private so that the student is not embarrassed.
C— provide direction and guidance to improve performance.

Answer (C) is correct (6095). *(AIH Chap 6)*
A critique should improve a student's performance and provide something constructive with which (s)he can work on and build. It should provide direction and guidance to improve performance.
Answer (A) is incorrect because a comprehensive critique is not necessarily a long one, nor must it treat every aspect of the performance in detail. The instructor must decide whether the greater benefit will come from discussing a few major points or a number of minor points. Answer (B) is incorrect because a critique may be conducted in private or before the entire class. A critique presented before the entire class can be beneficial to every student in the classroom as well as to the student who performed the exercise.

5.

6096. Which is true about an instructor's critique of a student's performance?

A— Praise for praise's sake is of value.
B— It should be constructive and objective.
C— It should treat every aspect of the performance in detail.

Answer (B) is correct (6096). *(AIH Chap 6)*
A critique must be constructive by explaining to the student how to capitalize on things which are done well and to use them to compensate for lesser accomplishments. A critique must also be objective by basing it on the performance as it was, not as it could have been.
Answer (A) is incorrect because praise for praise's sake is of no value if a student is not taught how to capitalize on things that are done well and to use them to compensate for lesser accomplishments. Answer (C) is incorrect because a comprehensive critique is not necessarily a long one, nor must it treat every aspect of the performance in detail. The instructor must decide whether the greater benefit will come from discussing a few major points or a number of minor points.

6.

6097. To be effective, a critique should

A— not contain negative remarks.
B— treat every aspect of the performance in detail.
C— be flexible enough to satisfy the requirements of the moment.

Answer (C) is correct (6097). *(AIH Chap 6)*
An effective critique is one that is flexible enough to satisfy the requirements of the moment. The instructor must fit the tone, technique, and content of the critique to the occasion and the student. Thus, the instructor is faced with the problem of what to say, what to omit, and what to minimize. The challenge of the critique is that the instructor must determine what to say at the proper moment.
Answer (A) is incorrect because a critique may contain negative remarks as long as they point toward improvement or a higher level of performance.
Answer (B) is incorrect because a comprehensive critique is not necessarily a long one, nor must it treat every aspect of the performance in detail. The instructor must decide whether the greater benefit will come from discussing a few major points or a number of minor points.

7.

6093. Which statement is true about instructors' critiques?

A— Instructors should rely on their personality to make a critique more acceptable.

B— A comprehensive critique should emphasize positive aspects of student performance.

C— Before students willingly accept their instructor's critique, they must first accept the instructor.

Answer (C) is correct (6093). *(AIH Chap 6)*
Students must have confidence in the instructor's qualifications, teaching ability, sincerity, competence, and authority before they will willingly accept their instructor's criticism. A critique holds little weight if the student has no respect for the instructor.
Answer (A) is incorrect because the effective critique is focused on student performance and should not reflect the personal opinions, likes, dislikes, and biases (i.e., personality) of the instructor. Answer (B) is incorrect because a comprehensive critique means that good and bad points are covered adequately, but not necessarily in exhaustive detail.

8.

6052. Which would more likely result in students becoming frustrated?

A— Giving the students meaningless praise.

B— Telling students their work is unsatisfactory with no explanation.

C— Covering up instructor mistakes or bluffing when the instructor is in doubt.

Answer (B) is correct (6052). *(AIH Chap 8)*
If a student has made an earnest effort but is told that the work is not satisfactory, with no other explanation, frustration occurs. On the other hand, if the student is briefed on the errors made and is told how to correct them, progress and accomplishment can be made.
Answer (A) is incorrect because giving meaningless praise is valueless, not frustrating, to a student. Answer (C) is incorrect because covering up instructor mistakes or bluffing when the instructor is in doubt results in destroying student confidence, not creating frustration.

7.2 Types of Testing

9.

6098b. Practical tests for pilot certification are

A— evaluation-referenced.

B— norm-referenced.

C— criterion-referenced.

Answer (C) is correct (6098b). *(AIH Chap 6)*
Criterion-referenced tests measure an applicant's performance against carefully written, measurable standards or criteria. Practical tests for pilot certification are criterion-referenced. The Practical Test Standards are the criteria.
Answer (A) is incorrect because practical tests are a form of evaluation, not evaluation-referenced. Evaluation-referenced is not a type of testing. Answer (B) is incorrect because norm-referenced testing measures a student's performance against that of other students; a practical test for pilot certification measures the applicant's performance against carefully written, measurable standards (the Practical Test Standards).

10.

6098c. The objective of the Practical Test Standards (PTS) is to ensure the certification of pilots at a high level of performance and proficiency, consistent with

A— the time available.

B— safety.

C— their abilities.

Answer (B) is correct (6098c). *(AIH Chap 6)*
The objective of the Practical Test Standards is to ensure the certification of pilots at a high level of performance and proficiency, consistent with safety.
Answer (A) is incorrect because the objective of the Practical Test Standards (PTS) is to ensure the certification of pilots at a high level of performance and proficiency, consistent with safety, not the time available. Answer (C) is incorrect because the objective of the Practical Test Standards (PTS) is to ensure the certification of pilots at a high level of performance and proficiency, consistent with safety, not their abilities.

11.
6124c. A pretest constructed to measure knowledge and skills necessary to begin a course is referred to as a

A— virtual-reality test.
B— norm-referenced test.
C— criterion-referenced test.

Answer (C) is correct (6124c). *(AIH Chap 8)*
A pretest is a criterion-referenced test constructed to measure the knowledge and skills that are necessary to begin a course. Criterion-referenced tests measure a student's performance against carefully written, measurable standards or criteria.
Answer (A) is incorrect because virtual reality is a potential future method of computer-based training (CBT) that can simulate environments very realistically. It is not a type of test. Answer (B) is incorrect because a pretest is a criterion-referenced test, not a norm-referenced test. Norm-referenced tests measure a student's performance against that of other students.

7.3 Oral Quizzing

12.
6100. One desirable result of proper oral quizzing by the instructor is to

A— reveal the effectiveness of the instructor's training procedures.
B— fulfill the requirements set forth in the overall objectives of the course.
C— reveal the essential information from which the student can determine progress.

Answer (A) is correct (6100). *(AIH Chap 6)*
One desirable result of proper oral quizzing by the instructor is that it reveals the effectiveness of the instructor's training procedures.
Answer (B) is incorrect because quizzing can only measure achievement, not fulfill the requirements, of the overall objectives of the course. Answer (C) is incorrect because an instructor should use the critique, not a quiz, to reveal the essential information from which the student can determine progress.

13.
6098a. Which is a valid reason for the use of proper oral quizzing during a lesson?

A— Promotes active student participation.
B— Identifies points that need less emphasis.
C— Helps the instructor determine the general intelligence level of the students.

Answer (A) is correct (6098a). *(AIH Chap 6)*
A valid reason for the use of proper oral quizzing during a lesson is to promote active student participation, which is important to effective teaching.
Answer (B) is incorrect because a valid reason for the use of proper oral quizzing during a lesson is that it identifies points which need more, not less, emphasis. Answer (C) is incorrect because a valid reason for the use of proper oral quizzing during a lesson is to check the students' comprehension of what has been learned, not their general intelligence level.

14.
6099. Proper oral quizzing by the instructor during a lesson can have which result?

A— Promotes effective use of available time.
B— Identifies points which need more emphasis.
C— Permits the introduction of new material not covered previously.

Answer (B) is correct (6099). *(AIH Chap 6)*
One desirable result of oral quizzing is that it helps the instructor identify points that need more emphasis. By noting students' answers, the instructor can quickly spot weak points in understanding and give these extra attention.
Answer (A) is incorrect because the use of a lesson plan, not oral quizzing, by the instructor will promote effective use of available time. Answer (C) is incorrect because the introduction of new material is accomplished during the presentation, not evaluation, step of the teaching process.

15.

6103. To be effective in oral quizzing during the conduct of a lesson, a question should

A— be of suitable difficulty for that stage of training.
B— include a combination of where, how, and why.
C— divert the student's thoughts to subjects covered in other lessons.

Answer (A) is correct (6103). *(AIH Chap 6)*
During oral quizzing, an effective question must present a challenge to the student. A question must be of suitable difficulty for the student at that particular stage of training. These types of questions stimulate learning.
Answer (B) is incorrect because an effective question should be limited to who, what, when, where, how, or why, not a combination. Answer (C) is incorrect because an effective question must apply to the subject of instruction, not divert the student's thoughts to subjects covered in other lessons.

16.

6101. During oral quizzing in a given lesson, effective questions should

A— be brief and concise.
B— provide answers that can be expressed in a variety of ways.
C— divert the student's thoughts to subjects covered in previous lessons.

Answer (A) is correct (6101). *(AIH Chap 6)*
During oral quizzing, an effective question should be brief and concise, but must also be clear and definite. Enough words must be used to establish the conditions or situations exactly, so that instructor and students will have the same mental picture.
Answer (B) is incorrect because all effective questions will have only one correct answer. A thought question will only have one correct answer, although it may be expressed in a variety of ways. Answer (C) is incorrect because an effective question must apply to the subject of instruction, not divert the student's thoughts to subjects covered in previous lessons.

17.

6102. In all quizzing as a portion of the instruction process, the questions should

A— include catch questions to develop the student's perceptive power.
B— call for specific answers and be readily evaluated by the instructor.
C— include questions with more than one central idea to evaluate how completely a student understands the subject.

Answer (B) is correct (6102). *(AIH Chap 6)*
In any kind of testing, questions should have one specific answer so that the instructor can readily evaluate the student's response. General questions tend to confuse rather than help, and unanswered questions serve no useful purpose at all.
Answer (A) is incorrect because catch questions should be avoided at all times. The students will feel they are engaged in a battle of wits with the instructor, and the whole significance of the subject of instruction will be lost. Answer (C) is incorrect because effective questions used in quizzing should center on only one central idea.

18.

6104. To answer a student's question, it is most important that the instructor

A— clearly understand the question.
B— have complete knowledge of the subject.
C— introduce more complicated information to partially answer the question, if necessary.

Answer (A) is correct (6104). *(AIH Chap 6)*
The answering of students' questions can be an effective teaching method. To answer a student's question, it is most important that the instructor clearly understands the question.
Answer (B) is incorrect because, while an instructor may have knowledge of a subject, occasionally a student will ask a question which the instructor cannot answer. The instructor should admit not knowing the answer, and should promise to get the answer or help the student to find it. Answer (C) is incorrect because introducing more complicated information to partially answer the question is normally unwise. Doing so would confuse the student and complicate the learning tasks at hand.

7.4 Types of Written Test Questions

19.
6112. What is a characteristic of supply-type test items?

A— They are easily adapted to testing knowledge of facts and details.

B— Test results would be graded the same regardless of the student or the grader.

C— The same test graded by different instructors would probably be given different scores.

Answer (C) is correct (6112). *(AIH Chap 6)*
A characteristic of supply-type test items is that they cannot be graded with uniformity. The same test graded by different instructors would probably be assigned different scores. The same test graded by the same instructor on consecutive days might be assigned two different scores. There is no assurance that the grade assigned is the grade deserved.
Answer (A) is incorrect because true-false, not supply-type, test items are easily adapted to testing knowledge of facts and details. Answer (B) is incorrect because selection-type, not supply-type, test items would be graded the same regardless of the student or the grader.

20.
6111. Which is the main disadvantage of supply-type test items?

A— They cannot be graded with uniformity.

B— They are readily answered by guessing.

C— They are easily adapted to statistical analysis.

Answer (A) is correct (6111). *(AIH Chap 6)*
The main disadvantage of supply-type test items is that they cannot be graded with uniformity. The same test graded by different instructors would probably be assigned different scores. The same test graded by the same instructor on consecutive days might be assigned two different scores. There is no assurance that the grade assigned is the grade deserved.
Answer (B) is incorrect because the main disadvantage of true-false, not supply-type, test items is they are readily answered by guessing. Answer (C) is incorrect because an advantage, not disadvantage, of selection-type, not supply-type, test items is that they are easily adapted to statistical analysis.

21.
6113. One of the main advantages of selection-type test items over supply-type test items is that the selection-type

A— decreases discrimination between responses.

B— would be graded objectively regardless of the student or the grader.

C— precludes comparison of students under one instructor with those under another instructor.

Answer (B) is correct (6113). *(AIH Chap 6)*
One of the main advantages of selection-type test items over supply-type test items is that the selection-type are graded objectively regardless of the student or grader.
Answer (A) is incorrect because an advantage of the selection-type test item over the supply-type test item is that more areas of knowledge can be tested in a given time, thus increasing, not decreasing, comprehensiveness, validity, and discrimination. Answer (C) is incorrect because an advantage of the selection-type test item over supply-type test item is the ability to compare, not to preclude comparison of, student performance under one instructor with those of another instructor.

22.
6115. Which statement is true about multiple-choice test items that are intended to measure achievement at a higher level of learning?

A— It is unethical to mislead students into selecting an incorrect alternative.

B— Some or all of the alternatives should be acceptable, but only one should be clearly better than the others.

C— The use of common errors as distracting alternatives to divert the student from the correct response is ineffective and invalid.

Answer (B) is correct (6115). *(AIH Chap 6)*
When multiple-choice test items are intended to measure achievement at a higher level of learning, some or all of the alternatives should be acceptable, but only one should be clearly better than the others. The instructions given should direct the student to select the best alternative.
Answer (A) is incorrect because when using multiple-choice test items the students are not supposed to guess the correct answer; they should select it only if they know it is correct. Thus, it is ethical, not unethical, to mislead students into selecting an incorrect alternative. Answer (C) is incorrect because when using multiple-choice test items, the use of common errors as distracting alternatives to divert the student from the correct response is effective, not ineffective, and valid, not invalid.

23.

6116. Which statement is true relative to effective multiple-choice test items?

A— Negative words or phrases need not be emphasized.
B— Items should call for abstract background knowledge.
C— Keep all alternatives of approximately equal length.

Answer (C) is correct (6116). *(AIH Chap 6)*
In preparing and reviewing the alternatives to a multiple-choice item, it is advisable to keep all alternatives approximately the same length. Research of instructor-made tests reveals that, in general, correct alternatives are longer than incorrect ones.
Answer (A) is incorrect because, when negative words or phrases are used, they should be emphasized in order to be effective. Answer (B) is incorrect because items should call for essential knowledge rather than for abstract background knowledge or unimportant facts.

24.

6110. Which type of test item creates the greatest probability of guessing?

A— True-false.
B— Supply-type.
C— Multiple-choice.

Answer (A) is correct (6110). *(AIH Chap 6)*
The true-false test item creates the greatest probability of guessing since the student always has a 50% chance of guessing correctly.
Answer (B) is incorrect because the true-false, not the supply-type, test item creates the greatest probability of guessing. Answer (C) is incorrect because the true-false, not the multiple-choice, test item creates the greatest probability of guessing.

25.

6114. Which is one of the major difficulties encountered in the construction of multiple-choice test items?

A— Adapting the items to statistical item analysis.
B— Keeping all responses approximately equal in length.
C— Inventing distractors which will be attractive to students lacking knowledge or understanding.

Answer (C) is correct (6114). *(AIH Chap 6)*
Three major difficulties are encountered in the construction of multiple-choice test items:

1. Development of a question or an item stem which can be expressed clearly without ambiguity.
2. Statement of an answer which cannot be refuted.
3. The invention of lures or distractors which will be attractive to those students who do not possess the knowledge or understanding necessary to recognize the correct answer.

Answer (A) is incorrect because it is a major advantage, not difficulty, for a multiple-choice test item to be well adapted to statistical item analysis. Answer (B) is incorrect because a principle, not difficulty, of constructing a multiple-choice test item is to keep all responses approximately equal in length.

26.

6117. In a written test, which type of selection-type test items reduces the probability of guessing correct responses?

A— Essay.
B— Matching.
C— Multiple-choice.

Answer (B) is correct (6117). *(AIH Chap 6)*
In a written test, matching test items reduces the probability of guessing correct responses compared to a series of multiple-choice items covering the same material, especially if alternatives are used more than once.
Answer (A) is incorrect because an essay question is a supply-type, not selection-type, test item. Answer (C) is incorrect because matching, not multiple-choice, test items reduce the probability of guessing correct responses.

7.5 Characteristics of a Good Test

27.
6106. A written test that has reliability

A— yields consistent results.
B— measures small differences in the achievement of students.
C— actually measures what it is supposed to measure and nothing else.

Answer (A) is correct (6106). *(AIH Chap 6)*
A written test that has reliability is one which yields consistent results.
Answer (B) is incorrect because a written test which shows discrimination, not reliability, measures small differences in the achievement of students. Answer (C) is incorrect because a written test which has validity, not reliability, actually measures what it is supposed to measure and nothing else.

28.
6105. A written test has validity when it

A— yields consistent results.
B— samples liberally whatever is being measured.

C— measures what it is supposed to measure and nothing else.

Answer (C) is correct (6105). *(AIH Chap 6)*
A written test has validity when it measures what it is supposed to measure and nothing else.
Answer (A) is incorrect because a written test has reliability, not validity, when it yields consistent results. Answer (B) is incorrect because a written test has comprehensiveness, not validity, when it samples liberally whatever is being measured.

29.
6109. A written test is said to be comprehensive when it

A— includes all levels of difficulty.

B— samples liberally whatever is being measured.
C— measures knowledge of the same topic in many different ways.

Answer (B) is correct (6109). *(AIH Chap 6)*
A written test is said to be comprehensive when it samples liberally whatever is being measured.
Answer (A) is incorrect because a written test shows discrimination, not comprehensiveness, when it includes all levels of difficulty. Answer (C) is incorrect because a written test shows discrimination, not comprehensiveness, when it measures knowledge of the same topic in many different ways.

30.
6107. The characteristic of a written test, which measures small differences in achievement between students, is its

A— validity.
B— reliability.

C— discrimination.

Answer (C) is correct (6107). *(AIH Chap 6)*
The characteristic of a written test which measures small differences in achievement between students is its discrimination.
Answer (A) is incorrect because a written test has validity when it measures what it is supposed to and nothing else, not when it measures small differences in achievement between students. Answer (B) is incorrect because a written test that has reliability is one which yields consistent results, not which measures small differences in achievement between students.

31.
6108. A written test having the characteristic of discrimination will

A— be easy to give and be easily graded.
B— distinguish between students both low and high in achievement.
C— include a representative and comprehensive sampling of the course objectives.

Answer (B) is correct (6108). *(AIH Chap 6)*
When a written test has the characteristic of discrimination, each item will distinguish between students who are low and students who are high in achievement of the course objectives.
Answer (A) is incorrect because a written test having the characteristic of usability, not discrimination, will be easy to give and be easily graded. Answer (C) is incorrect because a written test having the characteristic of comprehensiveness, not discrimination, will include a representative and comprehensive sampling of the course objectives.

7.6 Review and Evaluation

32.
6069. Evaluation of student performance and accomplishment during a lesson should be based on

A— objectives and goals established in the lesson plan.
B— performance of each student compared to an objective standard.
C— each student's ability to make an objective evaluation of their own progress.

Answer (A) is correct (6069). *(AIH Chap 4)*
    The evaluation of student performance and accomplishment during a lesson should be based on the objectives and goals that were established in the instructor's lesson plan.
    Answer (B) is incorrect because a critique, not an evaluation, is based on comparing a student's performance to an objective standard. Answer (C) is incorrect because a student's own evaluation can only be subjective, not objective. Only the instructor can provide a realistic evaluation of performance and progress.

33.
6067. Which statement is true regarding student evaluation?

A— The student's own evaluations can only be objective.
B— Evaluation of the student's learning should be an integral part of each lesson.
C— If deficiencies or faults not associated with the present lesson are revealed, they should be corrected immediately.

Answer (B) is correct (6067). *(AIH Chap 4)*
    Review and evaluation should be an integral part of each classroom or flight lesson. At the end of each class period, the instructor should review what has been covered during the lesson and require the students to demonstrate the extent to which the lesson objectives have been met. Evaluation can be formal (performance, written tests) or informal (oral quiz or guided discussion).
    Answer (A) is incorrect because the student's own evaluations can only be subjective, not objective. Answer (C) is incorrect because, if deficiencies or faults not associated with the present lesson are revealed, they should be noted and pointed out. Corrective measures that are practicable at the time should be taken immediately, but more thorough remedial actions must be included in future lesson plans.

34.
6118. Which type test is desirable for evaluating training that involves an operation, procedure, or process?

A— Oral.
B— Performance.
C— Proficiency.

Answer (B) is correct (6118). *(AIH Chap 6)*
    Performance testing is desirable for evaluating training that involves an operation, procedure, or process. This method of evaluation is particularly suited to the measurement of a student's ability in performing a task, either mental or physical.
    Answer (A) is incorrect because performance, not oral, testing is desirable for evaluating training that involves an operation, procedure, or process. Answer (C) is incorrect because there is no proficiency-type test in evaluation, only oral, written, or performance.

END OF CHAPTER

APPENDIX A
FUNDAMENTALS OF INSTRUCTING
PRACTICE TEST

The following 50 questions have been randomly selected from the 192 fundamental of instructing questions in the FAA's flight and ground instructor test bank. Topical coverage in this practice test is similar to that of the FAA knowledge test. Use the correct answer listing on page 102 to grade your practice test.

1.
6001. A change in behavior as a result of experience can be defined as

A— learning.
B— knowledge.
C— understanding.

2.
6004. Individuals make more progress learning if they have a clear objective. This is one feature of the principle of

A— primacy.
B— readiness.
C— willingness.

3.
6007. Things most often repeated are best remembered because of which principle of learning?

A— Principle of effect.
B— Principle of recency.
C— Principle of exercise.

4.
6010. Which principle of learning often creates a strong impression?

A— Principle of primacy.
B— Principle of intensity.
C— Principle of readiness.

5.
6013. Instruction, as opposed to the trial and error method of learning, is desirable because competent instruction speeds the learning process by

A— motivating the student to a better performance.
B— emphasizing only the important points of training.
C— teaching the relationship of perceptions as they occur.

6.
6016. The factor which contributes most to a student's failure to remain receptive to new experiences and which creates a tendency to reject additional training is

A— basic needs.
B— element of threat.
C— negative self-concept.

7.
6019. In the learning process, fear or the element of threat will

A— narrow the student's perceptual field.
B— decrease the rate of associative reactions.
C— cause a student to focus on several areas of perception.

8.
6022. Which statement is true concerning motivations?

A— Motivations must be tangible to be effective.
B— Motivations may be very subtle and difficult to identify.
C— Negative motivations often are as effective as positive motivations.

9.
6025. Which is generally the more effective way for an instructor to properly motivate students?

A— Maintain pleasant personal relationships with students.
B— Provide positive motivations by the promise or achievement of rewards.
C— Reinforce their self-confidence by requiring no tasks beyond their ability to perform.

10.
6028. During the flight portion of a practical test, the examiner simulates complete loss of engine power by closing the throttle and announcing "simulated engine failure." What level of learning is being tested?

A— Application.
B— Correlation.
C— Understanding.

11.
6031. The best way to prepare a student to perform a task is to

A— explain the purpose of the task.
B— provide a clear, step-by-step example.
C— give the student an outline of the task.

12.
6034. According to one theory, some forgetting is due to the practice of submerging an unpleasant experience into the subconscious. This is called

A— blanking.
B— immersion.
C— repression.

13.
6037. Responses that produce a pleasurable return are called

A— reward.
B— praise.
C— positive feedback.

14.
6040a. To ensure proper habits and correct techniques during training, an instructor should

A— use the building block technique of instruction.
B— repeat subject matter the student has already learned.
C— introduce challenging material to continually motivate the student.

15.
6043. Which of the student's human needs offer the greatest challenge to an instructor?

A— Social.
B— Egoistic.
C— Self-fulfillment.

16.
6046. When a student asks irrelevant questions or refuses to participate in class activities, it usually is an indication of the defense mechanism known as

A— flight.
B— aggression.
C— resignation.

17.
6049. When students display the defense mechanism called aggression, they

A— become visibly angry, upset, and childish.
B— may refuse to participate in class activities.
C— attempt to justify actions by asking numerous questions.

18.
6052. Which would more likely result in students becoming frustrated?

A— Giving the students meaningless praise.
B— Telling students their work is unsatisfactory with no explanation.
C— Covering up instructor mistakes or bluffing when the instructor is in doubt.

19.
6055. Student confidence tends to be destroyed if instructors

A— bluff whenever in doubt about some point.
B— continually identify student errors and failures.
C— direct and control the student's actions and behavior.

20.
6058. To communicate effectively, instructors must

A— recognize the level of comprehension.
B— provide an atmosphere which encourages questioning.
C— reveal a positive attitude while delivering their message.

21.
6061. By using abstractions in the communication process, the communicator will

A— bring forth specific items of experience in the minds of the receivers.
B— be using words which refer to objects or ideas that human beings can experience directly.
C— not evoke in the listener's or reader's mind the specific items of experience the communicator intends.

22.
6064. A communicator's words cannot communicate the desired meaning to another person unless the

A— words have meaningful referents.
B— words give the meaning that is in the mind of the receiver.
C— listener or reader has had some experience with the objects or concepts to which these words refer.

23.
6067. Which statement is true regarding student evaluation?

A— The student's own evaluations can only be objective.
B— Evaluation of the student's learning should be an integral part of each lesson.
C— If deficiencies or faults not associated with the present lesson are revealed, they should be corrected immediately.

24.
6070. To enhance a student's acceptance of further instruction, the instructor should

A— keep the student informed of the progress made.
B— continually prod the student to maintain motivational levels.
C— establish performance standards a little above the student's actual ability.

25.
6073. The method of arranging lesson material from the simple to complex, past to present, and known to unknown, is one that

A— creates student thought pattern departures.
B— shows the relationships of the main points of the lesson.
C— requires students to actively participate in the lesson.

26.
6076. The first step in preparing a lecture is to

A— research the subject.
B— develop the main ideas or key points.
C— establish the objective and desired outcome.

27.
6079. What is one advantage of a lecture?

A— Uses time economically.
B— Excellent when additional research is required.
C— Allows for maximum attainment of certain types of learning outcomes.

28.
6082a. Which teaching method is most economical in terms of the time required to present a given amount of material?

A— Briefing.
B— Teaching lecture.
C— Demonstration/performance.

29.
6085. In a guided discussion, learning is achieved through the

A— skillful use of questions.
B— use of questions, each of which contains several ideas.
C— use of reverse questions directed to the class as a whole.

30.
6088. When it appears students have adequately discussed the ideas presented during a guided discussion, one of the most valuable tools an instructor can use is

A— a session of verbal testing.
B— a written test on the subject discussed.
C— an interim summary of what the students accomplished.

31.
6091a. What is the last step in the demonstration/performance method?

A— Summary.
B— Evaluation.
C— Student performance.

32.
6094. When an instructor critiques a student, it should always be

A— done in private.
B— subjective rather than objective.
C— conducted immediately after the student's performance.

33.
6097. To be effective, a critique should

A— not contain negative remarks.
B— treat every aspect of the performance in detail.
C— be flexible enough to satisfy the requirements of the moment.

34.
6100. One desirable result of proper oral quizzing by the instructor is to

A— reveal the effectiveness of the instructor's training procedures.
B— fulfill the requirements set forth in the overall objectives of the course.
C— reveal the essential information from which the student can determine progress.

35.
6103. To be effective in oral quizzing during the conduct of a lesson, a question should

A— be of suitable difficulty for that stage of training.
B— include a combination of where, how, and why.
C— divert the student's thoughts to subjects covered in other lessons.

36.
6106. A written test that has reliability

A— yields consistent results.
B— measures small differences in the achievement of students.
C— actually measures what it is supposed to measure and nothing else.

37.
6109. A written test is said to be comprehensive when it

A— includes all levels of difficulty.
B— samples liberally whatever is being measured.
C— measures knowledge of the same topic in many different ways.

38.
6113. One of the main advantages of selection-type test items over supply-type test items is that the selection-type

A— decreases discrimination between responses.
B— would be graded objectively regardless of the student or the grader.
C— precludes comparison of students under one instructor with those under another instructor.

39.
6117. In a written test, which type of selection-type test items reduces the probability of guessing correct responses?

A— Essay.
B— Matching.
C— Multiple-choice.

40.
6121. Instructional aids used in the teaching/learning process should not be used

A— as a crutch by the instructor.
B— for teaching more in less time.
C— to visualize relationships between abstracts.

41.
6123a. Which statement is true regarding true professionalism as an instructor?

A— Anything less than sincere performance destroys the effectiveness of the professional instructor.
B— To achieve professionalism, actions and decisions must be limited to standard patterns and practices.
C— A single definition of professionalism would encompass all of the qualifications and considerations which must be present.

42.
6126. What should an instructor do with a student who assumes that correction of errors is unimportant?

A— Divide complex flight maneuvers into elements.
B— Try to reduce the student's overconfidence to reduce the chance of an accident.
C— Raise the standard of performance for each lesson, demanding greater effort.

43.
6130. When under stress, normal individuals usually react

A— by showing excellent morale followed by deep depression.
B— by responding rapidly and exactly, often automatically, within the limits of their experience and training.
C— inappropriately such as extreme overcooperation, painstaking self-control, and inappropriate laughing or singing.

44.
6134. The basic demonstration/performance method of instruction consists of several steps in proper order. They are

A— instructor tells--student does; student tells--student does; student does--instructor evaluates.
B— instructor tells--instructor does; student tells--instructor does; student does--instructor evaluates.
C— instructor tells--instructor does; student tells--instructor does; student tells--student does; student does--instructor evaluates.

45.
6138. During integrated flight instruction, the instructor must be sure the student

A— develops the habit of looking for other traffic.
B— is able to control the aircraft for extended periods under IMC.
C— can depend on the flight instruments when maneuvering by outside references.

46.
6142. Students quickly become apathetic when they

A— realize material is being withheld by the instructor.
B— understand the objectives toward which they are working.
C— recognize that the instructor is not adequately prepared.

47.
6146. Development and assembly of blocks of learning in their proper relationship will provide a means for

A— both the instructor and student to easily correct faulty habit patterns.
B— challenging the student by progressively increasing the units of learning.
C— allowing the student to master the segments of the overall pilot performance requirements individually and combining these with other related segments.

48.
6150a. Which statement is true regarding lesson plans?

A— Lesson plans should not be directed toward the course objective; only to the lesson objective.
B— A well-thought-out mental outline of a lesson may be used any time as long as the instructor is well prepared.
C— Lesson plans help instructors keep a constant check on their own activity as well as that of their students.

49.
6154. (Refer to figure 1 below.) Section A is titled:

A— Overview.
B— Objective.
C— Introduction.

50.
6158. (Refer to figure 1 below.) Section C is titled:

A— Schedule.
B— Overview.
C— Training Schedule.

LESSON GROUND REFERENCE MANEUVERS **STUDENT** _____ **DATE** _____

A _____ TO DEVELOP THE STUDENT'S SKILL IN PLANNING AND FOLLOWING A PATTERN OVER THE GROUND COMPENSATING FOR WIND DRIFT AT VARYING ANGLES.

B _____ USE OF GROUND REFERENCES TO CONTROL PATH. OBSERVATION AND CONTROL OF WIND EFFECT. CONTROL OF AIRPLANE ATTITUDE, ALTITUDE, AND HEADING.

C _____ PREFLIGHT DISCUSSION. : 10
INSTRUCTOR DEMONSTRATIONS. : 25
STUDENT PRACTICE. : 45
POSTFLIGHT CRITIQUE. : 10

D _____ CHALKBOARD FOR PREFLIGHT DISCUSSION. IFR VISOR FOR MANEUVERS REVIEWED.

E _____ PREFLIGHT – DISCUSS LESSON OBJECTIVE. DIAGRAM "S" TURNS, EIGHTS ALONG A ROAD, AND RECTANGULAR COURSE ON A CHALKBOARD.

INFLIGHT – DEMONSTRATE ELEMENTS. DEMONSTRATE FOLLOWING A ROAD, "S" TURNS, EIGHTS ALONG A ROAD, AND RECTANGULAR COURSE. COACH STUDENT PRACTICE.

POSTFLIGHT – CRITIQUE STUDENT PERFORMANCE AND MAKE STUDY ASSIGNMENT.

F _____ PREFLIGHT – DISCUSS LESSON OBJECTIVE AND RESOLVE QUESTIONS.

INFLIGHT – REVIEW PREVIOUS MANEUVERS INCLUDING POWER-OFF STALLS AND FLIGHT AT MINIMUM CONTROLLABLE AIRSPEED. PERFORM EACH NEW MANEUVER AS DIRECTED.

POSTFLIGHT – ASK PERTINENT QUESTIONS.

G _____ STUDENT SHOULD DEMONSTRATE COMPETENCY IN MAINTAINING ORIENTATION, AIRSPEED WITHIN 10 KNOTS, ALTITUDE WITHIN 100 FEET, AND HEADINGS WITHIN 10 DEGREES, AND IN MAKING PROPER CORRECTION FOR WIND DRIFT.

FIGURE 1.—Lesson Plan.

CORRECT ANSWER LISTING -- PRACTICE TEST

Ques.	Ans.	Page	Ques.	Ans.	Page	Ques.	Ans.	Page	Ques.	Ans.	Page	Ques.	Ans.	Page
1.	A	24	11.	B	33	21.	C	49	31.	B	63	41.	A	51
2.	B	24	12.	C	29	22.	C	49	32.	C	86	42.	C	40
3.	C	24	13.	B	29	23.	B	94	33.	C	87	43.	B	39
4.	A	25	14.	A	30	24.	A	86	34.	A	89	44.	C	64
5.	C	27	15.	C	45	25.	B	72	35.	A	90	45.	A	66
6.	C	37	16.	B	38	26.	C	59	36.	A	93	46.	C	52
7.	A	27	17.	B	38	27.	A	58	37.	B	93	47.	C	71
8.	B	47	18.	B	88	28.	B	58	38.	B	91	48.	C	77
9.	B	46	19.	A	52	29.	A	61	39.	B	92	49.	B	74
10.	B	31	20.	C	48	30.	C	62	40.	A	79	50.	A	76

APPENDIX B
REPRINTS FROM THE FAA'S
AVIATION INSTRUCTOR'S HANDBOOK

The FAA's *Aviation Instructor's Handbook* (FAA-H-8083-9) consists of 11 chapters, which are briefly outlined in Chapters 2 through 7 of this book. Chapters 8, 9, and 10 are reprinted for your reference as you prepare for your FAA knowledge test and your FAA practical test. These chapters may also be useful to you whether you are an active flight instructor or are becoming a flight instructor.

Chapter 8: Instructor Responsibilities and Professionalism
Chapter 9: Techniques of Flight Instruction
Chapter 10: Planning Instructional Activity

They are reprinted beginning on the next page and continue through page 148.

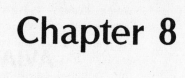

Chapter 8

Instructor Responsibilities and Professionalism

Students look to aviation instructors as authorities in their respective areas. It is important that aviation instructors not only know how to teach, but they also need to project a knowledgeable and professional image. In addition, aviation instructors are on the front lines of efforts to improve the safety record of the industry. This chapter addresses the scope of responsibilities for aviation instructors and enumerates methods they can use to enhance their professional image and conduct.

AVIATION INSTRUCTOR RESPONSIBILITIES

The job of an aviation instructor, or any instructor, is to teach. Previous chapters have discussed how people learn, the teaching process, and teaching methods. As indicated, the learning process can be made easier by helping students learn, providing adequate instruction, demanding adequate standards of performance, and emphasizing the positive. [Figure 8-1]

RESPONSIBILITIES FOR ALL AVIATION INSTRUCTORS

- Helping Students Learn
- Providing Adequate Instruction
- Demanding Adequate Standards of Performance
- Emphasizing the Positive

Figure 8-1. There are four main responsibilities for aviation instructors.

HELPING STUDENTS LEARN

Learning should be an enjoyable experience. By making each lesson a pleasurable experience for the student, the instructor can maintain a high level of student motivation. This does not mean the instructor must make things easy for the student or sacrifice standards of performance to please the student. The student will experience satisfaction from doing a good job or from successfully meeting the challenge of a difficult task.

The idea that people must be led to learning by making it easy is a fallacy. People are not always attracted to something simply because it is pleasant and effortless. Though they might initially be drawn to less difficult tasks, they ultimately devote more effort to activities that bring rewards, such as self-enhancement and personal satisfaction. People want to feel capable; they are proud of the successful achievement of difficult goals.

Learning should be interesting. Knowing the objective of each period of instruction gives meaning and interest to the student as well as the instructor. Not knowing the objective of the lesson often leads to confusion, disinterest, and uneasiness on the part of the student.

Learning to fly should provide students with an opportunity for exploration and experimentation. As part of this, students should be allowed time to explore and evaluate the various elements of each lesson. This encourages them to discover their own capabilities and it helps build self-confidence. Since students learn at different rates and in different ways, it usually is necessary to adjust presentations for some students.

Learning to fly should be a habit-building period during which students devote their attention, memory, and judgment to the development of correct habit patterns. Any objective other than to learn the right way is likely to make students impatient. The instructor should keep the students focused on good habits both by example and by a logical presentation of learning tasks.

Because aviation instructors have full responsibility for all phases of required training, they must be clear regarding the objectives. For ground and flight training, the objectives reflect the knowledge and skill required to train safe pilots who can complete the knowledge and practical tests for the appropriate certificate or rating. In the case of the flight student studying for the practical test, the objectives will come from the practical test standards (PTS) for the desired certificate or rating. Maintenance students will likewise be facing objectives aligned with the knowledge tests and the Oral and Practical. After the objectives have been established, the sequence of training, teaching methods, and related activities must be organized to best achieve them.

To accomplish these objectives, instructors need to take specific actions. The following measures should result in a positive and efficient learning experience.

• Devise a plan of action.

• Create a positive student-instructor relationship.

• Present information and guidance effectively.

• Transfer responsibility to the student as learning occurs.

• Evaluate student learning and thereby measure teaching effectiveness.

As noted in the list, the instructor must devise a plan of action, and present information and guidance effectively. Knowing the objectives is one part of accomplishing these tasks and knowing the student is the other. For example, the plan of action for a lesson on reciprocating engines for maintenance students would be different for a student transitioning from automotive maintenance than it would for a student with no maintenance background. In theory, the transitioning student would have less need for basic information. The best way to confirm this is with a pretest. Until the students are tested, the instructor does not know for sure where each student stands in relation to the objectives. A **pretest** is a criterion-referenced test constructed to measure the knowledge and skills that are necessary to begin the course. Pretests also may be used to determine the student's current level of knowledge and skill in relation to the material that will be presented in the course.

The pretest measures whether or not the student has the prerequisite knowledge and skills necessary to proceed with the course of instruction. Examples of skills that might be required of a student pilot would be knowledge of basic math, understanding the English language, and having certain spatial skills to understand maps and the relationship of maps to the earth. A pretest can expose deficiencies in these and other areas. The instructor could then base the plan of action accordingly. In the extreme, it might be necessary for the prospective student to get more training or education before beginning flight training.

The second part of a pretest is measuring the level of knowledge or skill the student has in relation to the material that is going to be taught. Typically, one or two questions for each of the key knowledge areas or skills in the course are included. The instructor will then be able to identify how much the student knows and tailor the instruction accordingly. Knowing where a student is at the beginning helps the instructor present the information and offer guidance more effectively.

Helping the student learn does not mean that the instructor has the responsibility for performing learning tasks which students need to do for themselves. This is not effective instruction. The best instructors provide information, guidance, and opportunity for student learning, and support the student's motivation while they are in a learning situation.

PROVIDING ADEQUATE INSTRUCTION

The flight instructor should attempt to carefully and correctly analyze the student's personality, thinking, and ability. No two students are alike, and the same methods of instruction cannot be equally effective for each student. The instructor must talk with a student at some length to learn about the student's background, interests, temperament, and way of thinking. The instructor's methods also may change as the student advances through successive stages of training.

An instructor who has not correctly analyzed a student may soon find that the instruction is not producing the desired results. For example, this could mean that the instructor has analyzed a student as a slow thinker, who is actually a quick thinker but is hesitant to act. Such a student may fail to act at the proper time due to lack of self-confidence, even though the situation is correctly understood. In this case, instruction would obviously be directed toward developing student self-confidence, rather than drill on flight fundamentals. In another case, too much criticism may completely subdue a timid person, whereas brisk instruction may force a more diligent application to the learning task. A slow student requires instructional methods that combine tact, keen perception, and delicate handling. If such a student receives too much help and encouragement, a feeling of incompetence may develop.

A student whose slow progress is due to discouragement and a lack of confidence should be assigned subgoals that can be attained more easily than the normal learning goals. For this purpose, complex lessons can be separated into elements, and each element practiced until an acceptable performance is achieved before the whole maneuver or operation is attempted. As an example, instruction in S-turns may begin with consideration for headings only. Elements of altitude control, drift correction, and coordination can be introduced one at a time. As the student gains confidence and ability, goals should be increased in difficulty until progress is normal.

Students who are fast learners can also create problems for the instructor. Because they make few mistakes, they may assume that the correction of errors is unimportant. Such overconfidence may soon result in faulty performance. For such students, the instructor should constantly raise the standard of performance for each lesson, demanding greater effort. Individuals learn when they are aware of their errors. Students who are permitted to complete every flight lesson without corrections and guidance will not retain what they have practiced as well as those students who have their attention constantly directed to an analysis of their performance. On the other hand, deficiencies should not be invented solely for the students' benefit because unfair criticism immediately destroys their confidence in the instructor.

The demands on an instructor to serve as a practical psychologist are much greater than is generally realized. As discussed in Chapters 1 and 2, an instructor can meet this responsibility through a careful analysis of the students and through a continuing deep interest in them.

STANDARDS OF PERFORMANCE

Flight instructors must continuously evaluate their own effectiveness and the standard of learning and performance achieved by their students. The desire to maintain pleasant personal relationships with the students must not cause the acceptance of a slow rate of learning or substandard flight performance. It is a fallacy to believe that accepting lower standards to please a student will produce a genuine improvement in the student-instructor relationship. An earnest student does not resent reasonable standards that are fairly and consistently applied.

Instructors fail to provide competent instruction when they permit their students to get by with a substandard performance, or without learning thoroughly some item

of knowledge pertinent to safe piloting. More importantly, such deficiencies may in themselves allow hazardous inadequacies in student performance later on.

EMPHASIZING THE POSITIVE

Aviation instructors have a tremendous influence on their students' perception of aviation. The way instructors conduct themselves, the attitudes they display, and the manner in which they develop their instruction all contribute to the formation of either positive or negative impressions by their students. The success of an aviation instructor depends, in large measure, on the ability to present instruction so that students develop a positive image of aviation. [Figure 8-2]

Figure 8-2. Students learn more when instruction is presented in a positive manner.

Chapter 1 emphasized that a negative self-concept inhibits the perceptual process, that fear adversely affects the students' perceptions, that the feeling of being threatened limits the ability to perceive, and that negative motivation is not as effective as positive motivation. Merely knowing about these factors is not enough. Instructors must be able to detect these factors in their students and strive to prevent negative feelings from becoming part of the instructional process.

Consider how the following scenario for the first lesson might impress a new student pilot without previous experience in aviation:

- An exhaustive indoctrination in preflight procedures with emphasis on the extreme precautions which must be taken before every flight because ". . . mechanical failures in flight are often disastrous."

- Instruction in the extreme care which must be taken in taxiing an airplane, because ". . . if you go too fast, it's likely to get away from you."

- A series of stalls, because ". . . this is how so many people lose their lives in airplanes."

- A series of simulated forced landings, because ". . . one should always be prepared to cope with an engine failure."

These are a series of new experiences that might make the new student wonder whether or not learning to fly is a good idea. The stall series may even cause the student to become airsick. In contrast, consider a first flight lesson in which the preflight inspection is presented to familiarize the student with the airplane and its components, and the flight consists of a perfectly normal flight to a nearby airport and return. Following the flight, the instructor can call the student's attention to the ease with which the trip was made in comparison with other modes of transportation, and the fact that no critical incidents were encountered or expected.

This by no means proposes that preflight inspections, stalls, and emergency procedures should be omitted from training. It only illustrates the positive approach in which the student is not overwhelmed with the critical possibilities of aviation before having an opportunity to see its potential and pleasurable features. The introduction of emergency procedures after the student has developed an acquaintance with normal operations is not so likely to be discouraging and frightening, or to inhibit learning by the imposition of fear.

There is nothing in aviation that demands that students must suffer as part of their instruction. This has often been the case because of overemphasis on negative motivation and explanations. Every reasonable effort should be made to ensure that instruction is given under the most favorable conditions.

Although most student pilots have been exposed to air travel in one form or another, they may not have flown in light, training aircraft. Consequently, students may experience unfamiliar noises, vibrations, eerie sensations due to G-forces, or a woozy feeling in the stomach. To be effective, instructors cannot ignore the existence of these negative factors, nor should they ridicule students who are adversely affected by them. These negative sensations can usually be overcome by understanding and positive instruction.

When emphasizing to a student that a particular procedure must be accomplished in a certain manner, an instructor might be tempted to point out the consequences of doing it differently. The instructor may even tell the student that to do it otherwise is to flirt with disaster or to suffer serious consequences. Justifications such as these may be very convenient, and the instructor may consider the negative approach necessary to ensure that the point is committed to memory. However, the final test must be whether the stated reasons contribute to the learning situation.

Most new instructors tend to adopt those teaching methods used by their own instructors. These methods may or may not have been good. The fact that one has learned under one system of instruction does not mean that this is necessarily the best way it can be done, regardless of the respect one retains for the ability of their original instructor. Some students learn in spite of their instruction, rather than because of it. Emphasize the positive because positive instruction results in positive learning.

FLIGHT INSTRUCTOR RESPONSIBILITIES

All aviation instructors shoulder an enormous responsibility because their students will ultimately be flying and servicing or repairing aircraft. Flight instructors have some additional responsibilities including the responsibility of evaluating student pilots and making a determination of when they are ready to solo. Other flight instructor responsibilities are based on Title 14 of the Code of Federal Regulations (14 CFR) part 61, and advisory circulars (ACs). [Figure 8-3]

ADDITIONAL RESPONSIBILITIES FOR FLIGHT INSTRUCTORS

- **Evaluation of Student Piloting Ability**
- **Pilot Supervision**
- **Practical Test Recommendations**
- **Flight Instructor Endorsements**
- **Additional Training and Endorsements**
- **Pilot Proficiency**

Figure 8-3. The flight instructor has many additional responsibilities.

EVALUATION OF STUDENT PILOTING ABILITY

Evaluation is one of the most important elements of instruction. In flight instruction, the instructor initially determines that the student understands the procedure or maneuver. Then the instructor demonstrates the maneuver, allows the student to practice the maneuver under direction, and finally evaluates student accomplishment by observing the performance.

Evaluation of demonstrated ability during flight instruction must be based upon established standards of performance, suitably modified to apply to the student's experience and stage of development as a pilot. The evaluation must consider the student's mastery of the elements involved in the maneuver, rather than merely the overall performance.

Demonstrations of performance directly apply to the qualification of student pilots for solo and solo cross-country privileges. Also associated with pilot skill evaluations during flight training are the stage checks conducted in FAA-approved school courses and the practical tests for pilot certificates and ratings.

In evaluating student demonstrations of piloting ability, it is important for the flight instructor to keep the student informed of progress. This may be done as each procedure or maneuver is completed or summarized during postflight critiques. When explaining errors in performance, instructors should point out the elements in which the deficiencies are believed to have originated and, if possible, suggest appropriate corrective measures.

Correction of student errors should not include the practice of taking the controls away from students immediately when a mistake is made. Safety permitting, it is frequently better to let students progress part of the way into the mistake and find their own way out. It is difficult for students to learn to do a maneuver properly if they seldom have the opportunity to correct an error. On the other hand, students may perform a procedure or maneuver correctly and not fully understand the principles and objectives involved. When the instructor suspects this, students should be required to vary the performance of the maneuver slightly, combine it with other operations, or apply the same elements to the performance of other maneuvers. Students who do not understand the principles involved will probably not be able to do this successfully.

PILOT SUPERVISION

Flight instructors have the responsibility to provide guidance and restraint with respect to the solo operations of their students. This is by far the most important flight instructor responsibility because the instructor is the only person in a position to make the determination that a student is ready for solo operations. Before endorsing a student for solo flight, the instructor should require the student to demonstrate consistent ability to perform all of the fundamental

maneuvers. The student should also be capable of handling ordinary problems that might occur, such as traffic pattern congestion, change in active runway, or unexpected crosswinds. The instructor must remain in control of the situation. By requiring the first solo flight to consist of landings to a full stop, the instructor has the opportunity to stop the flight if unexpected conditions or poor performance warrant such action.

PRACTICAL TEST RECOMMENDATIONS

Provision is made on the airman certificate or rating application form for the written recommendation of the flight instructor who has prepared the applicant for the practical test involved. Signing this recommendation imposes a serious responsibility on the flight instructor. A flight instructor who makes a practical test recommendation for an applicant seeking a certificate or rating should require the applicant to thoroughly demonstrate the knowledge and skill level required for that certificate or rating. This demonstration should in no instance be less than the complete procedure prescribed in the applicable practical test standards (PTS).

A practical test recommendation based on anything less risks the presentation of an applicant who may be unprepared for some part of the actual practical test. In such an event, the flight instructor is logically held accountable for a deficient instructional performance. This risk is especially great in signing recommendations for applicants who have not been trained by the instructor involved. 14 CFR parts 61 and 141 require a minimum of three hours of flight training preparation within 60 days preceding the date of the test for a recreational, private, or commercial certificate. The same training requirement applies to the instrument rating. The instructor signing the endorsement is required to have conducted the training in the applicable areas of operation stated in the regulations and the PTS, and certify that the person is prepared for the required practical test. In most cases, the conscientious instructor will have little doubt concerning the applicant's readiness for the practical test.

FAA inspectors and designated pilot examiners rely on flight instructor recommendations as evidence of qualification for certification, and proof that a review has been given of the subject areas found to be deficient on the appropriate knowledge test. Recommendations also provide assurance that the applicant has had a thorough briefing on the practical test standards and the associated knowledge areas, maneuvers, and procedures. If the flight instructor has trained and prepared the applicant competently, the applicant should have no problem passing the practical test.

FLIGHT INSTRUCTOR ENDORSEMENTS

The authority and responsibility for endorsing student pilot certificates and logbooks for solo and solo cross-country flight privileges are granted in 14 CFR part 61. These endorsements are further explained in AC 61-65, *Certification: Pilots and Flight Instructors*. Failure to ensure that a student pilot meets the requirements of regulations prior to making endorsements allowing solo flight is a serious deficiency in performance for which an instructor is held accountable. Providing a solo endorsement for a student pilot who is not fully prepared to accept the responsibility for solo flight operations also is a breach of faith with the student.

Flight instructors also have the responsibility to make logbook endorsements for pilots who are already certificated. Included are additional endorsements for recreational, private, commercial, and instrument-rated pilots as well as flight instructors. Typical examples include endorsements for flight reviews, instrument proficiency checks, and the additional training required for high performance, high altitude, and tailwheel aircraft. Completion of prerequisites for a practical test is another instructor task that must be documented properly. Examples of all common endorsements can be found in the current issue of AC 61-65, Appendix 1. This appendix also includes references to 14 CFR part 61 for more details concerning the requirements that must be met to qualify for each respective endorsement. The examples shown contain the essential elements of each endorsement, but it is not necessary for all endorsements to be worded exactly as those in the AC. For example, changes to regulatory requirements may affect the wording, or the instructor may customize the endorsement for any special circumstances of the student. Any time a flight instructor gives ground or flight training, a logbook entry is required. [Figure 8-4]

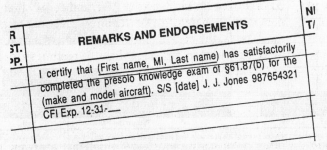

Figure 8-4. This is a sample logbook endorsement for presolo aeronautical knowledge.

14 CFR part 61 also requires that the instructor maintain a record in a logbook or some separate document that includes information on the type of endorsement, the name of the person receiving the endorsement, and the date of the endorsement. For a knowledge or practical test endorsement, the record must include the kind of test, the date, and the results. Records of endorsements must be maintained for at least three years.

FAA FORM 8710-1

After ensuring that an applicant for a certificate is prepared for the test and has met all the knowledge, proficiency, and experience requirements, it is advisable for the flight instructor to assist the applicant in filling out FAA Form 8710-1, *Airman Certificate and/or Rating Application*. The instructor's certification that the applicant is ready to take the test is on the reverse of the form, but the applicant will likely need the assistance of the instructor in filling out the front.

FAA Form 8710-1 comes with instructions attached for completing it. The example shown is for a private pilot applicant who received training under 14 CFR part 61. This is only an example, since the form is periodically revised to reflect changes in the applicable rules and regulations. If the current form is a later edition than shown here, the instructions must be read very carefully to ensure all areas of the form are filled out correctly. The example shown is annotated with additional guidance to clarify or reinforce certain areas that are frequently found incomplete by the FAA during the certification process. [Figure 8-5]

ADDITIONAL TRAINING AND ENDORSEMENTS

Flight instructors often provide required training and endorsements for certificated pilots. AC 61-98, *Currency and Additional Qualification Requirements for Certificated Pilots*, contains information to assist the instructor in providing training/endorsements for flight reviews, instrument proficiency checks, and transitions to other makes and models of aircraft. Included in the AC is general guidance in each of these areas, references to other related documents, and sample training plans that are pertinent to this type of training.

FLIGHT REVIEWS

The conduct of **flight reviews** for certificated pilots is not only a responsibility of the flight instructor, but it can also be an excellent opportunity to expand on the instructor's professional services. The flight review is intended to be an industry-managed, FAA-monitored currency program. The flight instructor must remember that the flight review is not a test or a check ride, but an instructional service designed to assess a pilot's knowledge and skills. As stated in 14 CFR part 61, no person may act as pilot in command of an aircraft unless a flight review has been accomplished within the preceding 24 calendar months.

Effective pilot refresher training must be based on specific objectives and standards. The objectives should

Type or print in ink when filling out 8710-1.

Spell out color.

Must include city or county and state within the U.S. Include city and country outside the U.S.

Middle name must be spelled out; if no middle name, the letters "NMN" must be indicated. DO NOT USE MIDDLE INITIAL.

Do not use P.O. Box or Rural Route, UNLESS a statement of physical location is provided.

Enter class shown on medical certificate (i.e. 1st, 2nd, 3rd), if required.

Items U. and V. DO NOT apply to alcohol related offenses (DWI or DUI).

Check that flight time is sufficient for certificate or rating.

Make sure applicant signs form.

Date signed by applicant should be within 60 days prior to date of practical test.

TYPE OR PRINT ALL ENTRIES IN INK

Form Approved OMB No: 2120-0021

Airman Certificate and/or Rating Application

U.S. Department of Transportation
Federal Aviation Administration

I. Application Information □ Student □ Recreational ☒ Private □ Commercial □ Airline Transport ☒ Instrument
□ Additional Aircraft Rating ☒ Airplane Single-Engine □ Airplane Multiengine □ Rotorcraft □ Glider □ Lighter-Than-Air
□ Flight Instructor ____ Initial ____ Renewal ____ Reinstatement □ Additional Instructor Rating □ Ground Instructor
□ Medical Flight Test □ Reexamination □ Reissuance of ____ Certificate □ Other ____

| A. Name (Last, First, Middle) Doe, John David | B. SSN (US Only) 223-45-6678 | C. Date of Birth Mo. Day Year 11/25/ | D. Place of Birth Bakersfield, CA |

E. Address (Please See Instructions Before Completing) 1234 North Street
F. Nationality (Citizenship) Specify ☒ USA □ Other ____
G. Do you read, speak and understand English? ☒ Yes □ No

City, State, Zip Code Alltown, PA 62534
H. Height 68 in. | I. Weight 165 Lbs. | J. Hair Blonde | K. Eyes Blue | L. Sex ☒ Male □ Female

M. Do you now hold, or have you ever held an FAA Pilot Certificate? ☒ Yes □ No
N. Grade Pilot Certificate Student | O. Certificate Number BB07138 | P. Date Issued 06-15-

Q. Do you hold a Medical Certificate? ☒ Yes □ No | R. Class of Certificate Third | S. Date Issued 6-15- | T. Name of Examiner Thomas C. Smith, MD

U. Have you been convicted for violation of Federal or State statutes relating to narcotic drugs, marijuana, or depressant or stimulant drugs or substances □ Yes ☒ No | V. Date of Final Conviction

W. Glider or Free Balloon Pilots only: *Medical Statement: I have no known physical defect which makes me unable to pilot a glider or free balloon.* | Signature | X. Date

II. Certificate or Rating Applied For on Basis of:

☒ A. Completion of Required Test
1. Aircraft to be used (if flight test required) Cessna 152 | 2a. Total time in this aircraft 55 hours | 2b. Pilot in command 24 hours

□ B. Military Competence Obtained in
1. Service | 2. Date Rated | 3. Rank or Grade and Service Number
4. Has flown at least 10 hours as pilot in command during the past 12 months in the following military aircraft.

□ C. Graduate of Approved Course
1. Name and Location of Training Agency or Training Center | 1a Certification Number
2. Curriculum From Which Graduated | 3. Date

□ D. Holder of Foreign License Issued By
1. Country | 2. Grade of License | 3. Number
4. Ratings

□ E. Completion of Air Carrier's Approved Training Program
1. Name of Air Carrier | 2. Date | 3. Which Curriculum □ Initial □ Upgrade □ Transition

III. Record of Pilot time *(Do not write in the shaded areas.)*

	Total	Instruction Received	Solo	Pilot in Command	Second in Command	Cross Country Instruction Received	Cross Country Solo	Cross Country Pilot in Command	Instrument	Night Instruction Received	Night Take-off/ Landing	Night Pilot in Command	Night Take-off/ Landing Pilot in Command	Number of Flights	Number of Aero-Tows	Number of Ground Launches	Number of Powered Launches	Number of Free Flights
Airplanes	55	31	24	24		5	12	12	3	4	12							
Rotor-craft																		
Gliders																		
Lighter than Air																		
Training Device																		
Simulator																		

IV. Have you failed a test for this certificate or rating? □ Yes ☒ No | **Within the Past 30 days?** □ Yes ☒ No

V. Applicant's Certification — I certify that all statements and answers provided by me on this application form are complete and true to the best of my knowledge, and I agree that they are to be considered as part of the basis for issuance of any FAA certificate to me. I have also read and understand the Privacy Act statement that accompanies this form.

Signature of Applicant *John David Doe* John David Doe | Date 04-12-

FAA Use Only

EMP	REG	D.O.	SEAL	CON	ISS	ACT	LEV	TR	S.N.	SRCH	RATE	RATING (1)

Figure 8-5. This sample FAA Form 8710-1 (front page) has been completed for a private pilot applicant.

Practical test date must be within 60 days after date of recommendation.

Full printed name should be included with signature.

Instructor's certificate must be current on date of recommendation.

Instructor's Recommendation

I have personally instructed the applicant and consider this person ready to take the test.

Date	Instructor's Signature		Certificate No:	Certificate Expires
4-11-	*James E. Jones* James E. Jones		1234567 CFI	05-31-

Air Agency's Recommendation

The applicant has successfully completed our _____ course, and is recommended for certification or rating without further _____ test.

Date	Agency Name and Number	Official's Signature
		Title

Designated Examiner's Report

☐ Student Pilot Certificate Issued *(Copy attached)*

☒ I have personally reviewed this applicant's pilot logbook, and certify that the individual meets the pertinent requirements of FAR 61 for the pilot certificate or rating sought.

☐ I have personally reviewed this applicant's graduation certificate, and found it to be appropriate and in order, and have returned the certificate.

☒ I have personally tested and/or verified this applicant in accordance with pertinent procedures and standards with the result indicated below.

        ☒ Approved—Temporary Certificate Issued *(Copy Attached)*

        ☐ Disapproved—Disapproval Notice Issued *(Copy Attached)*

Location of Test (Facility, City, State)	Duration of Test		
	Ground	Simulator	Flight
Alltown, PA	2.6	0	2.1

Certificate or Rating for Which Tested	Type(s) of Aircraft Used	Registration No.(s)
Private Pilot	Cessna 152	N12345

Date	Examiner's Signature		Certificate No.	Designation No.	Designation Expires
04-12-	Henry L. Smith *Henry L. Smith*		332345678	AE-01-1123	01-31-

Evaluator's Record For Airline Transport Certificate/Rating Only

	Inspector	Examiner	Signature	Date
Oral	☐	☐		
Approved Simulator/Training Device Check	☐	☐		
Aircraft Flight Check	☐	☐		
Advanced Qualification Program	☐	☐		

Inspector's Report

I have personally tested this applicant in accordance with or have otherwise verified that this applicant complies with pertinent procedures, standards, policies, and or necessary requirements with the result indicated below.

    ☐ **Approved**—Temporary Certificate Issued   ☐ **Disapproved**—Disapproval Notice Issued

Location of Test (Facility, City, State)	Duration of Test		
	Ground	Simulator	Flight

Certificate or Rating for Which Tested	Type(s) of Aircraft Used	Registration No.(s)

☐ Student Pilot Certificate issued	☐ Certificate or Rating Based on	☐ Instructor ☐ Flight ☐ Ground	
☐ Examiner's Recommendation	☐ Military Competence	☐ Renewal ☐ Approved	
☐ ACCEPTED ☐ REJECTED	☐ Foreign License	☐ Reinstatement ☐ Disapproved	
☐ Reissue or Exchange of Pilot Certificate	☐ Approved Course Graduate	**Instructor Renewal Based on**	
☐ Special medical test conducted—report forwarded to Aeromedical Certification Branch, AAM-130	☐ Other Approved FAA Qualification Criteria	☐ Activity ☐ Training Course	
	☐ Certificate Issued	☐ Acquaintance ☐ Test	
	☐ Certificate Denied		

Training Course (FIRC) Name	Graduation Certificate No.	Date

Date	Inspector's Signature	FAA District Office

Attachments:

☐ Student Pilot Certificate (copy)   ☒ Airmans Identification (ID)   ☐ Notice of Disapproval

☒ Report of Written Examination   Pennsylvania Drivers License   ☐ Superseded Pilot Certificate

☒ Temporary Pilot Certificate (copy)   Form of ID   ☐ Answer Sheet Graded

    223456678   ☐ Answer Sheet Graded (Foreign Instrument)

    Number

    11-25-

    Expiration Date

FAA Form 8710-1 (7-95) Supersedes Previous Edition

NSN: 0052-00-682-5006

☆ U.S. GOVERNMENT PRINTING OFFICE: 1997-668-106

Figure 8-5. This sample FAA Form 8710-1 (back page) has been completed for a private pilot applicant.

include a thorough checkout appropriate to the pilot certificate and aircraft ratings held, and the standards should be at least those required for the issuance of that pilot certificate. Before beginning any training, the pilot and the instructor should agree fully on these objectives and standards, and, as training progresses, the pilot should be kept appraised of progress toward achieving those goals.

AC 61-98, Chapter 1, provides guidance for conducting the flight review. Appendix 1 is a sample flight review plan and checklist. Appendix 2 is a sample list of flight review knowledge, maneuvers, and procedures. It contains recommended procedures and standards for general pilot refresher courses. At the conclusion of a successful flight review, the logbook of the pilot should be endorsed. [Figure 8-6]

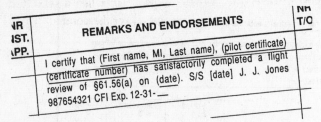

Figure 8-6. This sample logbook endorsement is for completion of a flight review.

INSTRUMENT PROFICIENCY CHECKS

Instrument rated pilots who have not met instrument currency requirements in the preceding six months or for six months thereafter are required by 14 CFR part 61 to pass an instrument proficiency check in order to regain their instrument flying privileges.

AC 61-98 contains guidance for the conduct of an **instrument proficiency check**, including a sample plan of action and checklist. When conducting an instrument proficiency check, the flight instructor should use the Instrument Rating Practical Test Standards as the primary reference for specific maneuvers and any associated tolerances. A pilot taking an instrument proficiency check should be expected to meet the criteria of the specific tasks selected in the Instrument Rating Practical Test Standards.

The flight instructor must hold aircraft and instrument ratings on his or her instructor certificate appropriate to the aircraft being flown. Part or all of the check may be conducted in a flight training device or flight simulator that meets 14 CFR section 141.41 requirements. The FAA FSDO having jurisdiction over the area where the device is used must specifically approve each flight training device or flight simulator. If planning to use a flight training device or flight simulator to conduct all or part of an instrument proficiency check, instructors should contact the local FSDO to verify the approval status of the device.

AIRCRAFT CHECKOUTS/TRANSITIONS

Certificated pilots look to flight instructors for **aircraft checkouts** and **transition training** including high performance airplanes, tailwheel airplanes, and aircraft capable of flight at high altitudes. The flight instructor who checks out and certifies the competency of a pilot in an aircraft for which a type rating is not required by regulations is accepting a major responsibility for the safety of future passengers. Many newer light airplanes are comparable in performance and complexity to transport airplanes. For these, the flight instructor's checkout should be at least as thorough as an official type rating practical test.

AC 61-98 provides a list of requirements for transitioning to other makes and models of aircraft along with a sample training plan. This AC also lists other publications that can be helpful in conducting checkouts. All checkouts should be conducted to the performance standards required by the appropriate practical test standards for the pilot certificate.

For the conduct of an aircraft checkout, it is essential that the flight instructor be fully qualified in the aircraft to be used and be thoroughly familiar with its operating procedures, approved flight manual, and operating limitations. An instructor who does not meet the recent flight experience prescribed by regulations for the aircraft concerned should not attempt to check out another pilot.

For the benefit of the pilot concerned, and for the instructor's protection in the case of later questions, the flight instructor should record in the pilot's logbook the exact extent of any checkout conducted. This can be done most easily by reference to the appropriate PTS.

In the event the instructor finds a pilot's performance to be insufficient to allow sign off, the pilot should be thoroughly debriefed on all problem areas, and further instruction scheduled. In some cases, a referral to another instructor may be appropriate.

PILOT PROFICIENCY

Professional flight instructors know the importance of maintaining knowledge and skill both as instructors and as pilots. Only by keeping themselves at top proficiency can they be true professionals. The flight instructor is at the leading edge of the aviation industry's efforts to improve aviation safety through additional training. One of the ways the FAA attempts to improve proficiency is through the requirement for having a flight review within the past 24 months. Another method of encouraging pilot proficiency is through provisions of AC 61-91, *Pilot Proficiency Award Program*.

The objective of the program is to provide pilots with the opportunity to establish and participate in a personal recurrent training program. It is open to all pilots holding a recreational pilot certificate or higher and a current medical certificate when required. Pilots of qualified ultralight vehicles are also eligible. For airplanes, the program requires three hours of flight training which includes one hour directed toward basic airplane control and mastery of the airplane; one hour devoted to patterns, approaches, and landings; and one hour of instrument training either in an airplane, approved flight training device, or flight simulator. The program also requires attending at least one sanctioned aviation safety seminar, or industry-conducted recurrent training program. AC 61-91 contains requirements for other categories/classes of aircraft, as well as additional detailed requirements for all aircraft.

Incentives to participate include distinctive pins and certificates of completion for Phases I through X. A certificate is awarded for Phases XI through XX. Work toward another phase can begin as soon as one phase is completed, but 12 months must pass between completion of one phase and application for the award of the next phase. Another incentive to participate is that the completion of a phase substitutes for the flight review and restarts the 24-month clock.

Flight instructors may also participate in the program. By giving instruction leading to phase completion for three pilots (nine hours of instruction) and attendance at a safety seminar or clinic, an instructor can earn Phases I through III. Phases IV through XX are each earned by completion of an evaluation or proficiency flight with a designated examiner or FAA inspector and attendance at a safety seminar or clinic.

Flight instructors can substantially improve their own proficiency and that of their students and other pilots by participating and encouraging participation in the Pilot Proficiency Award Program. When an instructor has conducted the appropriate training toward the completion of a phase, a logbook endorsement is required. [Figure 8-7]

NR IST. APP.	REMARKS AND ENDORSEMENTS	NR T/O
	I certify that (First name, MI, Last name), (pilot certificate) (certificate number) has satisfactorily completed Phase No. ___ of a WINGS program on (date). S.S [date] J. J. Jones 987654321 CFI Exp. 12-31-___	

Figure 8-7. This is an example of an instructor's logbook endorsement for a pilot who has completed a phase of training according to requirements of the Pilot Proficiency Award Program.

PROFESSIONALISM

The aviation instructor is the central figure in aviation training and is responsible for all phases of required training. The instructor must be fully qualified as an aviation professional, either as a pilot or aircraft maintenance technician; however, the instructor's ability must go far beyond this if the requirements of professionalism are to be met. Although the word "professionalism" is widely used, it is rarely defined. In fact, no single definition can encompass all of the qualifications and considerations that must be present before true professionalism can exist.

Though not all inclusive, the following list gives some major considerations and qualifications that should be included in the definition of professionalism.

- Professionalism exists only when a service is performed for someone, or for the common good.

- Professionalism is achieved only after extended training and preparation.

- True performance as a professional is based on study and research.

- Professionals must be able to reason logically and accurately.

- Professionalism requires the ability to make good judgmental decisions. Professionals cannot limit their actions and decisions to standard patterns and practices.

- Professionalism demands a code of ethics. Professionals must be true to themselves and to those they service. Anything less than a sincere performance is quickly detected, and immediately destroys their effectiveness.

Aviaton instructors should carefully consider this list. Failing to meet these qualities may result in poor performance by the instructor and students. Preparation and performance as an instructor with these qualities constantly in mind will command recognition as a professional in aviation instruction. Professionalism includes an instructor's public image.

SINCERITY

The professional instructor should be straightforward and honest. Attempting to hide some inadequacy behind a smokescreen of unrelated instruction will make it impossible for the instructor to command the respect and full attention of a student. Teaching an aviation student is based upon acceptance of the instructor as a competent, qualified teacher and an expert pilot or aircraft maintenance technician. Any facade of instructor pretentiousness, whether it is real or mistakenly assumed by the student, will immediately cause the student to lose confidence in the instructor and learning will be adversely affected.

ACCEPTANCE OF THE STUDENT

With regard to students, the instructor must accept them as they are, including all their faults and problems. The student is a person who wants to learn, and the instructor is a person who is available to help in the learning process. Beginning with this understanding, the professional relationship of the instructor with the student should be based on a mutual acknowledgement that the student and the instructor are important to each other, and that both are working toward the same objective.

Under no circumstance should the instructor do anything which implies degrading the student. Acceptance, rather than ridicule, and support rather than reproof will encourage learning. Students must be treated with respect, regardless of whether the student is quick to learn or is slow and apprehensive. Criticizing a student who does not learn rapidly is similar to a doctor reprimanding a patient who does not get well as rapidly as predicted.

PERSONAL APPEARANCE AND HABITS

Personal appearance has an important effect on the professional image of the instructor. Today's aviation customers expect their instructors to be neat, clean, and appropriately dressed. Since the instructor is engaged in a learning situation, the attire worn should be appropriate to a professional status. [Figure 8-8]

Figure 8-8. The aviation instructor should always present a professional appearance.

Personal habits have a significant effect on the professional image. The exercise of common courtesy is perhaps the most important of these. An instructor who is rude, thoughtless, and inattentive cannot hold the respect

of students, regardless of ability as a pilot or aviation maintenance technician. Personal cleanliness is important to aviation instruction. Frequently, an instructor and a student work in close proximity, and even little annoyances such as body odor or bad breath can cause serious distractions from learning the tasks at hand.

DEMEANOR

The attitude and behavior of the instructor can contribute much to a professional image. The instructor should avoid erratic movements, distracting speech habits, and capricious changes in mood. The professional image requires development of a calm, thoughtful, and disciplined, but not somber, demeanor.

The instructor should avoid any tendency toward frequently countermanding directions, reacting differently to similar or identical errors at different times, demanding unreasonable performance or progress, or criticizing a student unfairly. A forbidding or overbearing manner is as much to be avoided as is an air of flippancy. Effective instruction is best conducted in a calm, pleasant, thoughtful approach that puts the student at ease. The instructor must constantly portray competence in the subject matter and genuine interest in the student's well being.

SAFETY PRACTICES AND ACCIDENT PREVENTION

The safety practices emphasized by instructors have a long lasting effect on students. Generally, students consider their instructor to be a model of perfection whose habits they attempt to imitate, whether consciously or unconsciously. The instructor's advocacy and description of safety practices mean little to a student if the instructor does not demonstrate them consistently.

For this reason, instructors must meticulously observe the safety practices being taught to students. A good example is the use of a checklist before takeoff. If a student pilot sees the flight instructor start an airplane and take off without referring to a checklist, no amount of instruction in the use of a checklist will convince that student to faithfully use one when solo flight operations begin.

To maintain a professional image, a flight instructor must carefully observe all regulations and recognized safety practices during all flight operations. An instructor who is observed to fly with apparent disregard for loading limitations or weather minimums creates an image of irresponsibility that many hours of scrupulous flight instruction can never correct. Habitual observance of regulations, safety precautions, and the precepts of courtesy will enhance the instructor's image of professionalism. Moreover, such habits make the instructor more effective by encouraging students to develop similar habits.

The flight instructor must go beyond the requirements of developing technically proficient students who are knowledgeable in the areas of their equipment, flight procedures, and maneuvers. The flight instructor must not only teach students to know their own and their equipment's limitations, but must also teach them to be guided by those limitations. The flight instructor must make a strenuous effort to develop good judgment on the part of the students.

The aircraft maintenance instructor must similarly make the maintenance technician student aware of the consequences of safety in the work place. If a maintenance student observes the instructor violating safety practices such as not wearing safety glasses around hazardous equipment, the student will likely not be conscientious about using safety equipment when the instructor is not around.

PROPER LANGUAGE

In aviation instruction, as in other professional activities, the use of profanity and obscene language leads to distrust or, at best, to a lack of complete confidence in the instructor. To many people, such language is actually objectionable to the point of being painful. The professional instructor must speak normally, without inhibitions, and develop the ability to speak positively and descriptively without excesses of language.

The beginning aviation student is being introduced to new concepts and experiences and encountering new terms and phrases that are often confusing. Words such as "traffic," "stall," "elevator," and "lift" are familiar, but are given entirely new meanings. Coined words, such as VORTAC, UNICOM, and PIREP cause further difficulty. Phrases such as "clear the area," "monitor ATIS," or "lower the pitch attitude" are completely incomprehensible. The language is new and strange, but the words are a part of aviation and beginning students need to learn the common terms. Normally, they are eager to learn and will quickly adopt the terminology as part of their vocabulary. At the beginning of the student's training, and before each lesson during early instruction, the instructor should carefully define the terms and phrases that will be used during the lesson. The instructor should then be careful to limit instruction to those terms and phrases, unless the exact meaning and intent of any new expression are explained immediately.

Student errors and confusion can also result from using many of the colloquial expressions of aviation. These expressions are the result of the glamorous past of aviation and often are not understood even by long time aviators. Jargon such as ". . . throw the cobs to it," or ". . . firewall it," should be avoided. A phrase such as ". . . advance the power," would be preferable, since it has wider acceptance and understanding. In all cases, terminology should be explained to the student before it is used during instruction.

SELF-IMPROVEMENT

Professional aviation instructors must never become complacent or satisfied with their own qualifications and abilities. They should be constantly alert for ways to improve their qualifications, effectiveness, and the services they provide to students. Flight instructors are considered authorities on aeronautical matters and are the experts to whom many pilots refer questions concerning regulations, requirements, and new operating techniques. Likewise, aviation maintenance instructors are considered by maintenance students and other maintenance technicians to be a source of up-to-date information. They have the opportunity and responsibility of introducing new procedures and techniques to their students and other aviation professionals with whom they come in contact. Specific suggestions for self-improvement are discussed in Chapter 11.

MINIMIZING STUDENT FRUSTRATIONS

Minimizing student frustrations in the classroom, shop, or during flight training, is a basic instructor responsibility. By following some basic rules, instructors can reduce student frustrations and create a learning environment that will encourage rather than discourage learning. [Figure 8-9]

- **Motivate Students**
- **Keep Students Informed**
- **Approach Students As Individuals**
- **Give Credit When Due**
- **Criticize Constructively**
- **Be Consistent**
- **Admit Errors**

Figure 8-9. These are practical ways to minimize student frustration.

Motivate Students—More can be gained from wanting to learn than from being forced to learn. All too often students do not realize how a particular lesson or course can help them reach an important goal. When they can see the benefits or purpose of a lesson or course, their enjoyment and their efforts will increase.

Keep Students Informed—Students feel insecure when they do not know what is expected of them or what is going to happen to them. Instructors can minimize feelings of insecurity by telling students what is expected of them and what they can expect in return. Instructors should keep students informed in various ways, including giving them an overview of the course, keeping them posted on their progress, and giving them adequate notice of examinations, assignments, or other requirements.

Approach Students As Individuals—When instructors limit their thinking to the whole group without considering the individuals who make up that group, their efforts are directed at an average personality which really fits no one. Each group has its own personality that stems from the characteristics and interactions of its members. However, each individual within the group has a personality that is unique and that should be constantly considered.

Give Credit When Due—When students do something extremely well, they normally expect their abilities and efforts to be noticed. Otherwise, they may become frustrated. Praise or credit from the instructor is usually ample reward and provides an incentive to do even better. Praise pays dividends in student effort and achievement when deserved, but when given too freely, it becomes valueless.

Criticize Constructively—Although it is important to give praise and credit when deserved, it is equally important to identify mistakes and failures. It does not help to tell students that they have made errors and not provide explanations. If a student has made an earnest effort but is told that the work is unsatisfactory, with no other explanation, frustration occurs. Errors cannot be corrected if they are not identified, and if they are not identified, they will probably be perpetuated through faulty practice. On the other hand, if the student is briefed on the errors and is told how to correct them, progress can be made.

Be Consistent—Students want to please their instructor. This is the same desire that influences much of the behavior of subordinates toward their superiors in industry and business. Naturally, students have a keen interest in knowing what is required to please the instructor. If the same thing is acceptable one day and unacceptable the next, the student becomes confused. The instructor's philosophy and actions must be consistent.

Admit Errors—No one, including the students, expects an instructor to be perfect. The instructor can win the respect of students by honestly acknowledging mistakes. If the instructor tries to cover up or bluff, the students will be quick to sense it. Such behavior tends to destroy student confidence. If in doubt about some point, the instructor should admit it to the students.

ADDITIONAL RESPONSIBILITIES

This chapter has identified a number of areas necessary to maintain a professional appearance, demeanor, and attitude. In addition, the instructor has a number of responsibilities to the student, the public, and the FAA. Other areas aviation instructors should be deeply involved with include accident prevention and judgment training. Experience has shown that most accidents are the result of a chain of events. These events can be a mistake, but can also be a simple oversight, lack of awareness, or lack of a sense of urgency. The study of human factors in accidents is being taught throughout the aviation industry in an effort to understand why accidents occur and how training can prevent them. Concentration of this effort is in the area of how people make mistakes as a result of fatigue, stress, complacency, personal conflict, fear, or confusion. Human factors training also addresses the development of good judgment through the study of how and why people react to internal and external influences.

Flight instructors must incorporate aeronautical decision making (ADM) and judgment training into their instruction. This is a systematic approach to risk assessment and stress management in aviation. It shows how personal attitudes can influence decision making and how those attitudes can be modified to enhance safety in the cockpit. A number of FAA and industry references are available which provide instructors with methods for teaching ADM techniques and skills as a part of flight instruction. Aeronautical decision making and judgment training will be discussed more fully in Chapter 9.

Chapter 9

Techniques of Flight Instruction

In this chapter, the demonstration-performance method is applied to the telling-and-doing technique of flight instruction, as well as the integrated technique of flight instruction. This chapter also discusses positive exchange of flight controls, use of distractions, obstacles to learning encountered during flight training, and provides an overall orientation for teaching aeronautical decision making (ADM) and judgment.

THE TELLING-AND-DOING TECHNIQUE

This technique has been in use for a long time and is very effective in teaching physical skills. Flight instructors find it valuable in teaching procedures and maneuvers. The **telling-and-doing technique** is actually a variation of the demonstration-performance method. It follows the four steps of demonstration performance discussed in Chapter 5, except for the first step. In the telling-and-doing technique, the first step is preparation. This is particularly important in flight instruction because of the introduction of new maneuvers or procedures.

The flight instructor needs to be well prepared and highly organized if complex maneuvers and procedures are to be taught effectively. The student must be intellectually and psychologically ready for the learning activity. The **preparation** step is accomplished prior to the flight lesson with a discussion of lesson objectives and completion standards, as well as a thorough preflight briefing. Students need to know not only what they will learn, but also how they will learn it—that is, how the lesson will proceed and how they will be evaluated. The preparation phase also should include coverage of appropriate safety procedures.

INSTRUCTOR TELLS—INSTRUCTOR DOES

Presentation is the second step in the teaching process. It is a continuation of preparing the student, which began in the detailed preflight discussion, and now continues by a carefully planned demonstration and accompanying verbal explanation of the procedure or maneuver. While demonstrating inflight maneuvers, the instructor should explain the required power settings, aircraft attitudes, and describe any other pertinent factors that may apply. This is the only step in which the student plays a passive role. It is important that the demonstration conforms to the explanation as closely as possible. In addition, it should be demonstrated in the same sequence in which it was explained so as to avoid confusion and provide reinforcement. Since students generally imitate the instructor's performance, the instructor must demonstrate the skill exactly the way the students are expected to practice it, including all safety procedures that the students must follow. If a deviation does occur, the instructor should point it out and discuss any differences from the initial explanation.

Most physical skills lend themselves to a sequential pattern where the skill is explained in the same step-by-step order normally used to perform it. When the skill being taught is related to previously learned procedures or maneuvers, the known to unknown strategy may be used effectively. When teaching more than one skill at the same time, the simple-to-complex strategy works well. By starting with the simplest skill, a student gains confidence and is less likely to become frustrated when faced with building skills that are more complex.

Another consideration in this phase is the language used. Instructors should attempt to avoid unnecessary jargon and technical terms that are over the heads of their students. Instructors should also take care to clearly describe the actions that students are expected to perform. Communication is the key. It is neither appropriate nor effective for instructors to try to impress students with their expertise by using language that is unnecessarily complicated.

As an example, a level turn might be demonstrated and described by the instructor in the following way:

- Use outside visual references and monitor the flight instruments.

- After clearing the airspace around the airplane, add power slightly, turn the airplane in the desired direction, and apply a slight amount of back pressure on the yoke to maintain altitude. Maintain coordinated flight by applying rudder in the direction of the turn.

- Remember, the ailerons control the roll rate, as well as the angle of bank. The rate at which the airplane rolls depends on how much aileron deflection you use. How far the airplane rolls (steepness of the bank) depends on how long you deflect the ailerons, since the airplane continues to roll as long as the ailerons are deflected. When you reach the desired angle of bank, neutralize the ailerons and trim, as appropriate.

- Lead the roll-out by approximately one-half the number of degrees of your angle of bank. Use coordinated aileron and rudder control pressures as you roll out. Simultaneously, begin releasing the back pressure so aileron, rudder, and elevator pressures are neutralized when the airplane reaches the wings-level position.

- Leading the roll-out heading by one-half your bank angle is a good rule of thumb for initial training. However, keep in mind that the required amount of lead really depends on the type of turn, turn rate, and roll-out rate. As you gain experience, you will develop a consistent roll-in and roll-out technique for various types of turns. Upon reaching a wings-level attitude, reduce power and trim to remove control pressures.

STUDENT TELLS—INSTRUCTOR DOES

This is a transition between the second and third steps in the teaching process. It is the most obvious departure from the demonstration-performance technique, and may provide the most significant advantages. In this step, the student actually plays the role of instructor, telling the instructor what to do and how to do it. Two benefits accrue from this step. First, being freed from the need to concentrate on performance of the maneuver and from concern about its outcome, the student should be able to organize his or her thoughts regarding the steps involved and the techniques to be used. In the process of explaining the maneuver as the instructor performs it, perceptions begin to develop into insights. Mental habits begin to form with repetition of the instructions previously received. Second, with the student doing the talking, the instructor is able to evaluate the student's understanding of the factors involved in performance of the maneuver.

According to the principle of primacy, it is important for the instructor to make sure the student gets it right the first time. The student should also understand the correct sequence and be aware of safety precautions for each procedure or maneuver. If a misunderstanding exists, it can be corrected before the student becomes absorbed in controlling the airplane.

STUDENT TELLS—STUDENT DOES

Application is the third step in the teaching process. This is where learning takes place and where performance habits are formed. If the student has been adequately prepared (first step) and the procedure or maneuver fully explained and demonstrated (second step), meaningful learning will occur. The instructor should be alert during the student's practice to detect any errors in technique and to prevent the formation of faulty habits.

At the same time, the student should be encouraged to think about what to do during the performance of a maneuver, until it becomes habitual. In this step, the thinking is done verbally. This focuses concentration on the task to be accomplished, so that total involvement in the maneuver is fostered. All of the student's physical and mental faculties are brought into play. The instructor should be aware of the student's thought processes. It is easy to determine whether an error is induced by a misconception or by a simple lack of motor skills. Therefore, in addition to forcing total concentration on the part of the student, this method provides a means for keeping the instructor aware of what the student is thinking. The student is not only learning to do something, but he or she is learning a self-teaching process that is highly desirable in development of a skill.

The exact procedures that the instructor should use during student practice depends on factors such as the student's proficiency level, the type of maneuver, and the stage of training. The instructor must exercise good judgment to decide how much control to use. With potentially hazardous or difficult maneuvers, the instructor should be alert and ready to take control at any time. This is especially true during a student's first attempt at a particular maneuver. On the other hand, if a student is progressing normally, the instructor should avoid unnecessary interruptions or too much assistance.

A typical test of how much control is needed often occurs during a student's first few attempts to land an aircraft. The instructor must quickly evaluate the student's need for help, and not hesitate to take control, if required. At the same time, the student should be allowed to practice the entire maneuver often enough to achieve the level of proficiency established in the lesson objectives. Since this is a learning phase rather than an evaluation phase of the training, errors or unsafe practices should be identified and corrected in a positive and timely way. In some cases, the student will not be able to meet the proficiency level specified in the lesson objectives within the allotted time. When this occurs, the instructor should be prepared to schedule additional training.

STUDENT DOES—INSTRUCTOR EVALUATES

The fourth step of the teaching process is **review and evaluation**. In this step, the instructor reviews what has been covered during the instructional flight and determines to what extent the student has met the objectives outlined during the preflight discussion. Since the student no longer is required to talk through the maneuver during this step, the instructor should be satisfied that the student is well prepared and understands the task before starting. This last step is identical to the final step used in the demonstration-performance method. The instructor observes as the student performs, then makes appropriate comments.

At the conclusion of the evaluation phase, record the student's performance and verbally advise each student of the progress made toward the objectives. Regardless of how well a skill is taught, there may still be failures. Since success is a motivating factor, instructors should be positive in revealing results. When pointing out areas that need improvement, offer concrete suggestions that will help. If possible, avoid ending the evaluation on a negative note.

In summary, the telling and doing technique of flight instruction follows the four basic steps of the teaching process and the demonstration-performance method. However, the telling-and-doing technique includes specific variations for flight instruction. [Figure 9-1]

TEACHING PROCESS	DEMONSTRATION-PERFORMANCE METHOD	TELLING-AND-DOING TECHNIQUE
Preparation	Explanation	Preparation
Presentation	Demonstration	Instructor Tells Instructor Does
		Student Tells Instructor Does
Application	Student Performance Supervision	Student Tells Student Does
Review and Evaluation	Evaluation	Student Does Instructor Evaluates

Figure 9-1. This comparison of steps in the teaching process, the demonstration-performance method, and the telling-and-doing technique shows the similarities as well as some differences. The main difference in the telling-and-doing technique is the important transition, student tells—instructor does, which occurs between the second and third step.

INTEGRATED FLIGHT INSTRUCTION

Integrated flight instruction is flight instruction during which students are taught to perform flight maneuvers both by outside visual references and by reference to flight instruments. For this type of instruction to be fully effective, the use of instrument references should begin the first time each new maneuver is introduced. No distinction in the pilot's operation of the flight controls is permitted, regardless of whether outside references or instrument indications are used for the performance of the maneuver. When this training technique is used, instruction in the control of an airplane by outside visual references is integrated with instruction in the use of flight instrument indications for the same operations.

DEVELOPMENT OF HABIT PATTERNS

The continuing observance and reliance upon flight instruments is essential for efficient, safe operations. The habit of monitoring instruments is difficult to develop after one has become accustomed to relying almost exclusively on outside references.

General aviation accident reports provide ample support for the belief that reference to flight instruments is important to safety. The safety record of pilots who hold instrument ratings is significantly better than that of pilots with comparable flight time who have never received formal flight training for an instrument rating. Student pilots who have been required to perform all normal flight maneuvers by reference to instruments, as well as by outside references, will develop from the start the habit of continuously monitoring their own and the airplane's performance.

The early establishment of proper habits of instrument cross-check, instrument interpretation, and aircraft control will be highly useful to the student pilot. The habits formed at this time also will give the student a firm foundation for later training for an instrument rating.

ACCURACY OF FLIGHT CONTROL

During early experiments with the integrated technique of flight instruction, it was soon recognized that students trained in this manner are much more precise in their flight maneuvers and operations. This applies to all flight operations, not just when flight by reference to instruments is required.

Notable among student achievements are better monitoring of power settings and more accurate control of headings, altitudes, and airspeeds. As the habit of monitoring their own performance by reference to instruments is developed, students will begin to make corrections without prompting.

The habitual attention to instrument indications leads to improved landings because of more precise airspeed control. Effective use of instruments also results in superior cross-country navigation, better coordination, and generally, a better overall pilot competency level.

OPERATING EFFICIENCY

As student pilots become more proficient in monitoring and correcting their own flight technique by reference to flight instruments, the performance obtained from an airplane increases noticeably. This is particularly true of modern, complex, or high-performance airplanes, which are responsive to the use of correct operating airspeeds.

The use of correct power settings and climb speeds and the accurate control of headings during climbs result in a measurable increase in climb performance. Holding precise headings and altitudes in cruising flight will definitely increase average cruising performance.

The use of integrated flight instruction provides the student with the ability to control an airplane in flight for limited periods if outside references are lost. This ability could save the pilot's life and those of the passengers in an actual emergency.

During the conduct of integrated flight training, the flight instructor must emphasize to the students that the introduction to the use of flight instruments does not prepare them for operations in marginal weather or instrument meteorological conditions. The possible consequences, both to themselves and to others, of experiments with flight operations in weather conditions below VFR minimums before they are instrument rated, should be constantly impressed on the students.

PROCEDURES

The conduct of integrated flight instruction is simple. The student's first briefing on the function of the flight controls should include the instrument indications to be expected, as well as the outside references which should be used to control the attitude of the airplane.

Each new flight maneuver should be introduced using both outside references and instrument references. Students should develop the ability to maneuver an aircraft equally as well by instrument or outside references. They naturally accept the fact that the manipulation of the flight controls is identical, regardless of which references are used to determine the attitude of the airplane. This practice should continue throughout the student's flight instruction for all maneuvers. To fully achieve the demonstrated benefits of this type of training, the use of visual and instrument references must be constantly integrated throughout the training. Failure to do so will lengthen the flight instruction necessary for the student to achieve the competency required for a private pilot certificate.

PRECAUTIONS

The instructor must be sure that the students develop, from the start of their training, the habit of looking for other air traffic at all times. If students are allowed to believe that the instructor assumes all responsibility for scanning and collision avoidance procedures, they will not develop the habit of maintaining a constant vigilance, which is essential to safety. Any observed tendency of a student to enter flight maneuvers without first making a careful check for other air traffic must be corrected immediately.

In earlier stages of training, students may find it easier to perform flight maneuvers by instruments than by outside references. The fact that students can perform better by reference to instruments may cause them to concentrate most of their attention on the instruments, when they should be using outside references. This must not be allowed to continue, since it will cause considerable difficulty later in training while maneuvering by reference to ground objects. This tendency will also limit vigilance for other air traffic. The instructor should carefully observe the student's performance of maneuvers during the early stages of integrated flight instruction to ensure that this habit does not develop.

During the conduct of integrated flight instruction, the instructor should make it clear that the use of instruments is being taught to prepare students to accurately monitor their own and their aircraft's performance. The instructor must avoid any indication, by word or action that the proficiency sought is intended solely for use in difficult weather situations.

FLIGHT INSTRUCTOR QUALIFICATIONS

As a prerequisite, a flight instructor must be thoroughly familiar with the functions, characteristics, and proper use of all standard flight instruments. It is the personal responsibility of each flight instructor to maintain familiarity with current pilot training techniques and certification requirements. This may be done by frequent review of new periodicals and technical publications, personal contacts with FAA inspectors and designated pilot examiners, and by participation in pilot and flight instructor clinics. The application of outmoded instructional procedures, or the preparation of student pilots using obsolete certification requirements is inexcusable.

OBSTACLES TO LEARNING DURING FLIGHT INSTRUCTION

Certain obstacles are common to flight instruction and may apply directly to the student's attitude, physical condition, and psychological make-up. These are included in the following list:

- Feeling of unfair treatment;

- Impatience to proceed to more interesting operations;

- Worry or lack of interest;

- Physical discomfort, illness, and fatigue;

- Apathy due to inadequate instruction; and

- Anxiety.

UNFAIR TREATMENT

Students who believe that their instruction is inadequate, or that their efforts are not conscientiously considered and evaluated, will not learn well. In addition, their motivation will suffer no matter how intent they are on learning to fly. Motivation will also decline when a student believes the instructor is making unreasonable demands for performance and progress. [Figure 9-2]

Figure 9-2. The assignment of impossible or unreasonable goals discourages the student, diminishes effort, and retards the learning process.

Assignment of goals that the student considers difficult, but possible, usually provides a challenge, and promotes learning. In a typical flight lesson, reasonable goals are listed in the lesson objectives and the desired levels of proficiency for the goals are included in statements that contain completion standards.

IMPATIENCE

Impatience is a greater deterrent to learning pilot skills than is generally recognized. With a flight student, this may take the form of a desire to make an early solo flight, or to set out on cross-country flights before the basic elements of flight have been learned.

The impatient student fails to understand the need for preliminary training and seeks only the ultimate objective without considering the means necessary to reach it. With every complex human endeavor, it is necessary to master the basics if the whole task is to be performed competently and safely. The instructor can correct student impatience by presenting the necessary preliminary training one step at a time, with clearly stated goals for each step. The procedures and elements mastered in each step should be clearly identified in explaining or demonstrating the performance of the subsequent step.

Impatience can result from instruction keyed to the pace of a slow learner when it is applied to a motivated, fast learner. It is just as important that a student be advanced to the subsequent step as soon as one goal has been attained, as it is to complete each step before the next one is undertaken. Disinterest grows rapidly when unnecessary repetition and drill are required on operations that have already been adequately learned.

WORRY OR LACK OF INTEREST

Worry or lack of interest has a detrimental effect on learning. Students who are worried or emotionally upset are not ready to learn and derive little benefit from instruction. Worry or distraction may be due to student concerns about progress in the training course, or may stem from circumstances completely unrelated to their instruction. Significant emotional upsets may be due to personal problems, psychiatric disturbances, or a dislike of the training program or the instructor.

The experiences of students outside their training activities affect their behavior and performance in training; the two cannot be separated. When students begin flight training, they bring with them their interests, enthusiasms, fears, and troubles. The instructor cannot be responsible for these outside diversions, but cannot ignore them because they have a critical effect on the learning process. Instruction must be keyed to the utilization of the interests and enthusiasm students bring with them, and to diverting their attention from their worries and troubles to the learning tasks at hand. This is admittedly difficult, but must be accomplished if learning is to proceed at a normal rate.

Worries and emotional upsets that result from a flight training course can be identified and addressed. These problems are often due to inadequacies of the course or of the instructor. The most effective cure is prevention. The instructor must be alert to see that the students understand the objectives of each step of their training, and that they know at the completion of each lesson exactly how well they have progressed and what deficiencies are apparent. Discouragement and emotional upsets are rare when students feel that nothing is being withheld from them or is being neglected in their training.

PHYSICAL DISCOMFORT, ILLNESS, AND FATIGUE

Physical discomfort, illness, and fatigue will materially slow the rate of learning during both classroom instruction and flight training. Students who are not completely at ease, and whose attention is diverted by discomforts such as the extremes of temperature, poor ventilation, inadequate lighting, or noise and confusion, cannot learn at a normal rate. This is true no matter how diligently they attempt to apply themselves to the learning task.

A minor illness, such as a cold, or a major illness or injury will interfere with the normal rate of learning. This is especially important for flight instruction. Most illnesses adversely affect the acuteness of vision, hearing, and feeling, all of which are essential to correct performance.

Airsickness can be a great deterrent to flight instruction. A student who is airsick, or bothered with incipient airsickness, is incapable of learning at a normal rate. There is no sure cure for airsickness, but resistance or immunity can be developed in a relatively short period of time. An instructional flight should be terminated as soon as incipient sickness is experienced. As the student develops immunity, flights can be increased in length until normal flight periods are practicable.

Keeping students interested and occupied during flight is a deterrent to airsickness. They are much less apt to become airsick while operating the controls themselves. Rough air and unexpected abrupt maneuvers tend to increase the chances of airsickness. Tension and apprehension apparently contribute to airsickness and should be avoided.

The detection of student fatigue is important to efficient flight instruction. This is important both in assessing a student's substandard performance early in a lesson, and also in recognizing the deterioration of performance. Once fatigue occurs as a result of application to a learning task, the student should be given a break in instruction and practice. Fatigue can be delayed by introducing a number of maneuvers, which involve different elements and objectives.

Fatigue is the primary consideration in determining the length and frequency of flight instruction periods. The amount of training, which can be absorbed by one student without incurring debilitating fatigue, does not necessarily indicate the capacity of another student. Fatigue which results from training operations may be either physical or mental, or both. It is not necessarily a function of physical robustness or mental acuity. Generally speaking, complex operations tend to induce fatigue more rapidly than simpler procedures do, regardless of the physical effort involved. Flight instruction should be continued only as long as the student is alert, receptive to instruction, and is performing at a level consistent with experience.

APATHY DUE TO INADEQUATE INSTRUCTION

Students quickly become apathetic when they recognize that the instructor has made inadequate preparations for the instruction being given, or when the instruction appears to be deficient, contradictory, or insincere. To hold the student's interest and to maintain the motivation necessary for efficient learning, well-planned, appropriate, and accurate instruction must be provided. Nothing destroys a student's interest so quickly as a poorly organized period of instruction. Even an inexperienced student realizes immediately when the instructor has failed to prepare a lesson. [Figure 9-3]

Figure 9-3. Poor preparation leads to spotty coverage, misplaced emphasis, unnecessary repetition, and a lack of confidence on the part of the student. The instructor should always have a plan.

Instruction may be overly explicit and so elementary it fails to hold student interest, or it may be so general or complicated that it fails to evoke the interest necessary for effective learning. To be effective, the instructor must teach for the level of the student. The presentation must be adjusted to be meaningful to the person for whom it is intended. For example, instruction in the preflight inspection of an aircraft should be presented quite differently for a student who is a skilled aircraft maintenance technician compared to the instruction on the same operation for a student with no previous aeronautical experience. The inspection desired in each case is the same, but a presentation meaningful to one of these students would be inappropriate for the other.

Poor instructional presentations may result not only from poor preparation, but also from distracting mannerisms, personal untidiness, or the appearance of irritation with the student. Creating the impression of talking down to the student is one of the surest ways for an instructor to lose the student's confidence and attention. Once the instructor loses this confidence, it is difficult to regain, and the learning rate is unnecessarily diminished.

ANXIETY

Anxiety may place additional burdens on the instructor. This frequently limits the student's perceptive ability and retards the development of insights. The student must be comfortable, confident in the instructor and the aircraft, and at ease, if effective learning is to occur. Providing this atmosphere for learning is one of the first and most important tasks of the instructor. Although doing so may be difficult at first, successive accomplishments of recognizable goals and the avoidance of alarming occurrences or situations will rapidly ease the student's mind. This is true of all flight students, but special handling by the instructor may be required for students who are obviously anxious or uncomfortable.

POSITIVE EXCHANGE OF FLIGHT CONTROLS

Positive exchange of flight controls is an integral part of flight training. It is especially critical during the telling-and-doing technique of flight instruction. Due to the importance of this subject, the following discussion provides guidance for all pilots, especially student pilots, flight instructors, and pilot examiners, on the recommended procedure to use for the positive exchange of flight controls between pilots when operating an aircraft.

BACKGROUND

Incident/accident statistics indicate a need to place additional emphasis on the exchange of control of an aircraft by pilots. Numerous accidents have occurred due to a lack of communication or misunderstanding as to who actually had control of the aircraft, particularly between students and flight instructors.

Establishing the following procedure during the initial training of students will ensure the formation of a habit pattern that should stay with them throughout their flying careers. They will be more likely to relinquish control willingly and promptly when instructed to do so during flight training.

PROCEDURES

During flight training, there must always be a clear understanding between students and flight instructors of who has control of the aircraft. Prior to flight, a briefing should be conducted that includes the procedure for the exchange of flight controls. A positive three-step process in the exchange of flight controls between pilots is a proven procedure and one that is strongly recommended. When an instructor is teaching a maneuver to a student, the instructor will normally demonstrate the maneuver first, then have the student follow along on the controls during a demonstration and, finally, the student will perform the maneuver with the instructor following along on the controls. [Figure 9-4]

POSITIVE EXCHANGE OF FLIGHT CONTROLS
1. When the flight instructor wishes the student to take control of the aircraft, the instructor says to the student,   **"You have the flight controls."**
2. The student acknowledges immediately by saying,   **"I have the flight controls."**
3. The flight instructor again says,   **"You have the flight controls."**

Figure 9-4. During this procedure, a visual check is recommended to see that the other person actually has the flight controls. When returning the controls to the instructor, the student should follow the same procedure the instructor used when giving control to the student. The student should stay on the controls and keep flying the aircraft until the instructor says, "I have the flight controls." There should never be any doubt as to who is flying the aircraft.

Flight instructors should always guard the controls and be prepared to take control of the aircraft. When necessary, the instructor should take the controls and calmly announce, "I have the flight controls." If an instructor allows a student to remain on the controls, the instructor may not have full and effective control of the aircraft. Anxious students can be incredibly strong and usually exhibit reactions inappropriate to the situation. If a recovery is necessary, there is absolutely nothing to be gained by having the student on the controls and having to fight for control of the aircraft.

Students should never be allowed to exceed the flight instructor's limits. Flight instructors should not exceed their own ability to perceive a problem, decide upon a course of action, and physically react within their ability to fly the aircraft.

USE OF DISTRACTIONS

National Transportation Safety Board (NTSB) statistics reveal that most stall/spin accidents occured when the pilot's attention was diverted from the primary task of flying the aircraft. Sixty percent of stall/spin accidents occured during takeoff and landing, and twenty percent were preceded by engine failure. Preoccupation inside or outside the cockpit while changing aircraft configuration or trim, maneuvering to avoid other traffic or clearing hazardous obstacles during takeoff and climb could create a potential stall/spin situation.

The intentional practice of stalls and spins seldom resulted in an accident. The real danger was inadvertent stalls induced by distractions during routine flight situations.

Pilots at all skill levels should be aware of the increased risk of entering into an inadvertent stall or spin while performing tasks that are secondary to controlling the aircraft. The FAA has also established a policy for use of certain distractions on practical tests for pilot certification. The purpose is to determine that applicants possess the skills required to cope with distractions while maintaining the degree of aircraft control required for safe flight. The most effective training is the simulation of scenarios that can lead to inadvertent stalls by creating distractions while the student is practicing certain maneuvers.

The instructor should tell the student to divide his/her attention between the distracting task and maintaining control of the aircraft. The following are examples of distractions that can be used for this training:

- Drop a pencil. Ask the student to pick it up.

- Ask the student to determine a heading to an airport using a chart.

- Ask the student to reset the clock.

- Ask the student to get something from the back seat.

- Ask the student to read the outside air temperature.

- Ask the student to call the Flight Service Station (FSS) for weather information.

- Ask the student to compute true airspeed with a flight computer.

- Ask the student to identify terrain or objects on the ground.

- Ask the student to identify a field suitable for a forced landing.

- Have the student climb 200 feet and maintain altitude, then descend 200 feet and maintain altitude.

- Have the student reverse course after a series of S-turns.

AERONAUTICAL DECISION MAKING

Aeronautical decision making (ADM) is a systematic approach to the mental process used by aircraft pilots to consistently determine the best course of action in response to a given set of circumstances. The importance of teaching students effective ADM skills can not be overemphasized. The flight instructor can make a difference! While progress is continually being made in the advancement of pilot training methods, aircraft equipment and systems, and services for pilots, accidents still occur. Despite all the changes in technology to improve flight safety, one factor remains the same—the human factor. It is estimated that approximately 75% of all aviation accidents are **human factors** related.

Historically, the term **pilot error** has been used to describe the causes of these accidents. Pilot error means that an action or decision made by the pilot was the cause of, or contributing factor which lead to, the accident. This definition also includes the pilot's failure to make a decision or take action. From a broader perspective, the phrase "human factors related" more aptly describes these accidents since it is usually not a single decision that leads to an accident, but a chain of events triggered by a number of factors.

The **poor judgment chain**, sometimes referred to as the error chain, is a term used to describe this concept of contributing factors in a human factors related accident. Breaking one link in the chain normally is all that is necessary to change the outcome of the sequence of events. The best way to illustrate this concept to students is to discuss specific situations which lead to aircraft accidents or incidents. The following is an example of the type of scenario which can be presented to students to illustrate the poor judgment chain.

A private pilot, who had logged 100 hours of flight time, made a precautionary landing on a narrow dirt runway at a private airport. The pilot lost directional control during landing and swerved off the runway into the grass. A witness recalled later that the airplane appeared to be too high and fast on final approach, and speculated the pilot was having difficulty controlling the airplane in high winds. The weather at the time of the incident was reported as marginal VFR due to rain showers and thunderstorms. When the airplane was fueled the following morning, 60 gallons of fuel were required to fill the 62-gallon capacity tanks.

By discussing the events that led to this incident, instructors can help students understand how a series of judgmental errors contributed to the final outcome of this flight. For example, one of the first elements that affected the pilot's flight was a decision regarding the weather. On the morning of the flight, the pilot was running late, and having acquired a computer printout of the forecast the night before, he did not bother to obtain a briefing from flight service before his departure.

A flight planning decision also played a part in this poor judgment chain. The pilot calculated total fuel requirements for the trip based on a rule-of-thumb figure he had used previously for another airplane. He did not use the fuel tables printed in the pilot's operating handbook for the airplane he was flying on this trip. After reaching his destination, the pilot did not request refueling. Based on his original calculations, he believed sufficient fuel remained for the flight home.

Failing to recognize his own limitations was another factor that led the pilot one step closer to the unfortunate conclusion of his journey. In the presence of deteriorating weather, he departed for the flight home at 5:00 in the afternoon. He did not consider how fatigue and lack of extensive night flying experience could affect the flight. As the flight continued, the weather along the route grew increasingly hazardous. Since the airplane's fuel supply was almost exhausted, the pilot no longer had the option of diverting to avoid rapidly developing thunderstorms. With few alternatives left, he was forced to land at the nearest airfield available, a small private airport with one narrow dirt runway. Due to the gusty wind conditions and the pilot's limited experience, the approach and landing were difficult. After touchdown, the pilot lost directional control and the airplane finally came to a stop in the grass several yards to the side of the runway.

On numerous occasions during the flight, the pilot could have made effective decisions which may have prevented this incident. However, as the chain of events unfolded, each poor decision left him with fewer and fewer options. Teaching pilots to make sound decisions is the key to preventing accidents. Traditional pilot instruction has emphasized flying skills, knowledge of the aircraft, and familiarity with regulations. ADM training focuses on the decision-making process and the factors that affect a pilot's ability to make effective choices.

ORIGINS OF ADM TRAINING

The airlines developed some of the first training programs that focused on improving aeronautical decision making. Human factors-related accidents motivated the airline industry to implement **crew resource management (CRM)** training for flight crews. The focus of CRM programs is the effective use of all available resources; human resources, hardware, and information. Human resources include all groups routinely working with the cockpit crew (or pilot) who are involved in decisions which are required to operate a flight safely. These groups include, but are not limited to: dispatchers, cabin crewmembers, maintenance personnel, and air traffic controllers. Although the CRM concept originated as airlines developed ways of facilitating crew cooperation to improve decision making in the cockpit, CRM principles, such as workload management, situational awareness, communication, the leadership role of the captain, and crewmember coordination have direct application to the general aviation cockpit. This also includes single pilots since pilots of small aircraft, as well as crews of larger aircraft, must make effective use of all available resources—human resources, hardware, and information.

Crew resource management training has proven extremely successful in reducing accidents, and airlines typically introduce CRM concepts during initial indoctrination of new hires. Instructors in the general aviation environment can learn from this example when conducting ADM training. In the past, some students were introduced to ADM concepts toward the completion of their training or not at all. It is important that these concepts be incorporated throughout the entire training course for all levels of students; private, instrument, commercial, multi-engine, and ATP. Instructors, as well as students, also can refer to AC 60-22, *Aeronautical*

Decision Making, which provides background references, definitions, and other pertinent information about ADM training in the general aviation environment. [Figure 9-5]

THE DECISION-MAKING PROCESS

An understanding of the decision-making process provides students with a foundation for developing ADM skills. Some situations, such as engine failures, require a pilot to respond immediately using established procedures with little time for detailed analysis. Traditionally, pilots have been well trained to react to emergencies, but are not as well prepared to make decisions which require a more reflective response. Typically during a flight, the pilot has time to examine any changes which occur, gather information, and assess risk before reaching a decision. The steps leading to this conclusion constitute the decision-making process. When the decision-making process is presented to students, it is essential to discuss how the process applies to an actual flight situation. To explain the decision-making process, the instructor can introduce the following steps with the accompanying scenario that places the student in the position of making a decision about a typical flight situation.

DEFINING THE PROBLEM

Problem definition is the first step in the decision-making process. Defining the problem begins with recognizing that a change has occurred or that an expected

---

DEFINITIONS

ADM is a systematic approach to the mental process used by pilots to consistently determine the best course of action in response to a given set of circumstances.

ATTITUDE is a personal motivational predisposition to respond to persons, situations, or events in a given manner that can, nevertheless, be changed or modified through training as sort of a mental shortcut to decision making.

ATTITUDE MANAGEMENT is the ability to recognize hazardous attitudes in oneself and the willingness to modify them as necessary through the application of an appropriate antidote thought.

CREW RESOURCE MANAGEMENT (CRM) is the application of team management concepts in the flight deck environment. It was initially known as cockpit resource management, but as CRM programs evolved to include cabin crews, maintenance personnel, and others, the phrase crew resource management was adopted. This includes single pilots, as in most general aviation aircraft. Pilots of small aircraft, as well as crews of larger aircraft, must make effective use of all available resources; human resources, hardware, and information. A current definition includes all groups routinely working with the cockpit crew who are involved in decisions required to operate a flight safely. These groups include, but are not limited to: pilots, dispatchers, cabin crewmembers, maintenance personnel, and air traffic controllers. CRM is one way of addressing the challenge of optimizing the human/machine interface and accompanying interpersonal activities.

HEADWORK is required to accomplish a conscious, rational thought process when making decisions. Good decision making involves risk identification and assessment, information processing, and problem solving.

JUDGMENT is the mental process of recognizing and analyzing all pertinent information in a particular situation, a rational evaluation of alternative actions in response to it, and a timely decision on which action to take.

PERSONALITY is the embodiment of personal traits and characteristics of an individual that are set at a very early age and extremely resistant to change.

POOR JUDGMENT CHAIN is a series of mistakes that may lead to an accident or incident. Two basic principles generally associated with the creation of a poor judgment chain are: (1) One bad decision often leads to another; and (2) as a string of bad decisions grows, it reduces the number of subsequent alternatives for continued safe flight. ADM is intended to break the poor judgment chain before it can cause an accident or incident.

RISK ELEMENTS IN ADM take into consideration the four fundamental risk elements: the pilot, the aircraft, the environment, and the type of operation that comprise any given aviation situation.

RISK MANAGEMENT is the part of the decision making process which relies on situational awareness, problem recognition, and good judgment to reduce risks associated with each flight.

SITUATIONAL AWARENESS is the accurate perception and understanding of all the factors and conditions within the four fundamental risk elements that affect safety before, during, and after the flight.

SKILLS and PROCEDURES are the procedural, psychomotor, and perceptual skills used to control a specific aircraft or its systems. They are the stick and rudder or airmanship abilities that are gained through conventional training, are perfected, and become almost automatic through experience.

STRESS MANAGEMENT is the personal analysis of the kinds of stress experienced while flying, the application of appropriate stress assessment tools, and other coping mechanisms.

Figure 9-5. These terms are used in AC 60-22 to explain concepts used in ADM training.

change did not occur. A problem is perceived first by the senses, then is distinguished through insight and experience. These same abilities, as well as an objective analysis of all available information, are used to determine the exact nature and severity of the problem.

One critical error that can be made during the decision-making process is incorrectly defining the problem. For example, failure of a landing-gear-extended light to illuminate could indicate that the gear is not down and locked into place or it could mean the bulb is burned out. The actions to be taken in each of these circumstances would be significantly different. Fixating on a problem that does not exist can divert the pilot's attention from important tasks. The pilot's failure to maintain an awareness of the circumstances regarding the flight now becomes the problem. This is why once an initial assumption is made regarding the problem, other sources must be used to verify that the pilot's conclusion is correct.

While on a cross-country flight, you discover that your time en route between two checkpoints is significantly longer than the time you had originally calculated. By noticing this discrepancy, you have recognized a change. Based on your insight, cross-country flying experience, and your knowledge of weather systems, you consider the possibility that you have an increased headwind. You verify that your original calculations are correct and consider factors which may have lengthened the time between checkpoints, such as a climb or deviation off course. To determine if there is a change in the winds aloft forecast and to check recent pilot reports, you contact Flight Watch. After weighing each information source, you conclude that your headwind has increased. To determine the severity of the problem, you calculate your new groundspeed, and reassess fuel requirements.

CHOOSING A COURSE OF ACTION

After the problem has been identified, the pilot must evaluate the need to react to it and determine the actions which may be taken to resolve the situation in the time available. The expected outcome of each possible action should be considered and the risks assessed before the pilot decides on a response to the situation.

You determine your fuel burn if you continue to your destination, and consider other options, such as turning around and landing at a nearby airport that you have passed, diverting off course, or landing prior to your destination at an airport on your route. You must now consider the expected outcome of each possible

action and assess the risks involved. After studying the chart, you conclude that there is an airport which has fueling services within a reasonable distance ahead along your route. You can refuel there and continue to your destination without a significant loss of time.

IMPLEMENTING THE DECISION AND EVALUATING THE OUTCOME

Although a decision may be reached and a course of action implemented, the decision-making process is not complete. It is important to think ahead and determine how the decision could affect other phases of the flight. As the flight progresses, the pilot must continue to evaluate the outcome of the decision to ensure that it is producing the desired result.

To implement your decision, you plot the course changes and calculate a new estimated time of arrival, as well as contact the nearest flight service station to amend your flight plan and check weather conditions at your new destination. As you proceed to the airport, you continue to monitor your groundspeed, aircraft performance, and the weather conditions to ensure that no additional steps need to be taken to guarantee the safety of the flight.

To assist teaching pilots the elements of the decision-making process, a six-step model has been developed using the acronym "DECIDE." The DECIDE model has been used to instruct pilots of varying experience levels, as well as analyze accidents. [Figure 9-6]

DECIDE MODEL

Detect the fact that a change has occurred.
Estimate the need to counter or react to the change.
Choose a desirable outcome for the success of the flight.
Identify actions which could successfully control the change.
Do the necessary action to adapt to the change.
Evaluate the effect of the action.

Figure 9-6. During initial training, the DECIDE model can provide a framework for effective decision making.

RISK MANAGEMENT

During each flight, decisions must be made regarding events which involve interactions between the four **risk elements**—the pilot in command, the aircraft, the environment, and the operation. The decision-making process involves an evaluation of each of these risk

Figure 9-7. One of the most important decisions that the pilot in command must make is the go/no-go decision. Evaluating each of these risk elements can help the pilot decide whether a flight should be conducted or continued.

elements to achieve an accurate perception of the flight situation. [Figure 9-7]

To reinforce the risk elements and their significance to effective decision making, the instructor can ask the student to identify the risk elements for a flight. The student should also be able to determine whether the risks have been appropriately evaluated in the situation.

A pilot schedules to fly to a business appointment with a client in a nearby city. She is a noninstrument-rated private pilot with no experience in marginal weather conditions, although she did gain some attitude instrument flying experience during her private pilot flight training. She intends to fly in a small four-seat, single-engine airplane with standard communication and navigation equipment. However, the VOR receiver is inoperative. The pilot plans to leave in the morning and return early in the afternoon. When she receives her weather briefing, she is informed that marginal VFR conditions with possible icing in the clouds are forecast for late afternoon. Having been delayed at the office, the pilot departs later than planned. While en route, the pilot encounters low ceilings and restricted visibility and she becomes spatially disoriented due to continued flight by ground reference.

In this case, the pilot did not effectively evaluate the four risk elements when making decisions regarding this flight. When assessing her fitness as a pilot, she overestimated her flying abilities by attempting to fly in marginal VFR conditions. The capability of her airplane was not properly evaluated. The inoperative VOR receiver limits her options if she becomes lost, or is required to navigate with limited visual reference to the ground. In addition, her airplane did not contain sophisticated navigation equipment which may have helped her locate an airport in an emergency situation. The flying environment was less than optimal when she decided to depart despite the threat of marginal conditions. When faced with deteriorating weather, she did not enlist the assistance of air traffic control (ATC) or use her instruments as references to turn around. Since she was trying to reach her destination for a business appointment, the operation affected her decision to undertake and continue the flight.

ASSESSING RISK

Examining NTSB reports and other accident research can help students learn to assess risk more effectively. Instructors can point out the phases of flight when accidents are most likely to occur and when risk is the greatest. For example, the majority of accidents occur when approaching or departing airports. [Figure 9-8]

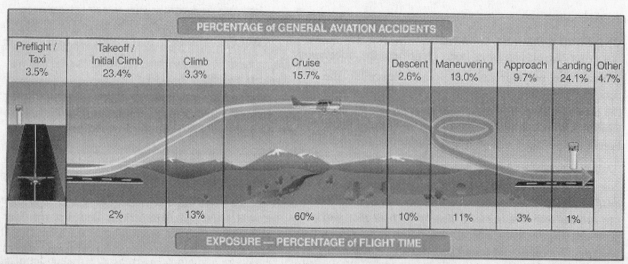

Figure 9-8. Workload is highest during takeoff and landing, which increases the chance of error.

Studies also indicate the types of flight activities that are most likely to result in the most serious accidents. The majority of fatal general aviation accident causes fall under the categories of maneuvering flight, approaches, takeoff/initial climb, and weather. Delving deeper into accident statistics can provide some important details that can help students understand the risks involved with specific flying situations. For example, maneuvering flight is one of the largest single producers of fatal accidents and many of these accidents are attributed to maneuvering during low, slow flight, often during buzzing or unauthorized aerobatics. Fatal accidents which occur during approach often happen at night or in IFR conditions. Takeoff/initial climb accidents frequently are due to the pilot's lack of awareness of the effects of density altitude on aircraft performance or other improper takeoff planning resulting in loss of control or stalls during, or shortly after takeoff. The majority of weather-related accidents occur after attempted VFR flight into IFR conditions.

In addition to discussing these facts, instructors can increase student awareness of these risks by setting positive examples. For instance, ensuring that students obtain weather briefings before every flight develops good habits and emphasizes the importance of the weather check. Instructors should take the time to discuss the conditions, and require the student to arrive at a go/no-go decision. Ignoring a marginal forecast or continuing a flight in poor weather may be sending the message that checking the weather serves no practical purpose. During the flight planning phase, the flight instructor can introduce situations that are different from those planned. The student should be asked to explain the possible consequences of each situation. Even if a flight lesson is canceled based on forecast conditions that never materialize, a lesson in judgment has been accomplished.

FACTORS AFFECTING DECISION MAKING

It is important to point out to students that being familiar with the decision-making process does not ensure that they will have the good judgment to be safe pilots. The ability to make effective decisions as pilot in command depends on a number of factors. Some circumstances, such as the time available to make a decision, may be beyond the pilot's control. However, a pilot can learn to recognize those factors that can be managed, and learn skills to improve decision-making ability and judgment.

PILOT SELF-ASSESSMENT

The pilot in command of an aircraft is directly responsible for, and is the final authority as to, the operation of that aircraft. In order to effectively exercise that responsibility and make effective decisions regarding the out-come of a flight, pilots must have an understanding of their limitations. A pilot's performance during a flight is affected by many factors, such as health, recency of experience, knowledge, skill level, and attitude.

Students must be taught that exercising good judgment begins prior to taking the controls of an aircraft. Often, pilots thoroughly check their aircraft to determine airworthiness, yet do not evaluate their own fitness for flight. Just as a checklist is used when preflighting an aircraft, a personal checklist based on such factors as experience, currency, and comfort level can help determine if a pilot is prepared for a particular flight. Specifying when refresher training should be accomplished, designating weather minimums which may be higher than those listed in Title 14 of the Code of Federal Regulations (14 CFR) part 91, and setting limitations regarding the amount of crosswind for takeoffs and landings are examples of elements which may be included on a personal checklist. Instructors set an example by having their own personal checklists and can help students create their own checklists. In addition to a review of personal limitations, pilots should use the I'M SAFE Checklist to further evaluate their fitness for flight. [Figure 9-9]

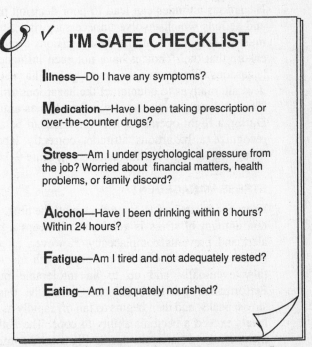

I'M SAFE CHECKLIST

Illness—Do I have any symptoms?

Medication—Have I been taking prescription or over-the-counter drugs?

Stress—Am I under psychological pressure from the job? Worried about financial matters, health problems, or family discord?

Alcohol—Have I been drinking within 8 hours? Within 24 hours?

Fatigue—Am I tired and not adequately rested?

Eating—Am I adequately nourished?

Figure 9-9. Prior to flight, pilots should assess their fitness, just as they evaluate the aircraft's airworthiness.

RECOGNIZING HAZARDOUS ATTITUDES

Being fit to fly depends on more than just a pilot's physical condition and recency of experience. For example, attitude will affect the quality of decisions. **Attitude** can be defined as a personal motivational predisposition to respond to persons, situations, or events in a given manner. Studies have identified five

---

THE FIVE HAZARDOUS ATTITUDES

1. Anti-Authority: "Don't tell me."	This attitude is found in people who do not like anyone telling them what to do. In a sense, they are saying, "No one can tell me what to do." They may be resentful of having someone tell them what to do, or may regard rules, regulations, and procedures as silly or unnecessary. However, it is always your prerogative to question authority if you feel it is in error.
2. Impulsivity: "Do it quickly."	This is the attitude of people who frequently feel the need to do something, anything, immediately. They do not stop to think about what they are about to do; they do not select the best alternative, and they do the first thing that comes to mind.
3. Invulnerability: "It won't happen to me."	Many people feel that accidents happen to others, but never to them. They know accidents can happen, and they know that anyone can be affected. They never really feel or believe that they will be personally involved. Pilots who think this way are more likely to take chances and increase risk.
4. Macho: "I can do it."	Pilots who are always trying to prove that they are better than anyone else are thinking, "I can do it –I'll show them." Pilots with this type of attitude will try to prove themselves by taking risks in order to impress others. While this pattern is thought to be a male characteristic, women are equally susceptible.
5. Resignation: "What's the use?"	Pilots who think, "What's the use?" do not see themselves as being able to make a great deal of difference in what happens to them. When things go well, the pilot is apt to think that it is good luck. When things go badly, the pilot may feel that someone is out to get me, or attribute it to bad luck. The pilot will leave the action to others, for better or worse. Sometimes, such pilots will even go along with unreasonable requests just to be a "nice guy."

Figure 9-10. Pilots should examine their decisions carefully to ensure that their choices have not been influenced by a hazardous attitude.

hazardous attitudes which can interfere with a pilot's ability to make sound decisions and exercise authority properly. [Figure 9-10]

Hazardous attitudes can lead to poor decision making and actions which involve unnecessary risk. Students must be taught to examine their decisions carefully to ensure that their choices have not been influenced by hazardous attitudes and they must be familiar with positive alternatives to counteract the hazardous attitudes. These substitute attitudes are referred to as antidotes. During a flight operation, it is important to be able to recognize a hazardous attitude, correctly label the thought, and then recall its antidote. [Figure 9-11]

STRESS MANAGEMENT

Everyone is stressed to some degree all the time. A certain amount of stress is good since it keeps a person alert and prevents complacency. However, effects of stress are cumulative and, if not coped with adequately, they eventually add up to an intolerable burden. Performance generally increases with the onset of stress, peaks, and then begins to fall off rapidly as stress levels exceed a person's ability to cope. The ability to make effective decisions during flight can be impaired by stress. Factors, referred to as stressors, can increase a pilot's risk of error in the cockpit. [Figure 9-12]

One way of exploring the subject of stress with a student is to recognize when stress is affecting performance. If a student seems distracted, or has a particularly difficult time accomplishing the tasks of the lesson, the instructor can query the student. Was the student uncomfortable or tired during the flight? Is there some stress in another aspect of the student's life that may be causing a distraction? This may prompt the student to

HAZARDOUS ATTITUDES	ANTIDOTES
Anti-Authority — Although he knows that flying so low to the ground is prohibited by the regulations, he feels that the regulations are too restrictive in some circumstances.	**Follow the rules. They are usually right.**
Impulsivity — As he is buzzing the park, the airplane does not climb as well as Steve had anticipated and without thinking, Steve pulls back hard on the yoke. The airspeed drops and the airplane is close to a stalling attitude as the wing brushes a power line.	**Not so fast. Think first.**
Invulnerability — Steve is not worried about an accident since he has flown this low many times before and he has not had any problems.	**It could happen to me.**
Macho — Steve often brags to his friends about his skills as a pilot and how close to the ground he flies. During a local pleasure flight in his single-engine airplane, he decides to buzz some friends barbecuing at a nearby park.	**Taking chances is foolish.**
Resignation — Although Steve manages to recover, the wing sustains minor damage. Steve thinks to himself, "It's dangerous for the power company to put those lines so close to a park. If somebody finds out about this I'm going to be in trouble, but it seems like no matter what I do, somebody's always going to criticize."	**I'm not helpless. I can make a difference.**

Figure 9-11. Students can be asked to identify hazardous attitudes and the corresponding antidotes when presented with flight scenarios.

STRESSORS

Physical Stress—Conditions associated with the environment, such as temperature and humidity extremes, noise, vibration, and lack of oxygen.

Physiological Stress—Physical conditions, such as fatigue, lack of physical fitness, sleep loss, missed meals (leading to low blood sugar levels), and illness.

Psychological Stress—Social or emotional factors, such as a death in the family, a divorce, a sick child, or a demotion at work. This type of stress may also be related to mental workload, such as analyzing a problem, navigating an aircraft, or making decisions.

Figure 9-12. The three types of stressors can affect a pilot's performance.

evaluate how these factors affect performance and judgment. The instructor should also try to determine if there are aspects of pilot training that are causing excessive amounts of stress for the student. For example, if the student consistently makes a decision not to fly, even though weather briefings indicate favorable conditions, it may be due to apprehension regarding the lesson content. Stalls, landings, or an impending solo flight may cause concern for the student. By explaining a specific maneuver in greater detail or offering some additional encouragement, the instructor may be able to alleviate some of the student's stress.

To help students manage the accumulation of life stresses and prevent stress overload, instructors can recommend several techniques. For example, including relaxation time in a busy schedule and maintaining a program of physical fitness can help reduce stress levels. Learning to manage time more effectively can help pilots avoid heavy pressures imposed by getting behind schedule and not meeting deadlines. While these pressures may exist in the workplace, students may also experience the same type of stress regarding their flight training schedule. Instructors can advise students to take assessments of themselves to determine their capabilities and limitations and then set realistic goals. In addition, avoiding stressful situations and encounters can help pilots cope with stress.

USE OF RESOURCES

To make informed decisions during flight operations, students must be made aware of the resources found both inside and outside the cockpit. Since useful tools and sources of information may not always be readily apparent, learning to recognize these resources is an essential part of ADM training. Resources must not only be identified, but students must develop the skills to evaluate whether they have the time to use a particular resource and the impact that its use will have upon the safety of flight. For example, the assistance of ATC may be very useful if a pilot is lost. However, in an emergency situation when action needs be taken quickly, time may not be available to contact ATC immediately. During training, instructors can routinely point out resources to students.

INTERNAL RESOURCES

Internal resources are found in the cockpit during flight. Since some of the most valuable internal resources are ingenuity, knowledge, and skill, pilots can expand cockpit resources immensely by improving their capabilities. This can be accomplished by frequently reviewing flight information publications, such as the CFRs and the AIM, as well as by pursuing additional training.

A thorough understanding of all the equipment and systems in the aircraft is necessary to fully utilize all resources. For example, advanced navigation and autopilot systems are valuable resources. However, if pilots do not fully understand how to use this equipment, or they rely on it so much that they become complacent, it can become a detriment to safe flight. To ensure that students understand the operation of various equipment, instructors must first be familiar with the components of each aircraft in which they instruct.

Checklists are essential cockpit resources for verifying that the aircraft instruments and systems are checked, set, and operating properly, as well as ensuring that the proper procedures are performed if there is a system malfunction or in-flight emergency. Students reluctant to use checklists can be reminded that pilots at all levels of experience refer to checklists, and that the more advanced the aircraft is, the more crucial checklists become. In addition, the POH, which is required to be carried on board the aircraft, is essential for accurate flight planning and for resolving in-flight equipment malfunctions. Other valuable cockpit resources include current aeronautical charts, and publications, such as the *Airport/Facility Directory*.

It should be pointed out to students that passengers can also be a valuable resource. Passengers can help watch for traffic and may be able to provide information in an irregular situation, especially if they are familiar with flying. A strange smell or sound may alert a passenger to a potential problem. The pilot in command should brief passengers before the flight to make sure that they are comfortable voicing any concerns.

EXTERNAL RESOURCES

Possibly the greatest external resources during flight are air traffic controllers and flight service specialists. ATC can help decrease pilot workload by providing traffic advisories, radar vectors, and assistance in emergency situations. Flight service stations can provide updates on weather, answer questions about airport conditions, and may offer direction-finding assistance. The services provided by ATC can be invaluable in enabling pilots to make informed in-flight decisions. Instructors can help students feel comfortable with ATC by encouraging them to take advantage of services, such as flight following and Flight Watch. If students are exposed to ATC as much as possible during training, they will feel confident asking controllers to clarify instructions and be better equipped to use ATC as a resource for assistance in unusual circumstances or emergencies.

Throughout training, students can be asked to identify internal and external resources which can be used in a variety of flight situations. For example, if a discrepancy is found during preflight, what resources can be used to determine its significance? In this case, the student's knowledge of the airplane, the POH, an instructor or another experienced pilot, or an aviation maintenance technician are resources which may help define the problem.

During cross-country training, students may be asked to consider the following situation. On a cross-country flight, you become disoriented. Although you are familiar with the area, you do not recognize any landmarks, and fuel is running low. What resources do you have to assist you? Students should be able to identify their own skills and knowledge, aeronautical charts, ATC, flight service, and navigation equipment as some of the resources that can be used in this situation.

WORKLOAD MANAGEMENT

Effective workload management ensures that essential operations are accomplished by planning, prioritizing, and sequencing tasks to avoid work overload. As experience is gained, a pilot learns to recognize future workload requirements and can prepare for high workload periods during times of low workload. Instructors can teach this skill by prompt-ing their students to prepare for a high workload. For example, when en route, the student can be asked to explain the actions that will need to be taken during the approach to the airport. The student should be able to describe the procedures for traffic pattern entry and landing preparation. Reviewing the appropriate chart and setting radio frequencies well in advance of when they will be needed helps reduce workload as the flight nears the airport. In addition, the student should listen to ATIS, ASOS, or AWOS, if available, and then monitor the tower frequency or CTAF to get a good idea of what traffic conditions to expect. Checklists should be performed well in advance so there is time to focus on traffic and ATC instructions. These procedures are especially important prior to entering a high-density traffic area, such as Class B airspace.

To manage workload, items should be prioritized. This concept should be emphasized to students and reinforced when training procedures are performed. For example, during a go-around, adding power, gaining airspeed, and properly configuring the airplane are priorities. Informing the tower of the balked landing should be accomplished only after these tasks are completed. Students must understand that priorities change as the situation changes. If fuel quantity is lower than expected on a cross-country flight, the priority can shift from making a scheduled arrival time at the destination, to locating a nearby airport to refuel. In an emergency situation, the first priority is to fly the aircraft and maintain a safe airspeed.

Another important part of managing workload is recognizing a work overload situation. The first effect of high workload is that the pilot begins to work faster. As workload increases, attention cannot be devoted to several tasks at one time, and the pilot may begin to focus on one item. When the pilot becomes task saturated, there is no awareness of inputs from various sources so decisions may be made on incomplete information, and the possibility of error increases. [Figure 9-13]

During a lesson, workload can be gradually increased as the instructor monitors the student's management of tasks. The instructor should ensure that the student has the ability to recognize a work overload situation. When becoming overloaded, the student should stop, think, slow down, and prioritize. It is important that the student understand options that may be available to decrease workload. For example, tasks, such as locating an item on a chart or setting a radio frequency, may be delegated to another pilot or passenger, an autopilot (if available) may be used, or ATC may be enlisted to provide assistance.

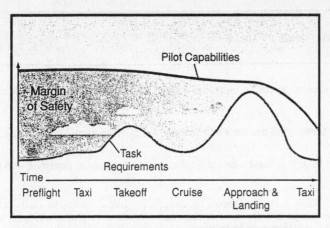

Figure 9-13. Accidents often occur when flying task requirements exceed pilot capabilities. The difference between these two factors is called the margin of safety. Note that in this idealized example, the margin of safety is minimal during the approach and landing. At this point, an emergency or distraction could overtax pilot capabilities, causing an accident.

SITUATIONAL AWARENESS

Situational awareness is the accurate perception of the operational and environmental factors that affect the aircraft, pilot, and passengers during a specific period of time. Maintaining situational awareness requires an understanding of the relative significance of these factors and their future impact on the flight. When situationally aware, the pilot has an overview of the total operation and is not fixated on one perceived significant factor. Some of the elements inside the aircraft to be considered are the status of aircraft systems, pilot, and passengers. In addition, an awareness of the environmental conditions of the flight, such as spatial orientation of the aircraft, and its relationship to terrain, traffic, weather, and airspace must be maintained.

To maintain situational awareness, all of the skills involved in aeronautical decision making are used. For example, an accurate perception of the pilot's fitness can be achieved through self-assessment and recognition of hazardous attitudes. A clear assessment of the status of navigation equipment can be obtained through workload management, and establishing a productive relationship with ATC can be accomplished by effective resource use.

OBSTACLES TO MAINTAINING SITUATIONAL AWARENESS

Fatigue, stress, and work overload can cause the pilot to fixate on a single perceived important item rather than maintaining an overall awareness of the flight situation. A contributing factor in many accidents is a distraction which diverts the pilot's attention from monitoring the instruments or scanning outside the aircraft. Many cockpit distractions begin as a minor

problem, such as a gauge that is not reading correctly, but result in accidents as the pilot diverts attention to the perceived problem and neglects to properly control the aircraft.

Complacency presents another obstacle to maintaining situational awareness. When activities become routine, the pilot may have a tendency to relax and not put as much effort into performance. Like fatigue, complacency reduces the pilot's effectiveness in the cockpit. However, complacency is harder to recognize than fatigue, since everything is perceived to be progressing smoothly. For example, cockpit automation can lead to complacency if the pilot assumes that the autopilot is doing its job, and does not crosscheck the instruments or the aircraft's position frequently. If the autopilot fails, the pilot may not be mentally prepared to fly the aircraft manually. Instructors should be especially alert to complacency in students with significant flight experience. For example, a pilot receiving a flight review in a familiar aircraft may be prone to complacency.

By asking about positions of other aircraft in the traffic pattern, engine instrument indications, and the aircraft's location in relationship to references on a chart, the instructor can determine if the student is maintaining situational awareness. The instructor can also attempt to focus the student's attention on an imaginary problem with the communication or navigation equipment. The instructor should point out that situational awareness is not being maintained if the student diverts too much attention away from other tasks, such as controlling the aircraft or scanning for traffic. These are simple exercises that can be done throughout flight training which will help emphasize the importance of maintaining situational awareness.

OPERATIONAL PITFALLS

There are a number of classic behavioral traps into which pilots have been known to fall. Pilots, particularly those with considerable experience, as a rule always try to complete a flight as planned, please passengers, meet schedules, and generally demonstrate that they have the right stuff. The basic drive to demonstrate the right stuff can have an adverse effect on safety, and can impose an unrealistic assessment of piloting skills under stressful conditions. These tendencies ultimately may bring about practices that are dangerous and often illegal, and may lead to a mishap. Students will develop awareness and learn to avoid many of these operational pitfalls through effective ADM training. The scenarios and examples provided by instructors during

OPERATIONAL PITFALLS

Peer Pressure—Poor decision making may be based upon an emotional response to peers, rather than evaluating a situation objectively.

Mind Set—A pilot displays mind set through an inability to recognize and cope with changes in a given situation.

Get-There-Itis—This disposition impairs pilot judgment through a fixation on the original goal or destination, combined with a disregard for any alternative course of action.

Duck-Under Syndrome—A pilot may be tempted to make it into an airport by descending below minimums during an approach. There may be a belief that there is a built-in margin of error in every approach procedure, or a pilot may want to admit that the landing cannot be completed and a missed approach must be initiated.

Scud Running—This occurs when a pilot tries to maintain visual contact with the terrain at low altitudes while instrument conditions exist.

Continuing Visual Flight Rules (VFR) into Instrument Conditions—Spatial disorientation or collision with ground/obstacles may occur when a pilot continues VFR into instrument conditions. This can be even more dangerous if the pilot is not instrument-rated or current.

Getting Behind the Aircraft—This pitfall can be caused by allowing events or the situation to control pilot actions. A constant state of surprise at what happens next may be exhibited when the pilot is getting behind the aircraft.

Loss of Positional or Situational Awareness—In extreme cases, when a pilot gets behind the aircraft, a loss of positional or situational awareness may result. The pilot may not know the aircraft's geographical location, or may be unable to recognize deteriorating circumstances.

Operating Without Adequate Fuel Reserves—Ignoring minimum fuel reserve requirements is generally the result of overconfidence, lack of flight planning, or disregarding applicable regulations.

Descent Below the Minimum En Route Altitude—The duck-under syndrome, as mentioned above, can also occur during the en route portion of an IFR flight.

Flying Outside the Envelope—The assumed high performance capability of a particular aircraft may cause a mistaken belief that it can meet the demands imposed by a pilot's overestimated flying skills.

Neglect of Flight Planning, Preflight Inspections, and Checklists—A pilot may rely on short- and long-term memory, regular flying skills, and familiar routes instead of established procedures and published checklists. This can be particularly true of experienced pilots.

Figure 9-14. All experienced pilots have fallen prey to, or have been tempted by, one or more of these tendencies in their flying careers.

ADM instruction should involve these pitfalls. [Figure 9-14]

EVALUATING STUDENT DECISION MAKING

A student's performance is often evaluated only on a technical level. The instructor determines whether maneuvers are technically accurate and that procedures are performed in the right order. Instructors must learn to evaluate students on a different level. How did the student arrive at a particular decision? What resources were used? Was risk assessed accurately when a go/no-go decision was made? Did the student maintain situational awareness in the traffic pattern? Was workload managed effectively during a cross-country? How does the student handle stress and fatigue?

Instructors should continually evaluate student decision-making ability and offer suggestions for improvement. It is not always necessary to present complex situations which require detailed analysis. By allowing students to make decisions about typical issues that arise throughout the course of training, such as their fitness to fly, weather conditions, and equipment problems, instructors can address effective decision making and allow students to develop judgment skills. For example, when a discrepancy is found during preflight inspection, the student should be allowed to initially determine the action to be taken. Then the effectiveness of the student's choice and other options that may be available can be discussed. Opportunities for improving decision-making abilities occur often during training. If the tower offers the student a runway that requires landing with a tailwind in order to expedite traffic, the student can be directed to assess the risks involved and asked to present alternative actions to be taken. Perhaps the most frequent choice that has to be made during flight training is the go/no-go decision based on weather. While the final choice to fly lies with the instructor, students can be required to assess the weather prior to each flight and make a go/no-go determination.

In addition, instructors can create lessons that are specifically designed to test whether students are applying ADM skills. Planning a flight lesson in which the student is presented with simulated emergencies, a heavy workload, or other operational problems can be valuable in assessing the student's judgment and decision-making skills. During the flight, performance can be evaluated on how effectively the student managed workload, or handled stress. While debriefing the student after the flight, the instructor can suggest ways that problems may have been solved more effectively, how tasks might have been prioritized differently, or other resources that could have been used to improve the situation.

Chapter 10

Planning Instructional Activity

This chapter is oriented to the beginning instructor who may be instructing independently outside of a formal training organization such as a pilot school. Independent instructors who learn to plan instructional activity effectively can provide high-quality training on an individual basis.

Any instructional activity must be well planned and organized if it is to proceed in an effective manner. Much of the basic planning necessary for the flight and ground instructor is provided by the knowledge and proficiency requirements published in Title 14 of the Code of Federal Regulations (14 CFR), approved school syllabi, and the various texts, manuals, and training courses available. This chapter reviews the planning required by the professional aviation instructor as it relates to four key topics—course of training, blocks of learning, training syllabus, and lesson plans.

COURSE OF TRAINING

In education, a course of training may be defined as a complete series of studies leading to attainment of a specific goal. The goal might be a certificate of completion, graduation, or an academic degree. For example, a student pilot may enroll in a private pilot certificate course, and upon completion of all course requirements, be awarded a graduation certificate. A course of training also may be limited to something like the additional training required for operating high-performance airplanes.

Other terms closely associated with a course of training include curriculum, syllabus, and training course outline. In many cases, these terms are used interchangeably, but there are important differences.

A **curriculum** may be defined as a set of courses in an area of specialization offered by an educational institution. A curriculum for a pilot school usually includes courses for the various pilot certificates and ratings. A syllabus is a summary or outline of a course of study. In aviation, the term "training syllabus" is commonly used. In this context, a **training syllabus** is a step-by-step, building block progression of learning with provisions for regular review and evaluations at prescribed stages of learning. The syllabus defines the unit of training, states by objective what the student is expected to accomplish during the unit of training, shows an organized plan for instruction, and dictates the evaluation process for either the unit or stages of learning. And, finally, a **training course outline**, within a curriculum, may be described as the content of a particular course. It normally includes statements of objectives, descriptions of teaching aids, definitions of evaluating criteria, and indications of desired outcome.

OBJECTIVES AND STANDARDS

Before any important instruction can begin, a determination of objectives and standards is necessary. Considerable theory regarding objectives and standards has been included in previous chapters. The theory described performance-based objectives as they relate to development of individual lessons and test items. The desired level of learning should also be incorporated into the objectives. In addition, level-of-learning objectives may apply to one or more of the three domains of learning—cognitive (knowledge), affective (attitudes, beliefs, and values), and psychomotor (physical skills). Normally, aviation training aspires to a level-of-learning at the application level or higher.

Standards are closely tied to objectives, since they include a description of the desired knowledge, behavior, or skill stated in specific terms, along with conditions and criteria. When a student is able to perform according to well-defined standards, evidence of learning is apparent. Comprehensive examples of the desired learning outcomes, or behaviors, should be included in the standards. As indicated in Chapter 1, standards for the level-of-learning in the cognitive and psychomotor domains are easily established. However, writing standards to evaluate a student's level-of-learning or overt behavior in the affective domain (attitudes, beliefs, and values) is more difficult.

The overall objective of an aviation training course is usually well established, and the general standards are included in various rules and related publications. For example, eligibility, knowledge, proficiency, and experience requirements for pilots and maintenance students are stipulated in the regulations, and the standards are published in the applicable practical test standards (PTS) or Oral and Practical Tests (O&P). It should be noted, though, that the PTS and O & P standards are limited to the most critical job tasks. Certification tests do not represent an entire training syllabus.

A broad, overall objective of any pilot training course is to qualify the student to be a competent, efficient, safe pilot for the operation of specific aircraft types under stated conditions. The established criteria or standards to determine whether the training has been adequate are the passing of knowledge and practical tests required by 14 CFR for the issuance of pilot certificates. Similar objectives and standards are established for aviation maintenance technician (AMT) students. Professional instructors should not limit their objectives to meeting only the published requirements for pilot or AMT certification. Instructional objectives should also extend beyond those listed in official publications. Successful instructors teach their students not only how, but also why and when. Ultimately, this leads to sound judgment and decision-making skills.

BLOCKS OF LEARNING

After the overall training objectives have been established, the next step is the identification of the blocks of learning which constitute the necessary parts of the total objective. Just as in building a pyramid, some blocks are submerged in the structure and never appear on the surface, but each is an integral and necessary part of the structure. Stated another way, the various blocks are not isolated subjects but essential parts of the whole. During the process of identifying the blocks of learning to be assembled for the proposed training activity, the planner must also examine each carefully to see that it is truly an integral part of the structure. Extraneous blocks of instruction are expensive frills, especially in flight instruction, and detract from, rather than assist in, the completion of the final objective.

While determining the overall training objectives is a necessary first step in the planning process, early identification of the foundation blocks of learning is also essential. Training for any such complicated and involved task as piloting or maintaining an aircraft requires the development and assembly of many segments or blocks of learning in their proper relationships. In this way, a student can master the segments or blocks individually and can progressively combine these with other related segments until their sum meets the overall training objectives.

The blocks of learning identified during the planning and management of a training activity should be fairly consistent in scope. They should represent units of learning which can be measured and evaluated—not a sequence of periods of instruction. For example, the flight training of a private pilot might be divided into the following major blocks: achievement of the knowledge and skills necessary for solo, the knowledge and skills necessary for solo cross-country flight, and the knowledge and skills appropriate for obtaining a private pilot certificate. [Figure 10-1]

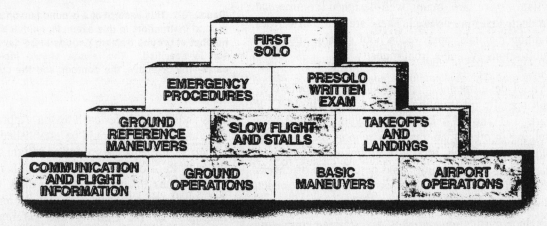

Figure 10-1. The presolo stage, or phase, of private pilot training is comprised of several basic building blocks. These blocks of learning, which should include coordinated ground and flight training, lead up to the first solo.

Use of the building block approach provides the student with a boost in self-confidence. This normally occurs each time a block is completed. Otherwise an overall goal, such as earning a private pilot certificate, may seem unobtainable. If the larger blocks are broken down into smaller blocks of instruction, each on its own is more manageable.

TRAINING SYLLABUS

There are a number of valid reasons why all aviation instructors should use a training syllabus. As technology advances, training requirements become more demanding. At the same time, new, and often more complicated rules continue to be proposed and implemented. In addition, the rules for instruction in other than an approved flight school are still quite specific about the type and duration of training. These factors, along with the continuing growth of aviation, add to the complexity of aviation training and certification. Instructors need a practical guide to help them make sure the training is accomplished in a logical sequence and that all of the requirements are completed and properly documented. A well organized, comprehensive syllabus can fulfill these needs.

SYLLABUS FORMAT AND CONTENT

The format and organization of the syllabus may vary, but it always should be in the form of an abstract or digest of the course of training. It should contain blocks of learning to be completed in the most efficient order.

Since a syllabus is intended to be a summary of a course of training, it should be fairly brief, yet comprehensive enough to cover essential information. This information is usually presented in an outline format with lesson-by-lesson coverage. Some syllabi include tables to show recommended training time for each lesson, as well as the overall minimum time requirements. [Figure 10-2]

While many instructors may develop their own training syllabi, there are many well-designed commercial products that may be used. These are found in various training manuals, approved school syllabi, and other publications available from industry.

Syllabi developed for approved flight schools contain specific information that is outlined in 14 CFR parts 141 and 147. In contrast, syllabi designed for training in other than approved schools may not provide certain details such as enrollment prerequisites, planned completion times, and descriptions of checks and tests to measure student accomplishments for each stage of training.

Since effective training relies on organized blocks of learning, all syllabi should stress well-defined objec-

---

STAGE I
GROUND LESSON 2

LESSON OBJECTIVES:
The objective of this lesson is for the student to learn important safety of flight considerations and become thoroughly familiar with airports, including marking and lighting aids. The student also will learn the significance of airspace divisions and how to use the radio for communications. In addition, the student will understand the capabilities and use of radar and other ATC services.

Content:
Introduce:
Section A—"Safety of Flight"
— Visual Scanning
— Collision Avoidance Precautions
— Blind Spots and Aircraft Design
— Right-of-Way Rules
— Minimum Safe Altitudes
— VFR Cruising Altitudes
— Special Safety Considerations
Section B—"Airports"
— Controlled and Uncontrolled Airports
— Runway and Taxiway Markings
— Airport Signs
— Wind Direction Indicators
— Segmented Circle
— Noise Abatement Procedures
— Airport Lighting
Section C—"Airspace"
— Cloud Clearance and Visibility
— Special Use and Other Airspace Areas
Section D—"Radio Communications"
— VHF Communications Equipment
— Coordinated Universal Time
— Radio Procedures
— Common Traffic Advisory Frequency
— Flight Service Stations
Section E—"Radar and ATC Services"
— Radar
— Transponder
— FAA Radar Systems

Completion Standards:
The student will complete Private Pilot Exercises 2A, 2B, 2C, 2D, and 2E with a minimum passing score of 80%, and the instructor will review each incorrect response to ensure understanding before the student progresses to Ground Lesson 3.

Figure 10-2. This excerpt of a ground lesson shows a unit of ground instruction. In this example, neither the time nor the number of ground training periods to be devoted to the lesson is specified. The lesson should include three key parts—the objective, the content, and the completion standards.

---

tives and standards for each lesson. Appropriate objectives and standards should be established for the overall course, the separate ground and flight segments, and for each stage of training. Other details may be added to a syllabus in order to explain how to use it and describe the pertinent training and reference materials. Examples of the training and reference materials include textbooks, video, compact disks, exams, briefings and instructional guides.

HOW TO USE A TRAINING SYLLABUS

Any practical training syllabus must be flexible, and should be used primarily as a guide. When necessary, the order of training can and should be altered to suit the progress of the student and the demands of special circumstances. For example, previous experience or different rates of learning often will require some alteration or repetition to fit individual students. The syllabus also should be flexible enough so it can be adapted to weather variations, aircraft availability, and scheduling changes without disrupting the teaching process or completely suspending training.

In departing from the order prescribed by the syllabus, however, it is the responsibility of the instructor to consider how the relationships of the blocks of learning are affected. It is often preferable to skip to a completely different part of the syllabus when the conduct of a scheduled lesson is impossible, rather than proceeding to the next block, which may be predicated completely on skills to be developed during the lesson which is being postponed.

Each approved training course provided by a certificated pilot school should be conducted in accordance with a training syllabus specifically approved by the Federal Aviation Administration (FAA). At certificated schools, the syllabus is a key part of the training course outline. The instructional facilities, airport, aircraft, and instructor personnel must be able to support the course of training specified in the syllabus. Compliance with the appropriate, approved syllabus is a condition for graduation from such courses. Therefore, effective use of a syllabus requires that it be referred to throughout the entire course of training. Both the instructor and the student should have a copy of the approved syllabus. However, as previously mentioned, a syllabus should not be adhered to so stringently that it becomes inflexible or unchangeable. It must be flexible enough to adapt to special needs of individual students.

Ground training lessons concentrate on the cognitive domain of learning. A typical lesson might include several knowledge areas. Many of these knowledge areas are directly or indirectly concerned with safety, aeronautical decision making, and judgment. These subjects tend to be closely associated with the affective domain of learning. Thus, instructors who find a way to stress safety, ADM, and judgment, along with the traditional aviation subjects, can favorably influence a student's attitude, beliefs, and values.

Flight training lessons also include knowledge areas, but they generally emphasize the psychomotor domain of learning. In addition, the affective domain of learning is also important in flight training. A student's attitude, especially toward flight safety, ADM, and judgment, should be a major concern of the instructor. [Figure 10-3]

STAGE I
FLIGHT LESSON 4
DUAL — LOCAL (1.0)

Note: A view-limiting device is required for the .2 hours of dual instrument time allocated to Flight Lesson 4.

LESSON OBJECTIVES:
• Practice the maneuvers listed for review to gain additional proficiency and demonstrate the ability to recognize and recover from stalls.
• The student will also receive instruction and practice in the maneuvers and procedures listed for introduction, including emergency operations and additional practice of airplane control by instrument reference (IR).
• Instructor may demonstrate secondary, accelerated maneuver, crossed-control, and elevator trim stalls.
• Emphasis will be on procedures related to airport operations, steep turns, slow flight, stalls, and stall recovery.

CONTENT:
INTRODUCE:
☐ Systems and Equipment Malfunctions
☐ Emergency Procedures
☐ Emergency Descent
☐ Emergency Approach and Landing
☐ Emergency Equipment and Survival Gear
☐ Climbing and Descending Turns (VR) (IR)

REVIEW:
☐ Airport and Runway Markings and Lighting
☐ Airspeed and Configuration Changes
☐ Flight at Approach Speed
☐ Flight at Various Airspeeds From Cruise to Slow Flight
☐ Maneuvering During Slow Flight
☐ Power-Off Stalls
☐ Power-On Stalls
☐ Normal Takeoffs and Landings
☐ Collision Avoidance Precautions
☐ Traffic Patterns

COMPLETION STANDARDS:
• Display increased proficiency in coordinated airplane attitude control during basic maneuvers.
• Perform unassisted takeoffs.
• Demonstrate correct communications and traffic pattern procedures.
• Landings completed with instructor assistance.
• Demonstrate basic understanding of steep turns, slow flight, stalls, stall recovery, and emergency operations.
• Complete demonstrated stalls
• Indicate basic understanding of airplane control by use of the flight instruments.

Figure 10-3. A flight training lesson, like a ground training lesson, should include an objective, content, and completion standards. More than one objective could, and often does, apply to a single flight lesson.

Individual flight lessons are much like ground lessons. Organization and format are similar. The lesson shown in figure 10-3 is an example showing the main elements.

A syllabus should include special emphasis items that have been determined to be cause factors in aircraft accidents or incidents. For example, the instructor should emphasize collision and wake turbulence avoidance procedures throughout a student's flight training.

A syllabus lesson may include several other items that add to or clarify the objective, content, or standards. A lesson may specify the recommended class time, reference or study materials, recommended sequence of training, and study assignment for the next lesson. Both ground and flight lessons may have explanatory information notes added to specific lessons. [Figure 10-4]

TYPICAL SYLLABUS NOTES

- Students should read Chapter 1 of the textbook prior to Ground Lesson 1.

- All preflight duties and procedures will be performed and evaluated prior to each flight. Therefore, they will not appear in the content outlines.

- The notation VR or IR is used to indicate maneuvers which should be performed by both visual references and instrument references during the conduct of integrated flight instruction.

- A view-limiting device is required for the .2 hours of dual instrument time allocated to Flight Lesson 4.

- The demonstrated stalls are not a proficiency requirement for private pilot certification. The purpose of the demonstrations is to help the student learn how to recognize, prevent, and if necessary, recover before the stall develops into a spin. These stalls should not be practiced without a qualified flight instructor. In addition, some stalls may be prohibited in some airplanes.

Figure 10-4. Information in the form of notes may be added to individual ground or flight lessons in a syllabus when they are necessary.

While a syllabus is designed to provide a road map showing how to accomplish the overall objective of a course of training, it may be useful for other purposes. As already mentioned, it can be used as a checklist to ensure that required training has successfully been completed. Thus, a syllabus can be an effective tool for record keeping. Enhanced syllabi, which also are designed for record keeping, can be very beneficial to the independent instructor.

This record-keeping function is usually facilitated by boxes or blank spaces adjacent to the knowledge areas, procedures, or maneuvers in a flight lesson. Most syllabi introduce each procedure or maneuver in one flight lesson and review them in subsequent lessons. Some syllabi also include provisions for grading student performance and recording both ground and flight training time. Accurate record keeping is necessary to keep both the student and the instructor informed on the status of training. These records also serve as a basis for endorsements and recommendations for knowledge and practical tests.

Another benefit of using a syllabus is that it helps in development of lesson plans. A well constructed syllabus already contains much of the essential information that is required in a lesson plan, including objectives, content, and completion standards.

LESSON PLANS

A **lesson plan** is an organized outline for a single instructional period. It is a necessary guide for the instructor in that it tells what to do, in what order to do it, and what procedure to use in teaching the material of a lesson. Lesson plans should be prepared for each training period and be developed to show specific knowledge and/or skills to be taught.

A mental outline of a lesson is not a lesson plan. A lesson plan should be put into writing. Another instructor should be able to take the lesson plan and know what to do in conducting the same period of instruction. When putting it in writing, the lesson plan can be analyzed from the standpoint of adequacy and completeness.

PURPOSE OF THE LESSON PLAN

Lesson plans are designed to assure that each student receives the best possible instruction under the existing conditions. Lesson plans help instructors keep a constant check on their own activity, as well as that of their students. The development of lesson plans by instructors signifies, in effect, that they have taught the lessons to themselves prior to attempting to teach the lessons to students. An adequate lesson plan, when properly used, should:

- Assure a wise selection of material and the elimination of unimportant details.

- Make certain that due consideration is given to each part of the lesson.

- Aid the instructor in presenting the material in a suitable sequence for efficient learning.

- Provide an outline of the teaching procedure to be used.

- Serve as a means of relating the lesson to the objectives of the course of training.

- Give the inexperienced instructor confidence.

- Promote uniformity of instruction regardless of the instructor or the date on which the lesson is given.

CHARACTERISTICS OF A WELL-PLANNED LESSON

The quality of planning affects the quality of results. Successful professionals understand the price of excellence is hard work and thorough preparation. The effective instructor realizes that the time and energy spent in planning and preparing each lesson is well worth the effort in the long run.

A complete cycle of planning usually includes several steps. After the objective is determined, the instructor must research the subject as it is defined by the objective. Once the research is complete, the instructor must determine the method of instruction and identify a useful lesson planning format. Other steps, such as deciding how to organize the lesson and selecting suitable support material also must be accomplished. The final steps include assembling training aids and writing the lesson plan outline. One technique for writing the lesson plan outline is to prepare the beginning and ending first. Then, complete the outline and revise as required. A lesson plan should be a working document that can and should be revised as changes occur or are needed. The following are some of the important characteristics that should be reflected in all well-planned lessons.

- **Unity**—Each lesson should be a unified segment of instruction. A lesson is concerned with certain limited objectives, which are stated in terms of desired student learning outcomes. All teaching procedures and materials should be selected to attain these objectives.

- **Content**—Each lesson should contain new material. However, the new facts, principles, procedures, or skills should be related to the lesson previously presented. A short review of earlier lessons is usually necessary, particularly in flight training.

- **Scope**—Each lesson should be reasonable in scope. A person can master only a few principles or skills at a time, the number depending on complexity. Presenting too much material in a lesson results in confusion; presenting too little material results in inefficiency.

- **Practicality**—Each lesson should be planned in terms of the conditions under which the training is to be conducted. Lesson plans conducted in an airplane or ground trainer will differ from those conducted in a classroom. Also, the kinds and quantities of instructional aids available have a great influence on lesson planning and instructional procedures.

- **Flexibility**—Although the lesson plan provides an outline and sequence for the training to be conducted, a degree of flexibility should be incorporated. For example, the outline of content may include blank spaces for add-on material, if required.

- **Relation to Course of Training**—Each lesson should be planned and taught so that its relation to the course objectives are clear to each student. For example, a lesson on short-field takeoffs and landings should be related to both the certification and safety objectives of the course of training.

- **Instructional Steps**—Every lesson, when adequately developed, falls logically into the four steps of the teaching process— preparation, presentation, application, and review and evaluation.

HOW TO USE A LESSON PLAN PROPERLY

- **Be Familiar with the Lesson Plan**—The instructor should study each step of the plan and should be thoroughly familiar with as much information related to the subject as possible.

- **Use the Lesson Plan as a Guide**—The lesson plan is an outline for conducting an instructional period. It assures that pertinent materials are at hand and that the presentation is accomplished with order and unity. Having a plan prevents the instructor from getting off the track, omitting essential points, and introducing irrelevant material. Students have a right to expect an instructor to give the same attention to teaching that they give to learning. The most certain means of achieving teaching success is to have a carefully thought-out lesson plan.

- **Adapt the Lesson Plan to the Class or Student**—In teaching a ground school period, the instructor may find that the procedures outlined in the lesson plan are not leading to the desired results. In this situation, the instructor should change the approach. There is no certain way of predicting the reactions of different groups of students. An approach that has been successful with one group may not be equally successful with another.

A lesson plan for an instructional flight period should be appropriate to the background, flight experience, and ability of the particular student. A lesson plan may have to be modified considerably during flight, due to deficiencies in the student's knowledge or poor mastery of elements essential to the effective completion of the lesson. In some cases, the entire lesson plan may have to be abandoned in favor of review.

• **Revise the Lesson Plan Periodically**—After a lesson plan has been prepared for a training period, a continuous revision may be necessary. This is true for a number of reasons, including availability or nonavailability of instructional aids, changes in regulations, new manuals and textbooks, and changes in the state-of-the-art among others.

LESSON PLAN FORMATS

The format and style of a lesson plan depends on several factors. Certainly the subject matter has a lot to do with how a lesson is presented and what teaching method is used. Individual lesson plans may be quite simple for one-on-one training, or they may be elaborate and complicated for large, structured classroom lessons. Preferably, each lesson should have somewhat limited objectives that are achievable within a reasonable period of time. This principle should apply to both ground and flight training. However, as previously noted, aviation training is not simple. It involves all three domains of learning, and the objectives usually include the higher levels of learning, at least at the application level.

In spite of need for varied subject coverage, diverse teaching methods, and relatively high level learning objectives, most aviation lesson plans have the common characteristics already discussed. They all should include objectives, content to support the objectives, and completion standards. Various authorities often divide the main headings into several subheadings, and terminology, even for the main headings, varies extensively. For example, completion standards may be called assessment, review and feedback, performance evaluation, or some other related term.

Commercially-developed lesson plans are acceptable for most training situations, including use by flight instructor applicants during their practical tests. However, all instructors should recognize that even well-designed preprinted lesson plans may need to be modified. Therefore, instructors are encouraged to use creativity when adapting preprinted lesson plans or when developing their own lesson plans for specific students or training circumstances.

As indicated by much of this discussion, the main concern in developing a lesson plan is the student. With this in mind, it is apparent that one format does not work well for all students, or for all training situations. Because of the broad range of aviation training requirements, a variety of lesson plans and lesson plan formats is recommended. Examples of various lesson plans and lesson plan formats are included in the following pages.

LESSON PLAN

Introduction (3 minutes)

ATTENTION: Relate aircraft accident in which a multi-engine airplane ran off the end of the runway. This could have been avoided by correctly computing the landing distance. Relate similar personal experience of the same type of mishap.

MOTIVATION: Tell students how landing distance can affect them (any aircraft, plus future application).

OVERVIEW: Explain what will be learned. Explain how the lesson will proceed. Define landing distance and explain the normal landing distance chart. Then, demonstrate how to solve for landing distance. The students will practice the procedure: at least once with supervision and at least once with as little help as possible. Next, the students will be evaluated according to the standards. Finally, the lesson will conclude with questions and answers, followed by a brief summary.

Body (29 minutes)

EXPLANATION DEMONSTRATION: (8 minutes) Define landing distance. Explain the normal landing distance chart to include the scale and interpolation. Ensure students can see demonstration and encourage questions. Demonstrate the procedure using °C with a headwind and °F with a tailwind. Show the normal landing distance chart with given data in the following order:
1. temperature
2. pressure altitude
3. gross weight
4. headwind-tailwind component
5. read ground roll distance from graph

PERFORMANCE SUPERVISION: (15 minutes) Review standards. Hand out chart and practice problems. Remind students to use a pencil, to make small tick marks, and to work as accurately as possible. Explain that they should follow the procedure on the chart to work the practice problems. Encourage students to ask questions. Check progress of each student continually so they develop skill proficiency within acceptable standards. Reteach any area(s) of difficulty to the class as they go along.

EVALUATION: (6 minutes) Review procedure again from the chart. Reemphasize standards of acceptable performance including time available. Prepare area for evaluation by removing the task step chart and practice problem sheets, and by handing out the evaluation problems. Ask students to work the three problems according to conditions and standards specified. Terminate evaluation after 6 minutes. Evaluate each student's performance and tactfully reveal results. Record results for use in reteaching any area(s) of difficulty in the summary.

Conclusion (3 minutes)

SUMMARY: Review lessons with emphasis on any weak area(s).

REMOTIVATION: Remind students that landing distance will be an important consideration in any aircraft they fly.

CLOSURE: Advise students that this lesson will be used as a starting point for the next lesson. Assign study materials for the next lesson.

This is an example of the lesson plan designed for a traditional ground school in a classroom environment.

Flight 6   Student:Judy Smith

DUAL-LOCAL
(7 to 10 knot crosswind conditions required)

SEQUENCE:
1.   Preflight Orientation
2.   Flight
3.   Postflight Evaluation

LESSON OBJECTIVE:
During the lesson, the student will review crosswind landing techniques in actual crosswind conditions and attempt to increase understanding and proficiency during their execution. The principle of a stabilized landing approach will be emphasized.

LESSON REVIEW:
1.   Slips
2.   Crosswind Landings

COMPLETION STANDARDS:
The student will demonstrate an understanding of how the slip is used to perform crosswind landings. In addition, the student will demonstrate safe crosswind landings in light crosswind conditions.

NOTES: Emphasize that the runway, airplane path, and longitudinal axis of airplane must be aligned at touchdown. Have the student establish a slip early on the final approach rather than crabbing and establishing slip just prior to touchdown. This should allow the student to concentrate on keeping the upwind wing low while maintaining runway alignment during the flare.

In this example, the lesson plan is specifically intended to help a student who is having difficulty with crosswind approaches and landings.

GROUND LESSON 8 — PCATD

OBJECTIVE

• Review of VOR concepts, intercepts, and tracks.

EMPHASIS

• Situational awareness; requires pilot constantly asking: Where am I? Where am I going? What am I going to do next?
• VOR utilization

SET-UP

• Choose an unfamiliar environment in which to fly (from the database map).
• Set airplane location off of a line between 2 NAVAID(s) about 40 miles apart (save as file for future use); configuration can be cruise flight or normal maneuvering flight regime.
• Utilize cockpit instrument check to set frequencies.
• Review terminology: bearing vs. radial, tracking inbound vs. outbound.

EXERCISES and MANEUVERS

• Determine position by orientation of TO/FROM and CDI centering; have student identify position on chart (paper) before looking at map screen, verify on map screen; discuss errors.
• Re-position airplane on the map screen, determine and note changes in CDI centering.
• Fly direct to selected NAVAID(s).
• Intercept a dictated radial:
    Tune/identify NAVAID(s).
    Determine location with respect to bearing by turning to the heading of course dictated; note on which side of airplane is desired course.
    Determine intercept angle and turn to intercept heading.
    Demonstrate bracketing techniques.

COMPLETION STANDARDS

• Correctly determine location and orientation TO/FROM NAVAID(s).
• Correctly determine appropriate intercept angle and heading.
• Recognize that the ability to track is heavily dependent on accurate maintenance of heading.
• Ability to visualize position.

This example lesson plan may be used for ground training in a personal computer-based aviation training device (PCATD) or a flight training device (FTD).

LESSON __Stalls__   STUDENT __Larry__   DATE __7-20__

OBJECTIVE

- To familiarize the student with the stall warnings and handling characteristics of the airplane as it approaches a stall. To develop the student's skill in recognition and recovery from stalls.

CONTENT

- Configuration of airplane for power-on and power-off stalls.
- Observation of airplane attitude, stall warnings, and handling characteristics as it approaches a stall.
- Control of airplane attitude, altitude, and heading.
- Initiation of stall recovery procedures.

SCHEDULE

- Preflight Discussion   :10
- Instructor Demonstrations   :25
- Student Practice   :45
- Postflight Critique   :10

EQUIPMENT

- Chalkboard or notebook for preflight discussion.

INSTRUCTOR'S ACTIONS

- Preflight — Discuss lesson objective.
- Inflight — Demonstrate elements. Demonstrate power-on and power-off stalls and recovery procedures. Coach student practice.
- Postflight — Critique student performance and assign study material.

STUDENT'S ACTIONS

- Preflight — Discuss lesson objective and resolve questions.
- Inflight — Review previous maneuvers including slow flight. Perform each new maneuver as directed.
- Postflight — Ask pertinent questions.

COMPLETION STANDARDS

- Student should demonstrate competency in controlling the airplane at airspeeds approaching a stall. Student should recognize and take prompt corrective action to recover from power-on and power-off stalls.

This is a typical lesson plan for flight training which emphasizes stall recognition and recovery procedures.

MULTI-ENGINE TRANSITION — LESSON THREE

OBJECTIVE: To complete the Baron systems instruction, review procedures for abnormal situations, including systems failures, and further review multi-engine aerodynamics and concepts. In addition, complete IFR proficiency in the ground trainer, and develop the pilot's skill and comfort operating the Baron in a variety of situations.

ELEMENTS:
- ground instruction
  - → systems
    - electrical
    - landing gear
  - → procedures
    - systems failures
    - other abnormal and emergency checklists
  - → multi-engine considerations / aerodynamics
    - zero sideslip
    - drag effects
- flight training device or flight simulator
  - → any further training needed on IFR skills
  - → utilize to practice engine failure after takeoff and single-engine go-around procedures
- flight
  - → engine failure on ground
  - → V_{MC} demo
  - → drag demo
  - → engine failure in cruise, descent
  - → systems failures including manual gear extension
  - → IFR procedures / single-engine approaches

COMPLETION STANDARDS: The lesson is complete when the student demonstrates understanding of all Baron systems and emergency procedures, and demonstrates a level of proficiency, as judged by the instructor, to cease training in the instrument ground trainer.

FURTHER STUDY: Baron POH (Chapter 3, Chapter 7)

This is a specialized flight training lesson plan for multi-engine transition.

LESSON PLAN
AVIATION MAINTENANCE TRAINING

INSTRUCTOR: William Brown

METHOD OF INSTRUCTION: Lecture, Audio Visuals, and Demonstration

TITLE: Flight line, Hangar, and Shop Safety

OBJECTIVE No 1: Recognize and neutralize or avoid (as appropriate) safety hazards that may be found in flight line, hangar, and maintenance shop areas.

OBJECTIVE No 2: Consistently apply safety practices on forming various aircraft maintenance functions.

MATERIALS YOU PLAN TO USE:

Visuals: Videos, overheads, and photographs showing safe and unsafe practices/conditions and their consequences.

Tools/Equipment: Power and hand tools, aircraft and aircraft systems, parts, and appliances, test and inspection tools, protective clothing and equipment, fire extinguishers, and chemicals commonly used in performing aircraft maintenance.

References: Material Safety Data Sheets (MSDS), aircraft maintenance manuals, government and industry published safety data, and equipment manufacturer's instructions.

PRESENTATION:

Topics/Steps: Personal Safey
Key Points:
1. Safety related terms.
2. General safety practices.
3. Causes of accidents.
4. Steps to be followed after an accident.
5. Accident report completion.

Flight Line, Shop, and Hangar Safety
Key Points:
1. Recognizing and identifying safety color codes and signs and their correct application.
2. Performing a safety inspection of flight line, hangar, and shop areas.
3. Identifying hazardous parts of various power tools.
4. Rules for safe use of hand and power tools and shop equipment.
5. Demonstrate proper use of power tools and shop equipment.

Chemical Safety
Key Points:
1. Using hazardous materials.
2. Using MSDS and manufacturer's instructions.

Fire Safety
Key Points:
1. Classes of fire.
2. Types of fire extinguishers and their inspection.
3. Matching fire extinguishing agents to classes of fires.
4. Proper techniques for using fire extinguishers.

PRACTICE: Identifying flight line, shop, and hangar safety hazards.
Safe use of hand and power tools, and flight line, shop, and hangar equipment.

ASSESSMENT: Written test covering category key points. Practical test covering practice items.

In this example, an aviation maintenance training lesson plan emphasizes safety.

APPENDIX C
GROUND SCHOOL COURSE SUGGESTIONS

The purpose of this appendix is to suggest ideas concerning marketing, organization, and presentation of ground schools for the private pilot knowledge test. We will appreciate any comments or suggestions you may have after reading this material, and so will other aviation professionals when we incorporate this information into subsequent editions. Please jot down notes on the last page of this book and send these to us at your convenience. Thank you.

RATIONALE FOR CONDUCTING A GROUND SCHOOL

1. **Aid to the industry.** General aviation (including flight instruction), while more financially sound than it has been in years, is still not normally a high-profit enterprise. A ground school is the first step into aviation for many students, who will one day become aircraft renters and owners, the people who sustain GA. While it will not generate large profits for a business on its own, a ground school sets the stage for a lasting relationship between a flight school/FBO and its students.

2. **Maintaining a professional level of currency and familiarity with aviation subjects.** Obtaining your flight and/or ground instructor certificate will keep you up to date on the CFRs and all other academic areas of flight. Additionally, teaching will challenge you to learn and understand a wide variety of material.

3. **Finding new customers.** Many flight instructors use ground schools as a source of student pilots.

4. **Public service.** Many flight and/or ground instructors provide ground schools to Civil Air Patrol (CAP) chapters, high school classes, etc., as a public service to young people.

5. **Personal employment.** Obtaining your flight and/or ground instructor certificate can lead to opportunities for part-time work at FBOs, community colleges, and adult education programs.

POTENTIAL SPONSORS OF GROUND SCHOOLS

1. **Community colleges.** Call your local junior college and ask if a ground school is offered. Ask what division it is in and call the Dean or Director to indicate your interest in teaching the ground school. While talking to the Dean or Director, you should obtain a course outline, as well as information on the cost and class schedule. The college may already have an instructor, but you should make known your interest in teaching in case there should be an opening.

   a.   Send us the Dean or Director's name and address and your own name and address. We will send him/her a complimentary copy of *Private Pilot and Recreational Pilot FAA Written Exam* and explain that it was at your suggestion. We will reiterate your interest in presenting a ground school.

2. **Local high school adult education centers.** Call all local high schools for more information.

3. **FBOs.** Inquire at your local airport, or check the Yellow Pages.

4. **Civil Air Patrol units.** Inquire at your local armed forces recruiting or training station for the name and telephone number of local CAP unit commanders (see the U.S. Government section of your telephone book). You can also find information about the CAP's aerospace education program at the Civil Air Patrol National Headquarters web site (www.capnhq.gov).

MARKETING GROUND SCHOOLS

The objective of marketing a ground school is to contact interested students if you are beginning a new ground school and to increase enrollment if you are associated with an existing ground school. The following are only a few suggestions.

1. **Classified ads in local newspapers.** Ads usually cost only a few dollars a day for a brief description that might read:

   "Private Pilot Ground School. 6 weeks in length, Tuesday and Thursday evenings, 7:00-9:00 p.m. Offered at (course location). Tuition, books, etc., $(your price). Call (instructor or sponsor name) at (phone number) after 7 p.m."

2. **Radio ads.** Call your local radio station and pay for an advertisement or, preferably, have it broadcast as a public service announcement. Provide the same information stated in the sample ad above.

3. **Posters.** Prepare posters and provide a telephone number, again with the above information. Post them at your local community college, university, airport, in stores, etc.

GROUND SCHOOL COURSE ORGANIZATION

We hope you will use *Pilot Handbook* and *Private Pilot and Recreational Pilot FAA Written Exam* for your ground school. Based on that presumption, it is probably easiest to follow our chapter organization, which is the same in both books, so you can use them together.

    Chapter 1 • Airplanes and Aerodynamics
    Chapter 2 • Airplane Instruments, Engines, and Systems
    Chapter 3 • Airports, Air Traffic Control, and Airspace
    Chapter 4 • Federal Aviation Regulations
    Chapter 5 • Airplane Performance and Weight and Balance
    Chapter 6 • Aeromedical Factors and Aeronautical Decision Making (ADM)
    Chapter 7 • Aviation Weather
    Chapter 8 • Aviation Weather Services
    Chapter 9 • Navigation: Charts, Publications, Flight Computers
    Chapter 10 • Navigation Systems
    Chapter 11 • Cross-Country Flight Planning

Pilot Handbook can be purchased for $13.95 retail, while *Private Pilot FAA Written Exam* sells for $15.95. Each book can be purchased at a discount if ordered in quantity. For instance, if you purchase four or more books and/or *FAA Test Prep* software ($49.95 retail), you can obtain a 40% discount by prepaying. Thus, you could package the books and software at your cost of $47.91 (or more), or include them in the cost of the ground school. Finally, you may wish to recommend the Gleim Private Pilot Kit (retail $119.95), which contains everything. Other purchase options are also available, including having your students order directly from us. To place an order or to obtain additional information, call us at (800) 87-GLEIM.

You will probably not have exactly 11 class sessions, which may necessitate combining chapters for various classes. Approximately 12 2-hr. sessions should be adequate if your course objective is to get your students ready for their pilot knowledge test. Even if you have 11 sessions, you may still want to combine certain chapters and spend more time on other chapters. As an example of how chapters might be combined, if you have a 5-week program that meets for 10 sessions, you might want to combine Chapters 9, 10, and 11. You could easily cover the Introduction in Session 1 and still use a good part of the session to get into Chapter 1. Then spend another entire meeting to finish Chapter 1.

If your course objective is to cover all the subjects in the amount of detail needed by proficient pilots (rather than simply to "teach the test"), 16 to 18 2-hr. sessions should be adequate. More time is needed for this comprehensive course because the FAA does not test every topic that your students need to know in order to be safe, capable pilots. Having 16 to 18 sessions will allow you to spend more than one session on the largest and most important chapters in *Pilot Handbook* (Chapters 1 through 4), and will allow you to spend extra time on challenging concepts like airspace and radio navigation. A comprehensive course outline might entail 2 sessions for the introduction and Chapter 1, 2 sessions for Chapter 2, 2 sessions for Chapter 3, 1 to 2 sessions for Chapter 4 (depending on how detailed you wish to get), 1 to 2 sessions for Chapter 5, and 1 session each for Chapters 6 through 11. Any extra time left in the course can be spent reviewing difficult topics and engaging in test-specific preparation.

Regardless of your course objective, you may wish to reserve 5 or 10 minutes at the end of each session for an overview and introduction of the material to be covered in the next session. That will help your students to study for the next session and help them understand it.

COURSE SYLLABUS AND HANDOUTS

1. At the beginning of the course, you should distribute an outline of the material to be covered in the course. It should show the meeting times, quiz schedule, and reading assignments for each session.

2. A suggested syllabus for a 9-week class (whose objective is to prepare students for the test) that meets for 3 hours one night per week is presented on the following page.

    a. Undoubtedly you will have to change the scheduling of topics. The topics have been overlapped so that you can talk about the same topic during two periods, i.e., you can provide double exposure. Introducing the topic the week before provides 3 weeks' coverage, which may be useful to your students.

3. Of course, the six chapters in this book will be helpful to you as general background in preparing and presenting your ground school.

GLEIM'S PRIVATE PILOT KIT

Gleim's Private Pilot Kit is designed to simplify and facilitate your students' flight and ground training. The Private Pilot Kit includes

- *Private Pilot FAA Written Exam*
- *Private Pilot Flight Maneuvers and Practical Test Prep*
- *Pilot Handbook*
- *FAR/AIM*
- *Private Pilot Syllabus and Logbook*
- Navigational plotter
- Flight computer
- *FAA Test Prep* software
- Flight bag

For ground training, your students will need to have at least a textbook (*Pilot Handbook*), a *FAR/AIM*, a means of test preparation (*Private Pilot FAA Written Exam* and/or *FAA Test Prep* software), a navigational plotter, and a flight computer. These items make up most of the Private Pilot Kit; the remaining items are primarily concerned with flight training. Because most people who take ground school courses intend to undertake flight training, it makes sense for your students to go ahead and obtain everything they will need at one time (at substantial savings) by purchasing the Private Pilot Kit.

ENROLLMENT PROCEDURES

1. You should make a list of the students and their telephone numbers so you can contact them in the event the classes need to be changed, rescheduled, etc.

    a. Note the form and date of their payment.

2. As each student enrolls, you can sell him/her a book (or give one to him/her if the book is included in the cost of the ground school course).

3. If you have a syllabus ready, distribute copies to your students and encourage them to do some study in advance.

SAMPLE COURSE SYLLABUS

COURSE SYLLABUS

Jonesville Community College
Evening Education Course 1121

PRIVATE PILOT GROUND SCHOOL
Summer Term A, 200X
June 1 - July 27

Tuesday evenings, 7:00 - 10:00 p.m.
North Campus, Building C, Room 171

INSTRUCTOR: Mr. Harold Gray, AGI
Office: (111) 555-5252
Home: (111) 555-2525

COURSE OBJECTIVE: Learn the material required by the FAA for the private pilot knowledge test (airplane) with the objective of each student passing the test.

CLASSROOM PROCEDURE: Lecture and guided discussion.

1. Each class will begin with a review and questions from the last class (approximately 5-15 minutes).

2. Next, there will be a brief overview and core concepts for the current evening's assignment, followed by class discussion and questions.

3. When appropriate, after the class break, an in-class quiz will be administered, self-graded, and analyzed through class discussion.

4. The last 15-30 minutes of each class session will be directed toward an overview and discussion of the next class's assignment.

5. Visual aids and handouts will be used as appropriate.

REQUIRED TEXT: *Private Pilot and Recreational Pilot FAA Written Exam*, by Irvin N. Gleim.

RECOMMENDED TEXT: *Pilot Handbook*, by Irvin N. Gleim.

These texts are available in the College Bookstore on the North Campus, which is open until 8:00 p.m. each Tuesday.

SCHEDULE

Class	Date	PPWE* Chapters	Topic
1	June 1	Introduction, 1	Introduction, Aerodynamic Theory
2	June 8	1, 2	Aerodynamics and Airplane Systems
3	June 15	2, 3	Airplane Systems, Airports, ATC
4	June 22	3, 4	Airspace, FARs
5	June 29	4, 5	FARs, Airplane Performance
6	July 6	5, 6	Weight and Balance, Aeromedical Factors
7	July 13	7, 8	Aviation Weather and Weather Services
8	July 20	9, 10, 11	Navigation, Cross-Country Flight
9	July 27		Review for pilot knowledge test

* PPWE = *Private Pilot and Recreational Pilot FAA Written Exam*

You may photocopy this syllabus and change it in any way you like.

4. With respect to requiring or recommending *Pilot Handbook* and *Aviation Weather and Weather Services*, you may proceed as follows:

    a. For each student, put one copy of each title on reserve in the bookstore of your choice.

    b. Get one copy of each book and pass them around to the class; indicate they can purchase another one from you, a local FBO, the bookstore you are using, or by calling Gleim Publications, Inc.

    c. Alternatively, have them order the book using our standard mail order brochure (let us know how many brochures you would like).

5. Note that you may wish to encourage each person who enrolls or even inquires about the program to invite friends to take the course with him/her. The idea is to build enrollment through enthusiasm for and interest in aviation.

THE FIRST CLASS SESSION

1. Preliminaries

    a. Arrive early with a supply of books, handouts, and your lecture notes for the first lecture.

    b. Begin by enrolling any students who show up at the first class without having already enrolled.

    c. Go over the roll and pass out the syllabus.

    d. Introduce yourself.

2. Student-Instructor Interaction

    a. Tell the students about your background, the origin of the course, your reasons for teaching, and any other relevant personal things.

    b. Tell the class that you need to learn more about them in order to teach effectively.

        1) Ask people to introduce themselves.

        2) Unless the class is too large, make notes on your roster to individualize participants and help you learn their names.

        3) Ask them why they are taking the course, if they have any flying experience, if they know anyone else who flies, if they have ever flown before in a small aircraft, etc.

    c. Such interaction is an ice-breaker, allowing you to get to know your students, and allowing them to get to know you and one another.

3. Discussion of Course Objective (FAA Private Pilot Knowledge Test)

    a. Display *Private Pilot and Recreational Pilot FAA Written Exam*.

    b. Point out that the textbook has the FAA questions reorganized by topic with answer explanations next to them.

    c. Indicate that the areas tested on the exam will be the topics specified on your syllabus (course outline), that the test will be only 60 questions, and that the students need to get only 42 questions correct to pass.

        1) This will be very easy because they will have gone over all possible test questions during your course (all of which appear in *Private Pilot and Recreational Pilot FAA Written Exam*), as well as additional material to help them learn how to fly safely.

    d. Explain the content of *Private Pilot and Recreational Pilot FAA Written Exam*.

        1) Explain that the Introduction is the current topic of discussion.

        2) Show them the organization of Chapters 1 through 11.

            a) Each chapter begins with an outline, module by module (topic by topic).

            b) Following the outlines are questions and answer explanations organized in the same modules and presented in the same order.

            c) Thus, the students are able to study and try to learn the material before they answer the questions. This format provides an extra level of reinforcement as they study the material.

4. Discussion of Course Objective (Comprehensive Coverage)

    a. Display *Pilot Handbook* and *Private Pilot and Recreational Pilot FAA Written Exam*.

    b. Explain that both books have the same chapter numbers and titles, so the content of each chapter number in both books will correspond.

        1) Explain that, because the chapters of these books are complementary, Chapters 1 through 4 of *Pilot Handbook* are disproportionately larger than their counterparts in *Private Pilot and Recreational Pilot FAA Written Exam*. Explain that this because there is a lot of material with which a safe pilot must be familiar that is not tested by FAA questions, and that much of this material happens to fit into the first 4 chapters.

        2) Explain that more time will therefore be spent on Chapters 1 through 4 of *Pilot Handbook*.

    c. Explain that, while your students will be well-prepared for their pilot knowledge test at the completion of this course, it is not your goal to simply "teach the test," and that you plan to give them a solid background in aviation topics.

        1) Explain that they will be expected to follow the progress of the course in *Private Pilot and Recreational Pilot FAA Written Exam* on their own and that you will primarily be teaching out of *Pilot Handbook*.

        2) Provide additional background about how to use *Private Pilot and Recreational Pilot FAA Written Exam* based on item 3. of this list.

LECTURE PRESENTATION

1. There are many ways to present a lecture, and you should use the method with which you feel most comfortable. The best method for you will be the best method for your students because you will perform better.

2. One approach to keep in mind is the idea of hitting the high points or key concepts.

    a. What are the basic or major concepts within any topic? These are generally outlined at the opening of each chapter in *Private Pilot and Recreational Pilot FAA Written Exam*.

    b. To amplify these concepts and provide additional discussion, consult *Pilot Handbook*, after which you can use additional examples from other textbooks, including the FAA/government textbooks.

3. A major objective of your lecture presentation is to make it interactive: the students must respond to you and participate.

    a. Learning is **not** a one-way communication from you to your students.

    b. You need to ask questions of individual students and of the class as a whole so that they can react and commit to an answer (silently or orally), and then get immediate feedback about the accuracy of their responses.

4. Have them work examples, e.g., provide them with a calculation and ask them to determine the answer.

    a. You could present a series of questions from the FAA written test (current or earlier test), take away the alternative answers, and have them work through a couple of exercises.

    b. You might also put these on overhead projectors.

5. Your preparation before class is very important. You should consult the lesson plan discussed in Appendix B of this book and review Chapter 5, Teaching Methods, beginning on page 53.

VISUAL AIDS

1. Visual aids include small model airplanes, film strips, slides, blackboard presentations, overhead projector pictures, etc.

2. Visual aids are most helpful in explaining ideas which are abstract when presented verbally (e.g., airspace).

3. You can bring items to class and pass them around, such as navigation tools/charts and operating manuals from airplanes.

4. Experiment with visual aids. Use them as attention getters or to break the pace of the normal presentation.

COURSE EVALUATIONS

1. At the end of the course, but before the session set aside for the FAA written test, you should administer a course evaluation.

    a. Your objective is to obtain feedback from your students about how the course can be improved in several aspects, including:

        1) Course organization
        2) Textbook(s)
        3) Lecture presentation
        4) Physical facilities

    b. Let the students know that you are seeking constructive criticism across many areas.

    c. Tell them that you do not want to make them ill at ease, so you are going to ask one member (tell them who) to hold the evaluations until the course is over.

    d. If the course is for grade credit, the evaluations should be held until after you have turned in the grades.

2. Please feel free to photocopy and modify the course evaluation illustrated below. Note that you should leave the back blank for additional written comments.

3. Remember that, at the conclusion of the last class session prior to your students' taking the FAA pilot knowledge test, you need to complete the Instructor Certification Form at the back of *Private Pilot and Recreational Pilot FAA Written Exam* for each student.

Date _____

(NAME OF COURSE)
GROUND SCHOOL EVALUATION FORM

This Ground School is being presented to aid you in your preparation for the FAA knowledge test. Please help us by answering the following questions, keeping in mind our objective: to help you prepare for the FAA knowledge test. Please check one response for each line. Return the completed form to the person designated to hold the evaluations until the completion of the last class (or after grades have been turned in).

Instructor	Excellent	Good	Adequate	Poor
1. Instructor presentation of material	—	—	—	—
2. Instructor knowledge of subject	—	—	—	—
3. Allocation of time to topics	—	—	—	—
4. Use of slides, boards, visual aids, etc.	—	—	—	—
5. Use of handouts, problems, etc.	—	—	—	—
6. Overall rating of instructor	—	—	—	—

Other questions

	Excellent	Good	Adequate	Poor
7. Classroom comfort	—	—	—	—
8. Progress of course as a whole	—	—	—	—
9. Outlines in *Private Pilot and Recreational Pilot FAA Written Exam*	—	—	—	—
10. Answer explanations in *Private Pilot and Recreational Pilot FAA Written Exam*	—	—	—	—
11. Overall rating of *Private Pilot and Recreational Pilot FAA Written Exam*	—	—	—	—

12. **Other comments.** Please explain "poor" responses and make any other suggestions you feel may be relevant in the space provided below and on the back of this sheet. **Thank you.**

HELPING YOUR STUDENTS SELECT A COMPUTER TESTING CENTER

1. Since most computer testing centers have limited seating, it is unlikely that you will be able to have all of your students take the test at the same time and place.

   a. Thus, you will need to help your students in the selection of a computer testing center.

2. Call each testing service to determine if any discounts are being offered and the payment policy. Explain your class situation (number of students, etc.)

   a. Some students may not have a credit card, so they need to select a computer testing center that will accept a check or cash at the time of the test.

      1) Some computer testing services may require that a check or money order be sent before the student can take the test.

   b. Make yourself available to assist your students as necessary.

3. Provide your students with the telephone numbers of the following computer testing services and the results of your inquiries.

    CATS   (800) 947-4228
    LASERGRADE   (800) 211-2754

4. Discuss the examination process and demonstrate testing procedures by using Gleim's *FAA Test Prep* software.

5. You, as a flight instructor, are required to maintain a record of each person for whom you sign a certification for a pilot knowledge test, including the kind of test, date of test, and the test result (FAR 61.189).

    a. An efficient way of obtaining test results is to preaddress and stamp one postcard for each student (include the student's name on the card) and explain why you need these returned.

        1) Hand them out on the exam day.
        2) Ask students to mail their numerical scores to you.
        3) List the student scores on your roster as they come in the mail.
        4) Call any individuals who have not submitted cards.

    b. You can use these pass rates in future advertising.

AN ALTERNATIVE APPROACH: EXPANDING YOUR MARKET

1. You may wish to broaden your ground school course so that it appeals to aviation enthusiasts interested in doing more than passing the FAA private pilot (airplane) knowledge test. If so, you need to

    a. Diversify your marketing plan and advertisements.
    b. Edit the suggested syllabus (make it more general).
    c. Prepare fewer class assignments focused on the FAA pilot knowledge test.

2. Can you prepare student pilots for the FAA pilot knowledge test **and** provide a general-interest aviation course?

    a. Many ground schools are so directed, especially at community colleges where a considerable number of enrollees do not take the FAA pilot knowledge test.

    b. One approach is to emphasize discussion of FAA test questions at the end (optional part) of each class; e.g., in a 100-minute class.

        1) The last 30 minutes might be restricted to discussion of FAA questions in *Private Pilot and Recreational Pilot FAA Written Exam*.

        2) The first 70 minutes would involve lecture discussion.

    c. Occasional questions might be discussed, but the emphasis would be on learning about airplanes, weather, and navigation rather than passing the FAA pilot knowledge test.

    d. In such a course, *Pilot Handbook* would be the required text instead of *Private Pilot and Recreational Pilot FAA Written Exam*, which can serve as the optional text.

3. With these general guidelines, we trust you will take the plunge and **start your class** (or at least begin to prepare for it) **right now**! It is fun, and it provides a valuable service -- teaching new aviation enthusiasts to **ENJOY FLYING -- SAFELY!**

CROSS-REFERENCES TO THE FAA PILOT KNOWLEDGE TEST QUESTION NUMBERS

Pages 159 and 160 contain the FAA fundamentals of instructing question numbers from the flight/ ground instructor knowledge test bank. The questions are numbered 6001 to 6160. To the right of each FAA question number, we have added the FAA's subject matter knowledge code (refer to page 10 in Chapter 1 for a complete listing and description of each). To the right of the subject matter knowledge code, we have listed our answer and our chapter and question number. For example, the FAA's question 6001 is cross-referenced to the FAA's subject matter knowledge code H201, "*Aviation Instructor's Handbook*, Chapter I, The Learning Process." The correct answer is A, and the question appears with answer explanations in our book under 2-1, which means it is reproduced in Chapter 2 as question 1.

The first line of each of our answer explanations in Chapters 2 through 7 contains

1. The correct answer
2. The FAA question number
3. A reference for the answer explanation, e.g., *AIH Chap I*.

Thus, our question numbers are cross-referenced throughout this book to the FAA question numbers, and these 2 pages cross-reference the FAA question numbers back to this book.

FAA Q. No.	FAA Subject Code	Gleim Answer	Gleim Chap/ Q. No.	FAA Q. No.	FAA Subject Code	Gleim Answer	Gleim Chap/ Q. No.	FAA Q. No.	FAA Subject Code	Gleim Answer	Gleim Chap/ Q. No.
6001	H201	A	2-1	6024	H203	C	4-10	6040c	H204	C	2-37
6002	H202	C	2-2	6025	H203	B	4-4	6040d	H204	C	2-38
6003	H202	C	2-3	6026	H203	A	4-6	6040e	H204	A	2-39
6004	H203	B	2-4	6027	H204	A	2-32	6040f	H204	B	2-40
6005	H203	A	2-6	6028	H204	B	2-33	6040g	H204	C	2-41
6006	H203	A	2-7	6029	H204	C	2-35	6041	H210	B	4-1
6007	H203	C	2-5	6030	H204	A	2-34	6042	H210	A	4-2
6008	H203	C	2-9	6031	H205	B	2-42	6043	H210	C	4-3
6009	H203	B	2-10	6032	H205	C	6-28	6044	H211	C	3-4
6010	H203	A	2-8	6033	H205	B	2-43	6045	H211	C	3-3
6011	H203	A	2-11	6034	H206	C	2-27	6046	H211	B	3-9
6012	H203	A	2-13	6035	H206	C	2-26	6047	H211	A	3-5
6013	H203	C	2-19	6036	H206	A	2-25	6048	H211	B	3-6
6014	H203	A	2-14	6037	H206	B	2-28	6049	H211	B	3-8
6015	H203	A	2-12	6038	H207	C	2-30	6050	H211	A	3-7
6016	H203	C	3-1	6039a	H207	B	2-29	6051	H211	B	3-10
6017	H203	A	2-17	6039b	H206	C	2-21	6052	H235	B	7-8
6018	H203	A	3-2	6039c	H206	A	2-22	6053	H235	A	4-7
6019	H203	A	2-15	6039d	H206	A	2-23	6054	H235	A	6-23
6020	H203	A	2-20	6039e	H206	C	2-24	6055	H235	A	4-30
6021	H203	B	2-18	6039f	H215	A	4-14	6056	H213	B	4-12
6022	H203	B	4-9	6040a	H207	A	2-31	6057	H213	C	4-16
6023	H203	B	4-5	6040b	H204	B	2-36	6058	H213	C	4-15

FAA Q. No.	FAA Subject Code	Gleim Answer	Gleim Chap/ Q. No.	FAA Q. No.	FAA Subject Code	Gleim Answer	Gleim Chap/ Q. No.	FAA Q. No.	FAA Subject Code	Gleim Answer	Gleim Chap/ Q. No.
6059	H213	B	4-13	6095	H226	C	7-4	6129d	H234	B	4-24
6060	H213	B	4-17	6096	H226	B	7-5	6129e	H234	B	4-27
6061	H214	C	4-21	6097	H226	C	7-6	6129f	H234	B	4-26
6062	H214	C	4-20	6098a	H227	A	7-13	6129g	H234	C	4-25
6063	H214	C	4-18	6098b	H227	C	7-9	6130	H212	B	3-11
6064	H214	C	4-19	6098c	H227	B	7-10	6131	H212	B	3-13
6065	H216	A	6-6	6099	H227	B	7-14	6132	H212	A	3-14
6066	H217	C	5-19	6100	H227	A	7-12	6133	H212	B	3-12
6067	H219	B	7-33	6101	H227	A	7-16	6134	H236	C	5-23
6068	H217	A	5-1	6102	H227	B	7-14	6135	H237	C	5-28
6069	H219	A	7-32	6103	H227	A	7-15	6136	H237	A	5-27
6070	H219	A	7-1	6104	H227	A	7-18	6137	H237	C	5-29
6071	H220	A	6-10	6105	H227	C	7-28	6138	H237	A	5-30
6072	H220	C	6-9	6106	H227	A	7-27	6139	H238	B	3-16
6073	H220	B	6-8	6107	H227	C	7-30	6140	H238	B	3-15
6074	H220	B	6-12	6108	H227	B	7-31	6141	H238	A	6-27
6075	H220	A	6-11	6109	H227	B	7-29	6142	H238	C	4-31
6076	H221	C	5-5	6110	H227	A	7-24	6143	H238	A	2-16
6077	H221	C	5-4	6111	H227	A	7-20	6144	H245	A	6-1
6078	H221	B	5-6	6112	H227	C	7-19	6145	H246	B	6-4
6079	H221	A	5-2	6113	H227	B	7-21	6146	H246	C	6-3
6080	H221	A	5-8	6114	H227	C	7-25	6147	H246	B	6-2
6081	H221	B	5-7	6115	H227	B	7-22	6148	H247	C	6-14
6082a	H221	B	5-3	6116	H227	C	7-23	6149	H247	C	6-5
6082b	H222	A	5-10	6117	H227	B	7-26	6150a	H248	C	6-22
6082c	H222	B	5-12	6118	H227	B	7-34	6150b	H248	C	6-7
6082d	H222	B	5-11	6119	H228	B	6-29	6150c	H248	C	6-25
6082e	H222	C	5-9	6120	H230	B	6-31	6151	H248	A	6-26
6083	H222	B	5-14	6121	H230	A	6-32	6152	H248	C	6-24
6084	H223	C	5-18	6122	H230	C	6-30	6153	H248	B	6-13
6085	H223	A	5-13	6123a	H235	A	4-28	6154	H32*	B	6-15
6086	H223	B	5-16	6123b	H235	B	4-29	6155	H32	A	6-16
6087	H223	A	5-15	6123c	H235	B	4-33	6156	H32	C	6-21
6088	H223	C	5-17	6124a	H233	A	4-11	6157	H32	C	6-19
6089	H224	C	5-20	6124b	H233	B	4-8	6158	H32	A	6-17
6090	H224	B	5-22	6124c	H233	C	7-11	6159	H32	B	6-18
6091a	H224	B	5-21	6125	H233	A	3-18	6160	H32	C	6-20
6091b	H225	C	5-24	6126	H233	C	3-17				
6091c	H225	B	5-25	6127	H233	C	4-32				
6091d	H225	B	5-26	6128	H233	B	5-32				
6092	H226	B	7-3	6129a	H233	B	5-31				
6093	H226	C	7-7	6129b	H234	C	4-23				
6094	H226	C	7-2	6129c	H234	C	4-22				

*Old Subject Matter Knowledge Code: Planning Instructional Activity

FOR CHOOSING GLEIM

Thank You

We dedicate ourselves to providing pilots with knowledge transfer systems, enabling them to pass the FAA pilot knowledge (written) tests and FAA practical (flight) tests. We solicit your feedback. Use the last page in this book to make notes as you use *Fundamentals of Instructing FAA Written Exam* and other Gleim products. Tear out the page and mail it to us when convenient. Alternatively, e-mail (irvin@gleim.com) or FAX (352-375-6940) your feedback to us.

GLEIM'S E-MAIL UPDATE SERVICE

update@gleim.com

Your message to Gleim must include (in the subject or body) the acronym for your book or software, followed by the edition-printing for books and version for software. The edition-printing is indicated on the book's spine and at the bottom right corner of the cover. The software version is indicated on the CD-ROM label.

	Written Exam Book	Software	Flight Maneuvers Book
Private Pilot	PPWE	FAATP PP	PPFM
Instrument Pilot	IPWE	FAATP IP	IPFM
Commercial Pilot	CPWE	FAATP CP	CPFM
Flight/Ground Instructor	FIGI	FAATP FIGI	FIFM
Fundamentals of Instructing	FOI	FAATP FOI	
Airline Transport Pilot	ATP	FAATP ATP	
Flight Engineer	FEWE	FAATP FEWE	

	Reference Book
Pilot Handbook	PH
Aviation Weather and Weather Services	AWWS
Private Pilot Syllabus and Logbook	PPSYL
FAR/AIM	FARAIM

EXAMPLES

For ***Fundamentals of Instructing***, seventh edition-first printing:

```
       To:   update@gleim.com
     From:   your e-mail address
  Subject:   FOI 7-1
```

For ***FAA Test Prep*** software, FOI, version 4.0:

```
       To:   update@gleim.com
     From:   your e-mail address
  Subject:   FAATP FOI 4-0
```

IT ONLY TAKES A MINUTE

If you do not have e-mail, have a friend send e-mail to us and print our response for you.

LESSON:

STUDENT: _____   **DATE:** _____

OBJECTIVE

ELEMENTS

SCHEDULE

EQUIPMENT

INSTRUCTOR'S ACTIONS

STUDENT'S ACTIONS

COMPLETION STANDARDS

PILOT KNOWLEDGE (WRITTEN EXAM) BOOKS AND SOFTWARE

Before pilots take their FAA pilot knowledge tests, they want to understand the answer to every FAA test question. Gleim's pilot knowledge test books are widely used because they help pilots learn and understand exactly what they need to know to pass. Each chapter opens with an outline of exactly what you need to know to pass the test. Additional information can be found in our reference books and flight maneuver/practical test prep books.

Use *FAA Test Prep* software with the appropriate Gleim book to prepare for success on your FAA pilot knowledge test.

PRIVATE PILOT AND RECREATIONAL PILOT FAA WRITTEN EXAM ($15.95)

The test for the private pilot certificate consists of 60 questions out of the 738 questions in our book. Also, the FAA's pilot knowledge test for the recreational pilot certificate consists of 50 questions from this book.

INSTRUMENT PILOT FAA WRITTEN EXAM ($18.95)

The test consists of 60 questions out of the 899 questions in our book. Also, become an instrument-rated flight instructor (CFII) or an instrument ground instructor (IGI) by taking the FAA's pilot knowledge test of 50 questions from this book.

COMMERCIAL PILOT FAA WRITTEN EXAM ($14.95)

The test consists of 100 questions out of the 595 questions in our book.

FUNDAMENTALS OF INSTRUCTING FAA WRITTEN EXAM ($12.95)

The test consists of 50 questions out of the 192 questions in our book. This test is required for any person to become a flight instructor or ground instructor. The test needs to be taken only once. For example, if someone is already a flight instructor and wants to become a ground instructor, taking the FOI test a second time is not required.

FLIGHT/GROUND INSTRUCTOR FAA WRITTEN EXAM ($14.95)

The test consists of 100 questions out of the 833 questions in our book. This book is to be used for the Flight Instructor--Airplane (FIA), Basic Ground Instructor (BGI), and the Advanced Ground Instructor (AGI) knowledge tests.

AIRLINE TRANSPORT PILOT FAA WRITTEN EXAM ($26.95)

The test consists of 80 questions each for the ATP Part 121, ATP Part 135, and the flight dispatcher certificate. Studying for the ATP will now be a learning and understanding experience rather than a memorization marathon -- at a lower cost and with higher test scores and less frustration!!

FLIGHT ENGINEER FAA WRITTEN EXAM ($26.95)

The FAA's flight engineer turbojet and basic knowledge test consists of 80 questions out of the 688 questions in our book. This book is to be used for the turbojet and basic (FEX) and the turbojet-added rating (FEJ) knowledge tests.

REFERENCE AND FLIGHT MANEUVERS/PRACTICAL TEST PREP BOOKS

Our Flight Maneuvers and Practical Test Prep books are designed to simplify and facilitate your flight training and will help prepare pilots for FAA practical tests as much as the Gleim written exam books help prepare pilots for FAA pilot knowledge tests. Each task, objective, concept, requirement, etc., in the FAA's practical test standards is explained, analyzed, illustrated, and interpreted so pilots will gain practical test proficiency as quickly as possible.

Private Pilot Flight Maneuvers and Practical Test Prep	368 pages	($16.95)
Instrument Pilot Flight Maneuvers and Practical Test Prep	432 pages	($18.95)
Commercial Pilot Flight Maneuvers and Practical Test Prep	336 pages	($14.95)
Flight Instructor Flight Maneuvers and Practical Test Prep	544 pages	($17.95)

PILOT HANDBOOK ($13.95)

A complete pilot ground school text in outline format with many diagrams for ease in understanding. This book is used in preparation for private, commercial, and flight instructor certificates and the instrument rating. A complete, detailed index makes it more useful and saves time. It contains a special section on biennial flight reviews.

AVIATION WEATHER AND WEATHER SERVICES ($18.95)

A complete rewrite of the FAA's *Aviation Weather 00-6A* and *Aviation Weather Services 00-45E* into a single easy-to-understand book complete with maps, diagrams, charts, and pictures. Learn and understand the subject matter much more easily and effectively with this book.

FAR/AIM ($14.95)

The purpose of this book is to consolidate the common Federal Aviation Regulations (FAR) parts and the *Aeronautical Information Manual* into one easy-to-use reference book. The Gleim book is better because of bigger type, better presentation, improved indexes, and full-color figures. FAR Parts 1, 43, 61, 67, 71, 73, 91, 97, 103, 105, 119, Appendices I and J of 121, 135, 137, 141, and 142 are included.

GLEIM'S PRIVATE PILOT KIT

Gleim's *Private Pilot FAA Written Exam* book, *Private Pilot Flight Maneuvers and Practical Test Prep*, *Pilot Handbook*, *FAR/AIM*, a combined syllabus/logbook, a flight computer, a navigational plotter, and a versatile, all-purpose flight bag. Our introductory price (substantial savings over purchasing items separately) is far lower than similarly equipped kits found elsewhere. The Gleim Kit retails for **$99.95**. Gleim's *FAR/AIM, Private Pilot Syllabus/Logbook*, flight computer, navigational plotter, and flight bag are also available for individual sale. See our order form for details.

Gleim Publications, Inc.
P.O. Box 12848
University Station
Gainesville, FL 32604

TOLL FREE: (800) 87-GLEIM
    or (800) 874-5346
LOCAL: (352) 375-0772
FAX: (352) 375-6940
INTERNET: www.gleim.com
E-MAIL: sales@gleim.com

Customer service is available:
8:00 a.m. - 7:00 p.m., Mon. - Fri.
9:00 a.m. - 2:00 p.m., Saturday
Please have your credit card ready
    or save time by ordering online.

GLEIM'S PRIVATE PILOT KIT

Includes everything you need to pass the FAA pilot knowledge (written) test and FAA practical (flight) test: Gleim's *Private Pilot FAA Written Exam* book; *Private Pilot Flight Maneuvers and Practical Test Prep*; *Pilot Handbook*; *FAR/AIM*; a combined syllabus/logbook; flight computer; navigational plotter; and an attractive, versatile, all-purpose flight bag. Our price is far lower than similarly equipped kits found elsewhere. ORDER TODAY!

BIG savings ➤

Original kit (with demo software) . . . . $ 99.95 _____
With CD-ROM (For Windows 95, Windows 98, or NT 4.0) . . . . $119.95 _____

FAA Test Prep Software

WRITTEN TEST BOOKS AND SOFTWARE		Books	CD-ROM‡	☐ free demo	Audio	☐ free demo	
Private/Recreational Pilot	Ninth Edition	☐ @ $15.95	☐ @ $49.95		☐ @ $60.00		_____
Instrument Pilot	Seventh Edition	☐ @ 18.95	☐ @ 59.95				_____
Commercial Pilot	Seventh Edition	☐ @ 14.95	☐ @ 59.95				_____
Fundamentals of Instructing . .	Seventh Edition	☐ @ 12.95	☐ @] $59.95 for both				_____
Flight/Ground Instructor	Sixth Edition	☐ @ 14.95					_____
Airline Transport Pilot	Fourth Edition	☐ @ 26.95	☐ @ 59.95				_____
Flight Engineer	First Edition	☐ @ 26.95	☐ @ 59.95				_____

‡CD-ROM version includes all questions, figures, charts, and outlines for each of the pilot knowledge tests. Must have Windows 95, Windows 98, or NT 4.0 or higher and a CD-ROM drive to use.

FLIGHT MANEUVERS/PRACTICAL TEST PREP BOOKS

Private Pilot Flight Maneuvers and Practical Test Prep . . . . (Third Edition) . . . . $16.95 _____
Instrument Pilot Flight Maneuvers and Practical Test Prep . . . . (Third Edition) . . . . 18.95 _____
Commercial Pilot Flight Maneuvers and Practical Test Prep . . . . . . (Third Edition) . . . . 14.95 _____
Flight Instructor Flight Maneuvers and Practical Test Prep . . . . (Second Edition) . . . . 17.95 _____

REFERENCE BOOKS AND SYLLABUS

FAR/AIM . . . . (Most Recent Edition) . . . . $14.95 _____
Aviation Weather and Weather Services . . . . (Third Edition) . . . . 22.95 _____
Pilot Handbook . . . . (Sixth Edition) . . . . 13.95 _____
Private Pilot Syllabus and Logbook . . . . 9.95 _____

OTHER

Flight Computer . . . . $ 9.95 _____
Navigational Plotter . . . . 5.95 _____
Flight Bag . . . . 29.95 _____

Shipping and Handling (nonrefundable): 1 item = $5; each additional item = $1 _____

Add applicable sales tax for shipments within the State of Florida.   Sales Tax _____

Please FAX or write for additional charges for outside the 48 contiguous United States.

Printed 12/00. Prices subject to change without notice.   **TOTAL** $_____

1. We process orders within 1 business day over 98.8% of the time. Call by noon for same-day service!

2. Please copy this order form for friends and others. Orders from individuals must be prepaid. No CODs.

3. Gleim Publications, Inc. guarantees the immediate refund of all resalable texts and unopened software and audiotapes returned in 30 days. Applies only to items purchased direct from Gleim. No refunds on shipping and handling.

4. If your local FBO or aviation bookstore does not stock the books you are ordering from us directly, please provide us with a name and address, so we can invite them to stock Gleim.

Name _____
    (please print)

Shipping Address _____
    (street address required for UPS)   Apt. #

_____

City _____ State _____ Zip _____

☐ VISA/MC/DISC ☐ Check/M.O.   Expiration Date (month/year) _____ / _____

Credit Card No. _____ - _____ - _____ - _____

Daytime Phone (_____) _____   Evening Phone (_____) _____

Signature _____   E-mail _____

INDEX

ABBREVIATIONS AND ACRONYMS
IN
FUNDAMENTALS OF INSTRUCTING

AC	Advisory Circular
AC Form	Airman Certification Form (i.e., AC Form 8080-2)
ADF	automatic direction finder
AGI	Advanced Ground Instructor
AIH	Aviation Instructor's Handbook
APS	Accident Prevention Specialist
ASR	Airport Surveillance Radar
ATC	Air Traffic Control
ATIS	Automatic Terminal Information Service
ATP	Airline Transport Pilot
BGI	Basic Ground Instructor
CAP	Civil Air Patrol
CFI	Certificated Flight Instructor
DF	direction finding
DME	distance measuring equipment
DUAT	Direct User Access Terminal
EAA	Experimental Aircraft Association
FAA	Federal Aviation Administration
FAR	Federal Aviation Regulation
FBO	Fixed-Base Operator
FOI	Fundamentals of Instructing
FSDO	Flight Standards District Office
GADO	General Aviation District Office (now called FSDO)
IFR	instrument flight rules
IGI	Instrument Ground Instructor
IMC	Instrument Meteorological Conditions
IR	instrument reference
NAFI	National Association of Flight Instructors
VFR	visual flight rules
VMC	Visual Meteorological Conditions
VOR	VHF omnidirectional range
VR	visual reference

Please forward your suggestions, corrections, and comments to **Irvin N. Gleim • c/o Gleim Publications, Inc. • P.O. Box 12848 • University Station • Gainesville, Florida • 32604** for inclusion in the next edition of *Fundamentals of Instructing FAA Written Exam*. Please include your name and address on the back of this page so we can properly thank you for your interest. Also, please refer to both the page number and the FAA question number for each item.

1. _____

2. _____

3. _____

4. _____

5. _____

6. _____

7. _____

8. _____

9. _____

10. _____

11. _____

12. _____

13. _____

14. _____

15. _____

16. _____

17. _____

Name: _____

Address: _____

City/State/Zip: _____

Telephone: Home: _____   Work: _____   Fax: _____

E-mail: _____